Crime Files Series

General Editor: **Clive Bloom**

Since its invention in the nineteenth century, detective fiction has never been more popular. In novels, short stories, films, radio, television and now in computer games, private detectives and psychopaths, prim poisoners and overworked cops, tommy gun gangsters and cocaine criminals are the very stuff of modern imagination, and their creators one mainstay of popular consciousness. Crime Files is a groundbreaking series offering scholars, students and discerning readers a comprehensive set of guides to the world of crime and detective fiction. Every aspect of crime writing, detective fiction, gangster movie, true-crime exposé, police procedural and post-colonial investigation is explored through clear and informative texts offering comprehensive coverage and theoretical sophistication.

Published titles include:

Maurizio Ascari
A COUNTER-HISTORY OF CRIME FICTION
Supernatural, Gothic, Sensational

Hans Bertens and Theo D'haen
CONTEMPORARY AMERICAN CRIME FICTION

Anita Biressi
CRIME, FEAR AND THE LAW IN TRUE CRIME STORIES

Ed Christian (*editor*)
THE POST-COLONIAL DETECTIVE

Paul Cobley
THE AMERICAN THRILLER
Generic Innovation and Social Change in the 1970s

Michael Cook
NARRATIVES OF ENCLOSURE IN DETECTIVE FICTION
The Locked Room Mystery

Barry Forshaw
DEATH IN A COLD CLIMATE
A Guide to Scandinavian Crime Fiction

Barry Forshaw
BRITISH CRIME FILM
Subverting the Social Order

Emelyne Godfrey
MASCULINITY, CRIME AND SELF-DEFENCE IN VICTORIAN LITERATURE

Emelyne Godfrey
FEMININITY, CRIME AND SELF-DEFENCE IN VICTORIAN LITERATURE
AND SOCIETY
From Dagger-Fans to Suffragettes

Christiana Gregoriou
DEVIANCE IN CONTEMPORARY CRIME FICTION

Lee Horsley
THE NOIR THRILLER

Merja Makinen
AGATHA CHRISTIE
Investigating Femininity

Fran Mason
AMERICAN GANGSTER CINEMA
From Little Caesar to Pulp Fiction

Fran Mason
HOLLYWOOD'S DETECTIVES
Crime Series in the 1930s and 1940s from the Whodunnit to Hard-boiled Noir

Linden Peach
MASQUERADE, CRIME AND FICTION
Criminal Deceptions

Steven Powell (*editor*)
100 AMERICAN CRIME WRITERS

Alistair Rolls and Deborah Walker
FRENCH AND AMERICAN NOIR
Dark Crossings

Susan Rowland
FROM AGATHA CHRISTIE TO RUTH RENDELL
British Women Writers in Detective and Crime Fiction

Adrian Schober
POSSESSED CHILD NARRATIVES IN LITERATURE AND FILM
Contrary States

Lucy Sussex
WOMEN WRITERS AND DETECTIVES IN NINETEENTH-CENTURY
CRIME FICTION
The Mothers of the Mystery Genre

Heather Worthington
THE RISE OF THE DETECTIVE IN EARLY NINETEENTH-CENTURY
POPULAR FICTION

R.A. York
AGATHA CHRISTIE
Power and Illusion

Crime Files
Series Standing Order ISBN 978–0–333–71471–3 (hardback)
978–0–333–93064–9 (paperback)
(*outside North America only*)

You can receive future titles in this series as they are published by placing a standing order. Please contact your bookseller or, in case of difficulty, write to us at the address below with your name and address, the title of the series and the ISBN quoted above.

Customer Services Department, Macmillan Distribution Ltd, Houndmills, Basingstoke, Hampshire RG21 6XS, England

---

British Crime Film

Subverting the Social Order

Barry Forshaw

First published 2012 by
PALGRAVE MACMILLAN

Palgrave Macmillan in the UK is an imprint of Macmillan Publishers Limited, registered in England, company number 785998, of Houndmills, Basingstoke, Hampshire RG21 6XS.

Palgrave Macmillan in the US is a division of St Martin's Press LLC, 175 Fifth Avenue, New York, NY 10010.

Palgrave Macmillan is the global academic imprint of the above companies and has companies and representatives throughout the world.

Palgrave® and Macmillan® are registered trademarks in the United States, the United Kingdom, Europe and other countries.

ISBN 978–0–230–30370–6   hardback
ISBN 978–1–137–00503–8   paperback

This book is printed on paper suitable for recycling and made from fully managed and sustained forest sources. Logging, pulping and manufacturing processes are expected to conform to the environmental regulations of the country of origin.

A catalogue record for this book is available from the British Library.

A catalog record for this book is available from the Library of Congress.

10 9 8 7 6 5 4 3 2 1
21 20 19 18 17 16 15 14 13 12

Printed and bound in Great Britain by
CPI Antony Rowe, Chippenham and Eastbourne

Contents

1
A Social History of the Crime Film

Is it possible to read a nation through its popular entertainment? With the growth of new critical theory, mainstream media ranging from television soap operas to comic books have been pressed into service as signifiers of the social and political ethos of individual countries, notably the USA. Needless to say, however much the illusion of verisimilitude is created by such entertainment media as film, in the final analysis the keyword remains illusion – any notions of reality are as false as those found in, say, reality TV – the careful organisation, staging and editing of events is directed towards one end: the presentation of a writer's or director's vision. Any truthfulness that may appear in the interstices is usually in the nature of a happy accident. To suggest, as this book will attempt to do, that Britain's long tradition of crime cinema may offer a more nuanced, intelligent and politically informed analysis of British society from the 1920s onwards than more overtly respectable 'heritage' cinema is something of a hostage to fortune – but there is a great deal of evidence to support this thesis, as I will attempt to show.

In many ways, the modest critical standing of much British crime cinema has afforded it a rich seam of possibilities. Genre cinema was for many years treated with critical disdain (consolidated by the fact that audiences – while enjoying it – regarded the field as nothing more than entertainment). But it didn't take long for intelligent filmmakers to utilise the language of classic crime cinema (gangsters, robberies, establishment-baiting policemen) in new and ingenious ways, frequently offering up a critique of

1

society by allusion. There is an interesting parallel here with the critical standing of literary crime fiction in Britain, which was similarly afforded little respect until such writers as P.D. James finessed the elements of psychology and characterisation first introduced by Golden Age novelists such as Dorothy L. Sayers, with the result that crime fiction on the printed page is now frequently reviewed in the broadsheets alongside more 'literary' genres. To some degree, there has been a parallel breakthrough for many filmmakers dealing in cinematic crime, but the level of acceptance has been more fitful. One of the principal aims of this book is to demonstrate the myriad ways in which British crime cinema is as worthy of serious critical attention as more self-consciously 'respectable' subjects. The most straightforward-seeming of films can furnish a revealing meta-text.

Throughout its long and colourful history, British crime cinema has encountered a series of problems peculiar to the genre. While the subject of the heist or ambitious robbery (in films such as Quentin Lawrence's *Cash on Demand* (1961) and Peter Yates' *Robbery* (1967)) has been relatively unproblematic, there are certain areas that proved to be incendiary when the films were examined by the British Board of Film Censors (the name of the organisation was changed in a piece of Orwellian rewriting to the British Board of Film Classification – appropriately, in 1984); and it is not hard to discern the reasons for the fuss. In the 1960s, the BBFC made little secret of the fact that it regarded its role as maintaining the rigid status quo of society as much as protecting the vulnerable public from sights that would cause offence or (worse still) inspire imitative behaviour. The 1961 Joseph Losey film *The Damned* featured scenes of gang violence in the original screenplay submitted to the Board and inspired a nannyish response. Registering unhappiness with the brutal young thugs, the Board was not persuaded by the filmmakers' stated aim of targeting an adult audience, pointing out that the offending sections would appeal to 'morons of a violent inclination' – revealingly talking about the sort of 'X'-certificate film patrons the Board wanted to protect. Interestingly, this protection extended into the political dimension, perhaps influenced by director Losey's recent pillorying by the House Un-American Activities Committee as part of its anti-communist initiatives (which had driven Losey to this country – and thereby facilitated the making of several classic British crime films, such as *Blind Date* (1959) and *The Criminal* (1960)). The Board took particular exception to the perceived left-leaning attitudes of the filmmakers involved in *The Damned* (not just Losey), identifying them as (most probably) 'ardent fellow travellers or fully paid-up members of the Communist Party' (BBFC internal report, 24 April 1961).

As so often in the history of British film censorship from the 1940s onwards, it is the potentially destabilising effect of popular cinema that has been seen to be as threatening as any graphic violence or sexuality (although the latter elements were clearly felt to be the vehicle through which anti-establishment sentiment was delivered, and crime films were firmly fixed in the popular imagination as depicting more explicit erotic activity and female nudity than more mainstream product). Britain's highly successful horror films were the target of much press hysteria (and swingeing cuts imposed before release, with pre-censorship at the script stage), but this strand of the popular cinema was generally dismissed as an example of the debasement of popular culture (exploited by cynical filmmakers), while British crime films – recognisably in settings much more like the real world than the castles and taverns of Transylvania – were far more subversive. The parallels with Hollywood and the Hays Code panics of the late 1930s could not be more pronounced: as with the Hollywood gangster movies of James Cagney, Humphrey Bogart *et al.*, the reason given for the strict monitoring of this product was its capacity for inspiring imitative behaviour when the gangsters were presented in glamorised fashion. Ironically, later films in which such charges might have had an iota of justification (Arthur Penn's *Bonnie and Clyde* (1967) or Brian De Palma's *Scarface* (1983)) did not have equivalents in the classic British crime films; even the most iconic of modern British gangster films, Mike Hodges' *Get Carter* (1971), casts a notably cold eye on its ruthless protagonist, however charismatically he is played by Michael Caine. The ideological distance between British filmmakers and their criminal subjects was not assessed by those who sought to neuter and homogenise crime cinema.

In terms of chronology, the most important changes in British commercial cinema took hold in the 1940s, with the relatively small number of films in the crime genre made in the 1930s fashioned along conventional lines. As such, this study will concentrate principally on the 1940s to the present day. But studying the British crime film from the mid-1940s to the present offers a microcosm of the events that shaped the nation, from the election of the post-war Labour government through the subsequent shift from middle-class drawing-room drama (and its attendant social strictures) to the new dominance of Northern-based realist drama (which was, nevertheless, often the product of impeccably middle-class artists such as Lindsay Anderson and Karel Reisz). This trajectory takes into account the changing view of class and a freeing-up of previously rigid sexual attitudes (attitudes embraced from press to pulpit, despite the realities of changing sexual behaviour). However, perhaps the most significant change in perception in the post-war years was the new, more jaundiced take on the establishment (be it the government, the legal profession or the conventional, hidebound moralism of the press). In this respect, the often iconoclastic impulses of popular entertainment such as the crime film could be read as a commentary on the shifting sands of moral viewpoints. And while the establishment might not always have recognised the taboo-busting strategies beneath the surface of popular narratives by filmmakers (usually, though not always, politically on the left), there was an uncomfortable awareness that something was going on under the attractive, dangerous sheen of the crime movie; less easy to target and censor than the increasingly more overt violence and sexuality of specific sequences, but more worrying because of its undefined nature.

By the late 1950s, comfortable middle-class cinema was under attack from a variety of directions. The growth of the British New Wave (more colloquially, kitchen-sink cinema, itself a development of the groundbreaking dramas performed at London's Royal Court Theatre, along with the working-class novels of such writers as Alan Sillitoe) offered one kind of destabilisation of the status quo, but these works frequently ended with the defeat of the blue-collar hero (in fact, this was part of a tradition extending as far back as Thomas Hardy's grim fate for the aspiring protagonist of *Jude the Obscure*). British crime cinema, however, offered something different: were audiences obliged to automatically disapprove of the lawbreaking anti-heroes in these films? Even without the moralistic imperatives of film censorship, it was axiomatic that criminals must be seen to be punished – or at least not rewarded for their lawbreaking activities. Filmmakers were well aware that the destruction of the central character in such films provided a satisfactory dramatic culmination (a paradigm here might be Robert Warshow's celebrated essay 'The Gangster as Tragic Hero' in *The Immediate Experience* (1962), which identified the struggle/success/destruction progression of the characters in crime films as a development of some of the narrative strategies of Shakespeare); it is perhaps no accident that one of the most intriguing of British crime films is Ken Hughes' modern-day Shakespearean drama *Joe Macbeth* (1955) – the Bard's notions of hubris transplanted into the present.

However, it would be too simplistic to say that disapproval of the crime genre was the prerogative of the right, a disapproval based on the idea that an anti-establishment critique was being freighted into popular entertainment (a syndrome that had actually happened in another field, when the 1960s television series *Robin Hood* employed writers who were *personae non gratae* in the USA in the McCarthy era). In fact, some of the most swingeing criticism of the crime field has come from the left. George Orwell's famously prissy outrage at the British author James Hadley Chase in Orwell's essay 'Raffles and Miss Blandish' (1944) was directed at what the author perceived as the 'depraved' nature of popular fiction such as that written by Chase, as opposed to the more innocent crime narratives of E.W. Hornung's master thief Raffles. Orwell's criticisms were applied verbatim to St John Legh Clowes' maladroit 1948 British film of the Chase novel. Ironically, this adaptation highlighted another recurrent strand of the British crime film: the attempt to produce a simulacra of American cinema by importing an American star and attempting to imitate – however crassly – the characteristics of the US product, in much the same way as many British readers had been fooled into thinking that James Hadley Chase was an American author.

The popularity of the British crime film rarely faltered over the years, even though the level of achievement within individual movies was widely disparate. Audiences were happy to recognise the familiar elements of the genre and applaud the novel uses to which they were put, whether the filmmakers involved were journeymen or major talents. Speaking of the latter, it is important to remember that one of the greatest of all English directors, Alfred Hitchcock, opted to utilise the crime form for some of the most personal and fully achieved works in the field. And regarding the Master of Suspense, it is worth noting that, although worldwide film criticism caught up with his achievement initially through the insights of French writers such as Truffaut, Godard and Chabrol (who championed him as something more than just a talented entertainer), opinionated English critics (such as the team who put together the highly influential – if sporadically published – journal *Movie*, essentially an English *Cahiers du Cinéma*) took a stand against the lazy view of the day (most notably espoused in the establishment magazine *Sight and Sound*) that the crime film was not worthy of serious consideration. Genre directors such as the otherwise ignored Seth Holt (whose *Nowhere to Go* (1958) was noted as a remarkable crime film) were celebrated by the magazine as a reaction against establishment neglect. But British films in this new pantheon were greatly outnumbered by the American product – *Movie's* first issue, in fact, was a broadside against the then-moribund state of British cinema. The current incarnation of *Sight and Sound,* however, reflects the 360° shift in attitudes to the crime film since that era: in the twenty-first century, genre product will be given quite as much attention as more worthy 'arthouse' material.

Of course, while good and bad crime cinema alike entertained audiences over the years, there is no question that the levelling effect of history has now identified a canon of films that are worthy of the critical acclaim commensurate with their popularity. And in many cases, the contribution of individual directors in the crime field has been comfortably ahead of their achievement in other fields, the possibilities of reinvigorating the familiar elements of the genre having created some of their most inventive and individual work (cf. Robert Hamer, Val Guest, Carol Reed, Ken Hughes, Vernon Sewell and Mike Hodges, among others).

To some degree, British crime film has had to overcome not just the disapprobation of moral guardians (both official and self-styled), but also what was (at least until the 1960s) something of an image problem: the notion that the English version of the classic American crime film was somehow twee, bloodless and etiolated. By the late 1960s non-cinéastes would be more than likely to think of the field – with a few exceptions – as hidebound and irrelevant, ephemeral products which had only a peripheral connection with the lives of real criminals – or real people. A series of unorthodox films (most notably Donald Cammell and Nicolas Roeg's phantasmagoric and hyper-violent *Performance* (1970)) were to bring about radical revisions of perception, setting the bar higher for any subsequent films (as well as extending the parameters of erotic activity and physical brutality). But this apparent breakthrough is not the whole story – looking beneath the sometimes deceptively sedate surfaces of earlier British crime movies reveals several unorthodox and subversive intelligences at work, reinventing the form in forceful and radical fashion.

Any study such as this cannot, of course, ignore the immense popularity of TV crime shows and their slew of tenacious detectives (usually derived from literary crime fiction, a field that gleaned levels of respectability considerably before the filmed variety). This book places the best work of such TV dramas in context. In fact, the dividing line between TV and film grows ever more tenuous, with a new adaptation of Mark Billingham's novel featuring his tough detective Tom Thorne (*Sleepyhead* (2010), starring David Morrissey) staged, shot on high-definition film and edited in exactly the same kinetic fashion as a cinema feature film. With a new TV frankness mirroring what is possible in the cinema today, the divisions between the various outlets for crime fiction are growing ever more blurred.

Themes and trends

The crime fiction movie is in the rudest of health, continuing to inspire some trenchant and accomplished work among the most ambitious filmmakers, who are as keen to incorporate political and social comment into their audience-pleasing narratives as any of their talented predecessors. It is a function of this book to identify and celebrate the most interesting work in the crime fiction genre, both past and present, along with a variety of key themes. From the cosy criminality of Basil Dearden's *The Blue Lamp* (1950, significant in its day, despite the now-quaint casting of the urbane Dirk Bogarde as the sullen teenage thug), through the intriguing take on class and social divisions thrown up in the same director's *The League of Gentlemen* (1960), to the critique of Thatcherite acquisitiveness and property speculation in John Mackenzie's state-of-the-nation crime epic *The Long Good Friday* (1979), the genre has never lacked for possibilities of keen insights into the society of the day (possibilities enthusiastically embraced by filmmakers keen to expand the potentialities of the genre). The treatment of juvenile delinquency has veered from the exploitative (as in Lewis Gilbert's *Cosh Boy* (1953)) to the sensitive (as in Sidney Furie's *The Leather Boys* (1963)), while violent criminal psychopathology in such films as Peter Medak's *The Krays* (1990) has been balanced by the nuanced (if forceful) treatment of compromised policemen in such films as Val Guest's *Hell is a City* (1959) and David Greene's *The Strange Affair* (1968) – all of which are addressed here.

Other topics discussed include censorship battles over contentious issues of sex in such films as Guy Hamilton's *The Party's Over* (1963) and changing attitudes to capital punishment (J. Lee Thompson's *Yield to the Night* (1956)).

Of course, the anti-heroes of the genre needed a new breed of actor to do them (rough) justice, and such edgy performers were to turn up in profusion, from the Celts Sean Connery and Stanley Baker to English actors such as John Mills and Tom Bell, greatly extending the parameters of the representation of masculinity in a variety of hard-hitting films.

While mainstream British cinema trod gingerly around such combustible subjects as paedophilia, miscegenation and homosexuality, the crime genre addressed these topics directly in such films as Basil Dearden's *Victim* (1961) and *Sapphire* (1959) and the long-unseen *Never Take Sweets from a Stranger* (Cyril Frankel, 1960), ostensibly set in Canada, but palpably English in conception and casting. Like most films discussed in this volume, the DVD revolution has made this intriguing film available again in an uncensored print.

The snobbery directed against British crime films has long been banished in the literary field, and the work of writers such as Graham Greene and Eric Ambler has been adapted with varying degrees of success; Greene's *Brighton Rock* enjoyed a creditable adaption by the Boulting Brothers in 1947, with Richard Attenborough terrifying as the sadistic Catholic killer Pinkie. The Boulting Brothers' version, despite its respectable literary antecedents, enjoyed unwelcome censor attention for its bloody razor-wielding assaults – and such attention is a recurrent theme in these pages (the modern version of *Brighton Rock*, directed by Rowan Joffe in 2010, enjoyed no such interference, being made in a more liberal era). But crime cinema is – and should be, for its own health – the cinema of the unacceptable.

Influence of the novel

Any social history of the British crime film (focusing on the variety of strategies used in order to address more radical notions than those in more 'reputable' mainstream cinema) could attain Proustian lengths – this study is relatively concise, but I trust that no worthwhile or ambitious films have escaped my critical net. And the fact that the genre continues to produce highly accomplished work on a regular basis is a real cause for celebration.

British Noir as a genre grew out of American hardboiled fiction of the 1930s and 1940s, initially engendered by such authors as Dashiell Hammett, Raymond Chandler and W.R. Burnett. It was essentially a product of the Second World War, though its antecedents preceded the war years. As with the American pulps, the protagonists were often solitary, conflicted men, customarily in thrall to femme fatales, with crime a social leveller that elided the upper crust and street life. Like its American counterpart, British Noir was emblematic of the anxieties and social upheavals of the era that produced it.

The 1930s were to prove a fecund period for ambitious British crime writers. One of the earliest novelists to write about crime and criminals in London was Hugh Desmond Clevely (1898–1964), whose novel *The Gang-Smasher* (1928) featured John Martinson, a tough and no-nonsense anti-hero up against the capital's ruthless crime bosses who was to reappear throughout the 1930s. Clevely, the son of a Bristol clergyman, was an unlikely creator of hardboiled fiction, but died in a grimly appropriate fashion, discovered face down in a weir on the River Stour in Dorset in May 1964, covered in blood. The mystery of his death was never solved.

The first significant British crime writer, however, was probably Peter Cheyney (1896–1951) whose signature character, Lemmy Caution, sported the two-fisted trappings of the pugnacious American private eye and is generally considered to be the template for Mickey Spillane's thick-ear detective character Mike Hammer. The effect of Cheyney's novel *This Man is Dangerous* (1936) was seismic; it was to be the inaugural book in a lengthy series about Caution (whose name was as notably inappropriate as Peter O'Donnell's Modesty Blaise was to be later), cutting a swathe through the crooked peddlers of drugs and prostitutes in the metropolitan underworld. Tut-tutting accusations of violence and brutality ensured that the novels enjoyed massive sales, and Cheyney was in fact the first British writer to successfully re-export hardboiled writing to its birthplace, America; his books enjoyed great success in the USA.

But the best-known (and most notorious) British author of crime fiction was James Hadley Chase (1906–1985), whose *No Orchids for Miss Blandish* (1939) is among the most famous titles in crime fiction, British or American. Inspired by a news story about the kidnapping of an American heiress and her savage mauling at the hands of her abductees (based in the book on the ruthless Ma Barker clan), the novel inspired outraged accusations of degeneracy and was, inevitably, a million-seller. Chase, whose birth name was René Lodge Brabazon Raymond, was the son of an army medical officer, who (inspired by the sales figures of American pulp writers and, notably, fellow British resident Peter Cheyney) decided to crack the lucrative hardboiled genre. George Orwell's famous criticism that reading *No Orchids* was like 'taking a header into a cesspool' helped ensure healthy sales, and Chase's subsequent novels (over 80 of them) similarly dispensed unabashed erotic and violent action for the delectation of readers. Most of these books were set in the USA, though Chase never visited the country and utilised atlases and travel guides for topography, while slang dictionaries helped with the language and idioms.

Similarly, the prodigious sales of Hank Janson (actually Stephen Daniel Francis, 1917–1989) made him one of the key British chroniclers of the gangster world in the 1940s and 1950s, with books that similarly upset the censors (an essential *sine qua non*) while delighting readers. Janson/Francis was born in Lambeth, south London, and came from a desperately poor tenement block upbringing, When he heard in 1946 that a paperback distributor was seeking writing to slake the demand for hardboiled crime fiction, 'Hank Janson' was born with such novels as *When Dames Get Tough*, inspired by the unabashed fare from the British James Hadley Chase and the American James M. Cain.

The most cultish of British Noir writers is unquestionably Gerald Kersh (1911–1968), who was initially undervalued after his death, with much of his writing out of print and difficult to track down. Born to an immigrant Jewish family in Teddington, Kersh nearly died of lung congestion when he was still a child. But it was in his boyhood that he first began to write. As a young man he asked the bestselling Edgar Wallace (who then enjoyed a superstar status) for advice, but received something of a dusty answer. However, Kersh's personal preoccupation with Soho's lowlifes and working girls (he haunted the area) provided him with plenty of colourful raw material. *Night and the City*, first published in 1938, tells of Harry Fabian, a bottom-feeding aspirant gangster and pimp who traverses a seamy Soho and is trying (among other things) to become a wrestling promoter by persuading a past-his-best wrestler back into the ring – with disastrous results. A sale of the film rights gleaned $40,000 for the author. (Kersh intensely disliked the script of the film that was ultimately made, but it is still a significant British Noir film.)

In 1947, the author created another distinctive piece of crime fiction with *Prelude to a Certain Midnight*, concerning the desperate search for a child-murderer – as dark a narrative as anything Kersh had written. Since his death, his reputation has flourished – though he is still largely unread.

Writers further up the ladder of literary acceptability also proved ingredients for the criminous mix that fuelled the British crime film – such as Graham Greene (1904–1991). Had Greene not been the author of the 'serious' novels (such as *A Burnt-Out Case* and *The Heart of the Matter*) which marked him out as one of the greatest of all English writers, his 'entertainments' (as he rather dismissively described them) would constitute a body of crime and thriller fiction almost without equal in the field. Early in his career, Greene introduced an element of the spy story into *The Confidential Agent* (1939), in which D, the agent of a Latin government (Republican Spain in all but name), figures in a narrative that was clearly influential on such later writers as John le Carré. The latter has long acknowledged Greene's considerable influence on his work. Greene's most celebrated crime novel, of course, is *Brighton Rock* (1938, with its psychotic young anti-hero Pinkie), which the author decided to move out of his 'entertainments' category. This sometimes slippery shifting of genres by the author was always a rather arbitrary endeavour: the moral concerns of the thrillers were often precisely those of the more serious books, while the pursuit narratives of the serious books (such as the whisky priest on the run in *The Power and the Glory* (1940)) had precisely the same visceral trajectory as the thrillers. But all the books have that dark and sardonic view of existence which quickly became identified as 'Greeneland', a queasy admixture of the seedy, the surrealistically funny and the dangerous. Two other crucial ingredients need to be identified in the Greene mix. One is the author's uneasy relationship with Catholicism (he converted under the influence of his wife's piety, but was never an unquestioning believer after the fashion of his correspondent and colleague Evelyn Waugh, who chastised Greene for his doubts). The other is that Greene's work is also distinguished by its frank and realistic depiction of the sexual relations between men and women – not, that is to say, in any graphic fashion, but with an unblinking assessment of the joys and despair concomitant with sexual passion.

Brighton Rock, with its brilliantly realised picture of a violent seaside underworld, is as strong a starting point for those new to Greene as anything he wrote, but such superbly honed thrillers as *The Ministry of Fear* (1943) demonstrate an authority and mastery of the narrative form that makes most practitioners look like mere journeymen. Despite the writer's long association with the cinema, the number of first-rate films associated with his work is relatively few (Carol Reed's *The Third Man*, of course, and Fritz Lang made a creditable stab at *The Ministry of Fear*), but rereading such exemplary novels as *The Quiet American* (1955, in which CIA double-dealing is the mainspring of the plot and the Vietnam conflict was introduced to many readers as a significant subject for a novel) is a salutary reminder that the best way to approach the writer is (unsurprisingly) through the books rather than the hit-or-miss films (the first cinematic version of *The Quiet American* downplayed the anti-American underpinnings of the book, and even though a later version did more justice to this theme, the author's particular tone of voice was once again lost). It might be argued that John le Carré and the playwright Harold Pinter adopted Greene's once-controversial (and sometimes over-splenetic) mistrust of all American foreign policy.

Greene's crime and thriller novels offer a wide panoply of pleasures, such as the wonderfully mordant humour of *Our Man in Havana* (1958, which drew on Greene's own experiences in the intelligence services), and it is notable that even in the twenty-first century all of his novels remain as vivid and involving as when they were first published. *Stamboul Train* (1932), for instance, is an exhilarating Hitchcockian adventure shot through with moral ambiguity, while *A Gun for Sale* (1936, with its chillingly drawn killer, Raven, and a political assassination that generates the threat of war) is far more than a period piece.

Of course, there are those readers who will find difficulties arising from the author's self-torturing Catholicism (a trait replicated in several of his protagonists), but Greene (unlike Waugh) was never an apologist for the Catholic Church. The acquisition of faith in his books is rarely a life-enhancing, positive experience. In fact, the overriding impression that the reader receives is that most of his heroes would be far better off without the dubious consolations of religion. And Greene himself was far too much of a self-confessed sensualist to be at ease with the anti-sex asceticism of the Catholic Church (it's possible to imagine Greene's wry response to the host of recent scandals involving priests), so agnostic readers need not allow these religious elements to prevent them from tackling one of the most considerable bodies of work (both the thrillers and literary novels) in English literature. And thriller readers will be doing themselves a considerable disservice if they read only the 'entertainments' – such books as *The Comedians* (1966) generate quite as much suspense as Greene's more avowedly generic novels (the latter may in fact be the best book for the novice Greeneian to tackle – this is the novel that made Haiti's dictator Papa Doc Duvalier very hot under the collar, a testament to its persuasiveness).

A relatively small number of crime novels have supplied material for the British cinema (a somewhat ironic situation, given the imposing wealth of excellent crime fiction written in the UK) – a situation which continues to this day, directors frequently showing a preference for original film material. In 1926, Alfred Hitchcock's inventive silent film *The Lodger* was derived from Marie Lowndes' tale of Jack the Ripper, while such films as 1933's *A Study in Scarlet* drew on the work of Sir Arthur Conan Doyle. The immensely prolific Edgar Wallace, now a dimly-remembered name for many modern readers, enjoyed a multiplicity of adaptations, with over 150 movies drawn from his work (the author was equally popular in Germany and enjoyed an even longer-lasting vogue in that country); Carol Reed made a distinctive adaptation of Gordon Wellesley's *Report on a Fugitive* (as *Night Train to Munich*) in 1940, while Arthur Woods' *They Drive by Night* in 1938 utilised a now-neglected book by James Curtis. However, of British novelists, Graham Greene provided particularly fecund material for the cinema industry, with such well-regarded films as *This Gun for Hire* (1942), *Went the Day Well?* (1942), *Ministry of Fear* (1944), *The Confidential Agent* (1945),

The Man Within (1947), *The Fallen Idol* (1948), *The Third Man* (1949), *The Heart of the Matter* (1953), *Our Man in Havana* (1959) and *The Quiet American* (1958), not to mention, of course, the twice-adapted *Brighton Rock*. In 1947, Anthony Kimmins created the memorable *Mine Own Executioner* from the book by the talented Nigel Balchin (who Kimmins wisely employed to write the screenplay). Michael Powell was to be attracted (some years later) to the author's *The Small Back Room*. 1950s filmmakers turned fruitfully to published novels for their inspiration; Vernon Sewell's *Soho Incident* (1956), for instance, did some justice to Robert Westerby's *Wide Boys Never Work*.

A certain level of economy and expertise (rather than inspiration) was a default mode of British crime film from the 1940s to the 1960s, as may be discerned in two examples: Lance Comfort's *Pit of Darkness* (1961) and – to a far lesser degree – in Norman Lee's *The Case of Charles Peace* (1949). Although neither film ever really rises above the quotidian, there are certain retrospective pleasures to be had in the sheer professionalism involved in turning out this kind of product (though the Lee film is generally stultifying and workaday, conforming to all the low expectations that are now the cinéaste's default verdict on most British 'B' films of this ilk – making the discovery of the better movies all the more cherishable). The former (and later) film, *Pit of Darkness*, is the livelier piece of work, with the reliable off-the-peg British actor William Franklyn as the amnesiac partner in a safe-making firm who is discovered unconscious on a Wapping bombsite (the film is a snapshot of the area, pre-expensive yuppie flats and gated hi-tech newspaper offices) with no recollection of his recent past. He finds out that his wife has hired a detective and that this man has been murdered. What's more, his own company has installed a safe in a large country house which has been scientifically burgled – and he is a logical suspect. What follows involves the working out of a complex (and unlikely) plot, handled with the kind of filmmaking nous that was Lance Comfort's stock-in-trade.

The workaday Norman Lee film *The Case of Charles Peace* (also a Butchers Films production and made at Merton Park studios) is based on a true story concerning a miscarriage of justice. While fireworks are never lit by either film (and Lee is largely content to move his actors around while simply keeping them in shot), there are incidental pleasures (at least in the Lance Comfort film), including the casting which can draw on the large coterie of character actors on which the British cinema has always been able to draw – *Pit of Darkness* boasts the matchless character actor Nigel Green in a part that will have viewers wishing he had been given more to do here than standard red herring duties.

The merest glance at the extensive range of British crime movies, however, demonstrates that even the most cursory excavation will unearth riches. Some remarkable films in the field are already celebrated (and have achieved cult status), while others remain unfairly neglected – as this book will show.

2
The Age of Austerity: Post-War Crime Films

Any examination of the changes in post-war British society as reflected in the nation's crime cinema must concentrate on the various social trends touched upon (sometimes obliquely) in the films: prostitution, black marketeering and the new questioning of the values of the professions and the establishment. It is possible to identify certain individual films as exemplars of this new awareness. Even in the late 1940s and early 1950s, signs could be detected of a loosening of conventional attitudes to sex, marriage, etc., despite the iron-clad moral codes of censors, local watch committees and important film producers such as the Presbyterian J. Arthur Rank, famous for insisting on outward rectitude. In light of these attitudes, the (hidden) subversive nature of some of the films is provocative.

In the immediate post-war years, there remained a firm distinction (in terms of the critical response) between two kinds of British film. The more respectable branch of national cinema was epitomised by adaptations of literary classics and films which had been injected with a conspicuous moral uplift (the latter to be found in – for instance – war films, which traded in British resilience and the value of communal effort in the face of foreign belligerence). All of these film enjoyed great popularity, but the cinema-going public consumed with equal avidness films which centred on criminals – or at least those individuals in pursuit of criminals. In the 1940s, of course, the habit of cinema attendance was so ingrained in the public that (to some degree) healthy box office was guaranteed for almost anything that played in the thriving cinemas of the day (before the destabilising onslaught of television in the 1950s and 1960s), and the popularity of the American crime film happily coexisted with the home-grown variety. Even maladroit British crime films (of which several are unapologetically discussed in this book) thrived in this climate, and audiences of the day responded to those elements which they felt to be a true representation of modern British life (although the enjoyable – if ludicrous – concoctions of Gainsborough studios, as represented by James Mason's sneer and Margaret Lockwood's cleavage, were catnip to the audiences). The all-powerful Rank Organisation reigned supreme and the flow of morally uplifting prestige productions was assiduously kept up, matching the stream of more populist, audience-pleasing material. Patriotism of a relatively unambiguous variety was to be found in Laurence Olivier's colourful adaptation of Shakespeare's *Henry V*, but such elements were absent from the crime films of the post-war years. In terms of the critical appraisal of genre product, there was little attempt to respond intelligently to the virtues of popular crime films, and in this respect the UK mirrored the establishment critical attitudes of the USA, with conspicuous 'prestige' productions afforded sober attention and respect. Only by the late 1950s (and via, among other things, the influence of the French critics who wrote in the influential *Cahiers du Cinéma*) were the directors of tough, transgressive crime movies being taken seriously, and the careers of such commercial (though exemplary) filmmakers as Don Siegel and Anthony Mann were finally given their due. So it is hardly surprising that the British equivalents of these directors were similarly neglected.

Personal elements and individual stylistic flourishes had to be shoehorned into commercial projects in both the UK and the USA by ambitious filmmakers in such a fashion that these flourishes did not draw attention to themselves but were always at the service of the material. However, critics have often underestimated the intelligence of cinema audiences and pointed to the taste for the banal that those audiences all too often demonstrated. As such, one fact was rarely remarked upon by critics of the day: the best of the British crime films, as well as being adroitly made pieces of popular entertainment, frequently incorporated elements of societal criticism that were not to be found in other popular product.

A curious Orwellian doublethink may be seen to be at work in the presentation of the English zeitgeist in many crime films. While the shibboleths of British society are generally presented as admirable and eternal (from the plucky industry of the working classes through the solid morality of the middle classes to a respect for the past and the eternal verities of the upper crust), the criminal impulse is generally presented as destabilising and dangerous. The latter is, however, also charged with energy and vitality. In this way, a distinctly mixed message is sent out: while the lawbreakers presented in these films invite the comeuppance that is their customary lot, their acts of transgression represent a dynamic response to society, however misguided. In some ways, this response – a crucial part of the appeal of crime fiction – finds its most potent realisation in the cinema rather than on the printed page, inasmuch as film is inevitably the more kinetic medium.

The family is often at the centre of many of these narratives and is usually presented in a sympathetic (if deeply unsexy) fashion. The lifestyle of a criminal – by corollary – frequently involves a seductive libidinal excess; it is possible for audiences (while paying lip service to the values of the family) to vicariously enjoy the sexual licence that it is so often a part of the film criminal's lifestyle. Certainly, the half-undressed girlfriends of the lawbreakers in British crime movies were customarily expected to show more flesh than their more conventional sisters, the 'good' girls. Occasionally, films appeared which suggested something destabilising beneath the surface of the English family or other placid inhabitants of this island – most famously, perhaps, in a non-crime film: Alberto Cavalcanti's celebrated Graham Greene adaptation *Went the Day Well?* (1942), in which the well-behaved, bourgeois residents of a British village are seen to be capable of massive violence against German invaders (to finesse the subversive nature of the film, even the reputable local squire is shown to be a quisling).

To some degree, a maintenance of the status quo relating to crime might be observed in the excellent Dickens adaptations directed by David Lean, particularly his *Great Expectations* (1946), in which the criminal Magwitch (while presented initially as threatening in the potentially throat-cutting, craggy form of Finlay Currie) ultimately behaves well. Here, Lean's film is perfectly at the service of Dickens' consistent ethos – everyone, from the rich to those on the fringes of society, should behave with humanity and charity. Such comforting notions, however, are largely absent from most British crime films.

Robert Hamer is now considered to be one of the greatest of British directors with an impressive (and highly individual) body of work before his career came to an all-too-sudden conclusion. One of his most celebrated films is the intelligent adaptation of Arthur La Bern's novel *It Always Rains on Sunday* that he made for Ealing Studios in 1947. Like many of the most intriguing of the studio's films, it is, to some degree, a subversion of the cosy Ealing ethos; despite the insistence of Michael Balcon that the majority of Ealing films present a certain roseate view of England, several directors were able to circumvent this stricture and produce something rich and strange. As long as an acknowledgement was made of the moral code of other Ealing films, it was occasionally possible to take a notably darker view of both British society and human existence – another example of this syndrome is Alexander Mackendrick's black comedy *The Ladykillers* (1955). Hamer's *It Always Rains on Sunday* could be one of the most astringent and least compromising films made by the studio, and was perhaps influenced by Italian neorealism in its unvarnished picture of crime and lives lived in quiet desperation. John McCallum plays Tommy Swann, a criminal specialising in smash-and-grab raids who breaks out of prison and makes tracks to his old territory, Bethnal Green. He is hoping to find shelter with Rose, an ex-lover (played by Googie Withers), but his thoughts are straying to the notion of a trip to Cape Town. Of course, nothing turns out as either Tommy or the self-deluding Rose expects. Initially, Rose, who nurtures memories of Tommy as a charismatic and well-dressed figure, is dismayed to discover the shabby criminal hiding out in her back garden, but decides to help him. However, his re-emergence into her life obliges her to confront everything that is negative and unfulfilling about her existence – principally her unstimulating marriage to the dull older widower George (played by Edward Chapman), not to mention conflicts with the latter's daughters and her own wayward son Alfie (who will before long turn to blackmail). Other characters are mixed into this ill-matched assembly, including a libidinous bandleader, a crooked spiv and a motley crew of criminals, both small and big time.

Hamer's merciless picture of the unsentimental reality behind the otherwise reassuring image of English community is unsparing, and what grants real verisimilitude here is the sharply observed period detail (including rationing and the unlovely sexual encounters between people who have very few options). But the director is not blind to the life-enhancing energy of the society he shows us and there are other pictures of working-class life (with a nice ear for the argot of the period – including the pervasive Jewish influence on speech patterns; the equivalent today might be that of black culture). The film effortlessly rises above most other similar fare and is even able to bear the tragic dimension that its director confers on the ill-fated lovers who are obliged to swap a romantic image of love for the cheerless realities of a life in which the next knock on the door may be that of the police. What's more, the location shooting in the film ensures that its interest as a historical document of London almost matches the dramatic values that Hamer finesses with such adroitness.

In the post-war period, the work in the UK of certain American directors (notably Joseph Losey) often demonstrated an intensity and readiness to move beyond the parameters of standard dramatic procedures. This adventurousness produced work which sometimes showed a more hysterical edge than British filmmakers were comfortable with. While the director Edward Dmytryk was nothing like as accomplished as Losey, he nevertheless demonstrated a readiness to confront such issues as the psychopathology of madness in a fashion that most UK directors of the 1940s and 1950s were eschewing. *Obsession* (1948) perhaps owes as much as anything else to the larger-than-life actor Robert Newton's readiness to suggest violent madness beneath a barely controlled surface. (To some degree, this was Newton's trademark – he was a menacing Bill Sykes in David Lean's film of *Oliver Twist* before his eye-rolling performance as Long John Silver in *Treasure Island* made him fodder for a million TV impersonators.)

The scenario of *Obsession* is worthy of Newton's characteristic intensity, playing a man discovering that his wife is having an affair. He imprisons her lover in a bomb-damaged house while slowly filling up a bathtub with nitric acid, transported in small measures (in a hot water bottle, no less). It's the sort of bizarre detail which would have appealed to the Anglophile crime writer Patricia Highsmith, who also enjoyed setting her cruel narratives in the otherwise sedate British middle-class world of manicured lawns and garden parties. But where Highsmith (herself a woman of fascinating conflicts) is happy to locate twisted psychopathology in the most ordinary-seeming of individuals, the casting of Newton in *Obsession* forces the audience to look upon the character *sub specie aeternitatis* – there is no question of identifying with the Newton figure, as Dmytryk presents him as a specimen, something 'other' from the audience, rather than as an identification figure for those who, prompted by jealousy, might jettison conventional notions of right and wrong. Impressive though the film is, finally it has very little to say beyond the relating of a grotesque and ingenious *conte cruel* – though the notion of bourgeois decorum is given a rattling. The director's other British film, *The End of the Affair* (an adaptation of the Graham Greene novel), once again demonstrated that the director had less-than-penetrating aperçus to impart about British life, with the latter film a heavily compromised version of Greene's original, fatally flawed by the casting of an American leading man, Van Johnson, who gave a colourless performance.

As English as *Obsession* is *Trent's Last Case* (Herbert Wilcox, 1952), a film which is both a rarity and a curio – a famous film of a famous crime novel (by E.C. Bentley) that has been difficult to see for years. The body of Manderson, an autocratic American financial tycoon, is found in the grounds of his Hampshire mansion, shot neatly in the left eye by a revolver that he had given his English secretary John Marlowe. The coroner's verdict is suicide, but Philip Trent – famed painter, newspaper reporter but above all, crime investigator – is uneasy. Sent down to cover the story, he soon concludes that Marlowe in fact killed Manderson – until a confrontation with the secretary at Manderson's widow's request soon reveals a piquant twist in the mystery. The appearance of a customarily operatic Orson Welles as Manderson totally unbalances the film, but in a pleasurably over-the-top fashion.

The necessity of importing American stars to ensure transatlantic sales produced interesting results in Wilcox's film, but other examples of the syndrome afforded intriguing clashes of accents and mores. Before the notorious and sexually provocative *Beat Girl* (1960, discussed later), the director Edmond T. Gréville had made an idiosyncratic and distinctive entry in the post-austerity crime genre with *Noose* (1948). This cynical piece began by showing a poster which read – with heavy irony – 'We work or we want' (a forlorn Central Office of Information attempt to alert the British to their parlous economic state in the late 1940s). In fact, the 'work' in this film (apart from the honest crust earned by a foolhardy journalist) consists of racketeering, smuggling, counterfeiting money and sundry other illegal enterprises. The film featured imported American character actor Joseph Calleia as the vicious Italian black marketeer Sugiani who is accruing considerable wealth from his illegal activities until a reporter (played by another American, Carole Landis) decides to target him. When another of Sugiani's victims is washed up from the River Thames, the reporter – realising that she is out of her depth – enlists the aid of her boyfriend Jumbo Hyde (a colourless Derek Farr) and a gang of boxers (the latter a signally unlikely plot device). The unusual material offered to Gréville here clearly inspired the director to adopt an unorthodox approach, and the standard devices of the genre are given an unusual – and even eccentric – spin. It must have inspired Gréville to realise that he had a particularly interesting cast: the always effectively sinister Calleia (an actor whose menacing physiognomy ensured that he usually played brutal characters such as the black marketeer here, though ill-advised humour constantly undercuts the threat); the brittle, vulnerable and (regrettably) short-lived Carole Landis (*Noose* was to be one of her last films); and, as a very camp, fast-talking, Max Miller-style spiv, Nigel Patrick (who makes the most of a colourfully written part here). The misjudged humour takes over completely in a ludicrous final mass knockabout fight (with 'wah-wah' trumpet scoring) and the film's sense of impeding violence is further undercut by censorship excisions: the black marketer's sexy, abused mistress slips his knuckle dusters on her own fingers to give him a taste of his own medicine – which goes unseen. The same is true of the brutal beating of the Farr character, who suddenly appears (inexplicably) in a bloody state. To say that the film has now acquired a cult reputation is not strictly speaking the case – despite the excavation process performed on neglected American 'B' movies, their British equivalents have remained under wraps until recently, but the greater availability of such material (via, for instance, home cinema DVD releases) has allowed a long overdue re-evaluation of unusual movies such as *Noose*.

Disparate acting styles (as in Gréville's film) were commonplace in British crime cinema, as demonstrated in John Gilling's bleak and energetic *The Challenge* (1960, aka *It Takes a Thief*, adapted from the director's own story), with the unlikely duo of the pneumatic and spectacularly cantilevered Jayne Mansfield (trying something different from her roles as a non-too-bright sex bomb in films for American directors such as Frank Tashlin) as the lover of the British Shakespearean actor Anthony Quayle (a notable King Lear at the

Old Vic), giving a relatively understated performance here (the internationalism of the film is further enhanced by the presence of the German actor Carl Möhner, here in a desperately under-written part), but Gilling does not allow his supranational cast to create the kind of Europudding production all too dispiritingly present in cinemas a decade or so later to undercut his sharply observed picture of London in the 1960s. Mansfield is encouraged to try something different by her director (closer, in fact, to the actress's own intelligence, which she was obliged to downplay in most of her films – but the commanding qualities that Barbara Stanwyck would have brought to the role are absent). Though the first shot – a bare-chested Quayle getting up from a bed as a half-dressed Mansfield, shot from above her breasts, pulls on her stockings – plays on audience expectations of the actress (and, *inter alia*, provides a more sexually-charged image than the chaste British cinema of the time was wont to trade in). Nevertheless, Mansfield does her best, playing the tough, proactive Billy in a notably tense drama. Billy is the ringleader of a band of thieves and, after an attempted heist goes wrong, her boyfriend/fall-guy Jim (played by Quayle) is captured. But before his arrest, he is able to stash the loot from a failed robbery in a secret hiding place, and Billy and her associates are desperately trying to track down the missing booty.

John Gilling's command of this material is exemplary (he was later to do some impressive work for the Hammer Film studios) and, against all the odds (a screenplay which is structurally all over the place and characters routinely behaving in a stupid or irrational fashion), Gilling cannily moderates between the strikingly different acting styles of his protagonists, rendering the character interaction as piquant as the unfurling of the standard 'failed heist' crime narrative. The attempt at American-style toughness is only fitfully successful, but *The Challenge* is more forceful than most bloodless British product of the day and even incorporates some sardonic commentary on trade union intransigence and self-interest in a subplot that echoes the social critiques of the Boulting Brothers.

3
Class and Crime: Social Divisions

There was a marked readjustment of class expectations in the post-war period, a syndrome that accelerated in the late 1950s and early 1960s with less of the emphasis by earlier films on establishment values. The notion of a disenchanted army officer reacting to his shabby treatment by organising a robbery (*The League of Gentlemen*), once almost unthinkable, was now the basis of a popular crime film. Films of this period also deal interestingly with the intersection of the classes in society. A new meritocracy of crime began to emerge, along with a carefully maintained, class-bound social order that was still maintained (even within the context of criminal enterprise).

The relative insularity of the British Isles was, of course, the perfect breeding ground for the class divisions which exist to this day, despite a fudging of the lines. While the British filmmakers of the 1940s were largely middle class, the underlying ethos of many of the films appeared to aspire to a higher social strata, though several of the best filmmakers attempted to find an honest, uncondescending response to characters lower down the social scale. The granting of a degree of nobility to the inarticulate classes was a mark of Italian neo-realist movement, but the use (by such directors as Roberto Rossellini and Vittorio De Sica) of non-professional actors was not a phenomenon repeated in the UK; a slew of highly capable character actors were able to convincingly create British working class protagonists (although, ironically, several were interlopers: John Mills, as authentic-seeming a squaddie as he was an officer-class type, was ineluctably a middle-class actor, and the all-purpose import Sidney James – the archetypal Cockney – was South African). While working-class and lower middle-class attitudes were treated in a variety of cosy and unchallenging dramas of the day, it was only the crime film genre which found uneasy common cause between the pressures of working-class life and the opportunities offered by lawbreaking. In this respect, British crime films were closer to the American product of the 1940s which demonstrated a similar readiness to draw such parallels.

Interestingly, several decades later, the crime writer P.D. James was to create something of a furore when a remark of hers resulted in an acrimonious argument between her crime-writing peers and it became necessary to take sides: pro- or anti-James. The interpretation put on James' remarks was that working-class people have fewer moral choices to make than members of the middle class, simply because of the more pressing exigencies of their day-to-day lives. The hot-tempered (and frequently ill-informed) disagreements over this issue (almost exclusively between middle-class crime writers burnishing either their own Home Counties or working-class credentials) would have seemed quaint to the British crime filmmakers of the 1940s and 1950s. Nuances of moral choice may have been discreet in this era, but the broader canvases tackled by such films allowed for similar points to be made, even if the final agenda of the filmmakers was to entertain rather than to instruct. These crime films incorporated (and embraced) such working-class values as stoicism and resistance in the face of adversity, while noting the destruction that was the inevitable final fate of overreaching protagonists who turned to crime. An argument, however, might be made that P.D. James' controversial observations have a relevance (and resonance) for crime films made before the 1980s.

These notions of restricted moral choice are often presented in British cinema of the 1940s as an intelligently argued proposition rather than a bowing to the ludicrous dictates of the Hays Code, which was still untouchable in the USA, dictating that all transgressors (whether in the criminal or the sexual arenas) were to come to a sticky end. An indicator of class is, of course, accent. Although the arch-received pronunciation accents of many of the British films of this period now present a problem for viewers in the twenty-first century, the truthfulness of the characterisation (despite the artifice) is often startling. And this, it should be pointed out, is before the British New Wave (and directors such as Karel Reisz and Jack Cardiff) hauled UK cinema into an uncompromising confrontation with issues of class and social mobility.

There is an interesting shift in terms of the trajectory for the working-class protagonists of British crime movies and later social climbers (such as the calculating Joe Lampton in Jack Clayton's film of John Braine's *Room at the Top* (1958)); all are doomed to failure, but that failure comes in different forms. For the anti-heroes of the British New Wave, it is social (and, often, sexual) advancement with a heavy price to be paid: the achievement of the dream catapults the protagonist into Thoreau's life of quiet desperation; and success achieved in the British crime film has one of two inevitable corollaries – prison or death. Only by the 1960s (and such films as *The Italian Job*) were the parameters extended; rewards are seldom granted, but crime can, occasionally, pay.

An examination of issues of class is sometimes central to the British crime film; central, in fact, in a fashion which is hardly to be found in anything other than the British New Wave/kitchen-sink dramas produced in the late 1950s and early 1960s by such companies as Bryanston. But any insights afforded by the genre are never foregrounded in any self-conscious fashion; the most pressing imperative for the makers of these films is to provide kinetic entertainment with the implicit promise to the audience that boundaries will be pushed, in terms both of the behaviour of the central characters and of what it is permissible to show the audience. In terms of censorship, crime films have always been ahead of the trend, always ready to upset the censors.

In the earlier days of the British cinema (from the 1930s onwards), working-class audiences were happy to identify with middle-class protagonists (played, typically, by such well-spoken, reined-in actors as Robert Donat) before a new breed of more proletarian-seeming actors changed the expectations of British viewers. A filmmaker prepared to accept this prelapsarian, middle-class attitude was himself closer to the working-class ethos (with a family background in 'trade'): Alfred Hitchcock, who was yet to cultivate his creepily avuncular public image and whose work (even as a young man) quickly established itself as *sui generis*.

Hitchcock was the first 'star' director of the British cinema and was fully cognisant of the marketability of his image. It might be argued that viewers whose acquaintance with the works of the

Leytonstone Master is confined to his American films – or at least his most celebrated British films (such as *The 39 Steps* and *The Lady Vanishes*) – would profit from seeing the early work of British cinema's most accomplished artist (apart, possibly, from Michael Powell, as discussed elsewhere). What's more, the sheer pleasure afforded by the very diverse movies of this period (not all in Hitchcock's later set-in-stone suspense mode) is considerable. Hitchcock directed his first feature film, *The Pleasure Garden*, in Germany in 1925 and was immediately acclaimed. Before he reached the age of 30, with several notable films under his belt, he was regarded as one of the most talented young film directors in all of Europe. The films of this period present as an invaluable introduction to the director's early career before he moved to Hollywood. And the Englishness of such films as *Blackmail* (1929), *Murder* (1930), *Rich and Strange* (1932), *Number Seventeen* (1932) and *Young and Innocent* (1937) is reflected in a variety of ways: his modest Leytonstone trade background instilled in him a caustic eye for the nuances of class division, studded throughout his films in a variety of fashions. Like the great English storyteller who was one of his predecessors in gripping an audience, Charles Dickens, Hitchcock admired middle-class characters with the sangfroid to move effortlessly across all social divisions: Derrick de Marney in *Young and Innocent* may have the plummy-voiced vowels of his public school, but sports an ease of manner that allows him access to all areas – very much as Robert Donat does in one of the director's English-period masterpieces, *The 39 Steps*. The latter is, of course, one of the favourites of aficionados of the director's British period and encapsulates all the virtues of the young director's pyrotechnic talent. It is a very free adaptation of John Buchan's classic novel (adding a sexual element), but it is none the worse for that. Interestingly, one of the great films of the director's American period, *North by Northwest*, is essentially a remake of the earlier classic with widescreen, colour and Cary Grant replacing Robert Donat.

By the mid-1960s, a variety of social types were being regularly presented on the screen with a degree of nuance and sophistication that had rarely been seen before. Middle-class morality (of the kind excoriated by George Bernard Shaw) was inevitably the norm, underpinning all – hardly surprising, given the background (and predilections) of the great majority of screenwriters – but such certitudes began to enjoy a rigorous reinvention as different kinds of writers (from different backgrounds) made their mark on the cinema. The middle classes themselves were now presented on screen in a variety of subcategories, such as the arrivistes who have moved upwards from manual jobs to middle management, with a certain limited degree of aspiration (even as late as 1964, the flexibility of movement across class strata was limited). And there were the more successful entrepreneurs from a manufacturing background who had been presented in a negative fashion in much late nineteenth-century drama – and continued to be so until they were afforded a degree of sympathy. Inevitably, there were the petty officials who were inevitably presented as overscrupulous and officious, concerned with nothing so much as keeping the lower orders in their place (such characters are still to be found in the work of such British directors as Ken Loach and are almost invariably presented in a scathingly reductive fashion when set against the more sympathetically presented working classes, however feckless the latter may be). These gradations were to be found in the crime cinema of the 1960s as well as more prestigious socially committed fare. The appeal of a new affluence and a burgeoning sexual freedom, destabilising the old certainties, were presented as attractive, albeit rife with moral danger. And the influence of the church still made itself felt tangentially, although that influence was to suffer fatal blows as more and more iconoclastic filmmakers moved into both genre cinema and drama.

In any discussion of the British character – of whatever class – it is necessary to point out a certain antithesis in the British spirit which sets the avoidance of unnecessary conflict against the bulldog spirit in which wrongs must be righted, whatever the physical risk. These paradoxical notions of Englishness are often a matter for quiet pride, in precisely the way that British emotional reserve is valued as more authentic and genuine than Latin demonstrativeness. But if these processes exist below a conscious level, that is not to deny their pervasiveness in the cinema, when an initial reluctance to engage in physical action is followed by a violent catharsis (the John Guillermin film *Never Let Go* is a salutary example here). Popular cinema can be as useful in pointing up such syndromes as more 'respectable' academic fare.

Thus, within the parameters of escapist entertainment, certain dichotomies in the English character can be profitably examined – for instance, an admiration for American recklessness can perfectly coexist with a coolly intellectual rejection of behaviour that is impulsive and unconsidered.

The problems for popular films lie in the barriers that prevent serious discussions in informed circles. Entertainments designed to be straightforward, unnuanced and physical rather than intellectual, and (according to more dismissive commentators) designed to appeal to the lowest common denominator merit only cursory examination. But any scrutiny of the best British crime films (and, for that matter, less successful work in the genre which can still be suggestive and interesting) might reveal a richness of texture and a range of reference that is as fecund as anything to be found in more rarefied art. Almost invariably, such films function best primarily on relatively basic levels (they would hardly be likely to be made if arty-farty considerations on the part of the director had been suspected in advance by hard-nosed producers with an eye on box office returns). Having said that, however, such directors as the American expats Joseph Losey and Cy Endfield (both shown the door in the USA) were able to enrich the textures of the commercial films they made while still delivering the exigencies (suspense, iron-clad storytelling values, etc.) that audiences primarily demanded. Any criticism which attempts to consider either the commercial or artistic aspects of the film in isolation is on a hiding to nowhere, and it is now a general critical consensus that the two elements should have a symbiotic relationship. Unlike much British film criticism of the 1970s – which simply neglected the films and directors who were being lionised by the more ambitious magazines – there is now a more balanced response to the achievement of filmmakers working within commercial parameters.

As a repository for socio-cultural observation, the British crime film offers haphazard results. Political insights, for instance, function better when integrated into commercial narrative strictures, but if there is a lesson to be learned from viewings of the genre, it is that there is everything to play for in extracting from these films something more than the simple entertainment ethos.

An air of disillusionment was to replace the pulse-racing qualities of the more straightforward entertainments in Alberto Cavalcanti's *They Made Me a Fugitive* (1947). Cavalcanti was (in his day) one of the unsung glories of the British cinema, producing quite the most chilling episode (that involving Michael Redgrave and a malevolent

ventriloquist's dummy) in the Ealing classic *Dead of Night*, but burnishing his impressive filmic credentials with such strong pieces as
They Made Me a Fugitive, a crime film sporting a gritty verisimilitude
that instantly sets it apart from most synthetic-seeming product of
the day. The cinematography perfectly captures the dark chiaroscuro
of the director's unforgiving vision and presents a cold-eyed picture
of British society in which non-achievers (or failures) are summarily
dealt with. Perhaps the picture of Britain which informs Cavalcanti's
film is a consequence of the director's outsider status, but a consideration of his entire career demonstrates that the film's truthfulness
and rigour is no fluke.

By a year later, a sophisticated examination of crime and notions of
'service' were to be found in *The Fallen Idol* (Carol Reed, 1948). Reed's
understated classic about a child's first glimpse into adult hypocrisy
was the first collaboration between the director and the writer Graham
Greene, and the duo would go on to work together (equally impressively) on *The Third Man* and *Our Man in Havana*. Reed was nominated
for a Best Director Oscar, and Greene for Best Screenplay for their
work on *The Fallen Idol*, which demonstrates the unique concatenation of talents that these two mavericks brought to British cinema;
intriguingly, the commentary on above-and-below stairs mindsets
produced aperçus on class and social divisions by Reed and Greene
that remain as cutting as anything by the just-around-the-corner
British New Wave (as exemplified by films based on the novels
of Alan Sillitoe or Stan Barstow), despite the upper middle-class
credentials of the director and writer. Based on the Greene story 'The
Basement Room', the film is told entirely from the perspective of a
young boy, Philippe (Bobby Henrey), who is the son of an ambassa-
dor. Phillipe idolises the likeable butler Baines (the impeccable Ralph
Richardson) whom he discovers is having an affair with the Embassy
typist (Michèle Morgan). Murder is a new ingredient introduced into
this incendiary equation, but the narrative is about the investing of
human trust – and its cost.

By the time of John Guillermin's *Town on Trial* (1956), issues of
class – on the peripheries in earlier films – were now up for grabs. An
intriguing grafting process may be seen to be at work in Guillermin's
film: at the centre is the classic hardboiled police detective (played
by John Mills at his most intransigent), but the presentation of the
seething eponymous British town appears to owe something to

Grace Metalious' scandalous community of Peyton Place, with its colourful array of simmering sexual transgression, corporate corruption and individual *mauvais fois*. Mills' tough cop's attempts to solve a crime open up unpleasant ramifications for many in the town, and his scattershot approach allows for a penetration of the various social strata (in much the same fashion as such literary American detectives as Ross Macdonald's Lew Archer made odysseys stretching from the cheap bars to the snooty country club). While the snarling hero's working-class credentials are posited as the reason for the acute dislike of the upper middle-class characters he interrogates, the film is hardly an encomium for the thrusting, iconoclastic qualities of the detective's background – the variety of social settings that Guillermin presents for us shows no favouritism, but *Town on Trial* wishes plagues on multiple houses. Perhaps the caustic social criticism articulated by the central character is thrown back upon him by the director's clear identification of the John Mills character as a damaged, unfulfilled figure; while another reading of the film might suggest that had the detective achieved the requisite social standing (or have been born into it like Elizabeth George's patrician copper Inspector Lynley), his confrontational manner would not have been so insistently present. But, given that the moneyed characters in the film are presented in such a uniformly unsympathetic fashion – and that the various sexual peccadilloes are not given an attractive gloss, *Town on Trial* might be read as something of a tabula rasa, in which each individual viewer takes from the film exactly what he or she wishes to. Such a view, however, probably overestimates the level of ambition on the part of Guillermin and his writers, Ken Hughes and Robert Westerby.

Guillermin's film was based on a Sunday newspaper series written by crime novelist Francis Durbridge under the title 'Nylon Murders', and the American note sounded in this original title was echoed in the US-style economy with which the film was made. Following up a murder in an English country town, Superintendent Halloran appears in the *de rigueur* trench coat and sporting the no-nonsense manner that audiences would expect from brusque British cops. But it becomes clear within a very short time that Mills is cannily investing this stock character with a richer inner life than audiences had any right to expect in the conventional-seeming context. It is clear that Halloran regards himself as someone who has pulled himself up by his own bootstraps and is bitterly aware that his progress up the professional ladder has been a slow and halting one. He is fully cognisant of the fact that his social background has constrained his chances and that those colleagues further up the social scale could expect quicker promotion (he points out bitterly that it has taken him ten years to reach even the middle-rung position he has attained). He is also a man without a family (they have been killed in the war) and this has left him with an anger which has no direction – and, what is more, is something that indirectly powers him in his job. He is notably gruff with everyone around him, particularly the suspects. Interestingly, though, the characterisation is fleshed out when he is allowed to develop a romantic attachment during the course of the narrative, and a further humanising factor is his barely concealed liking for children (not, thankfully, rendered in sentimental fashion). When so many British crime films presented police officers as utterly one-dimensional, clichéd figures – and complacently ensured that the police procedural aspects of the narrative were by far the least interesting things on view – it is a tribute to John Mills' performance in *Town on Trial* that his bitter copper is quite as interesting as the murder he is attempting to solve. *Town on Trial* demonstrated the omnipresence of the American model. The casting of the American character actor Charles Coburn was no doubt part of a strategy to make the film saleable abroad, but such is his unpleasant authority in the film (along with a determined attempt to integrate his accent and demeanour into the British background) that there is no sense of awkwardly shifting gears. The English social system is explored with a rigour previously more evident in the American models' examination of their society, but the unsparing attitudes to snobbishness and covetousness are very British. What is perhaps most overtly American about the film is the conspicuous level of energy and movement, and the barely contained visceral qualities which are more reminiscent of the American films of Fritz Lang than comparable British product of the time.

Similar ambition is certainly behind another British film of a slightly later period. Looking at *The League of Gentlemen* (Basil Dearden, 1960) today, it's a shame that this title is now so ineluctably associated with the eccentric TV comedy show that hijacked it – Dearden and (co-writer and co-star) Bryan Forbes' smart and intelligent British heist movie is as diverting and pointed as ever, with an acidulous commentary on class, the military and the professions in Britain to finesse the narrative. Dearden was always (even at his most accomplished) essentially a journeyman director, but Bryan Forbes' machine-tooled script drew a career-best job from him. Jack Hawkins excels as a former army officer bitter at being forced to retire early. Using his special access to top-secret military personnel files, he begins to plot a daring £1 million bank robbery and sets about gathering a highly skilled team of accomplices, drawn from various social strata (all of which are adroitly delineated). A who's who of 1960s cinema, the film's copper-bottomed cast includes Nigel Patrick (scene-stealing outrageously, as he so often did), Roger Livesey, an oleaginously spivvy Richard Attenborough and writer Bryan Forbes himself. *The League of Gentlemen* allows for a certain class solidarity among its disparate protagonists, but it is of a critical nature (as expressed in Forbes' sardonic screenplay). What is cogently represented is the working-class readiness to accept the upper-class, right-wing figures' cynical bending of the rules when it is in the latter's interest – such actions do not prompt disapproval in those lower down the social scale, but a wry, grudging admiration. Current attitudes to the officer class (in film terms at least) are generally unsympathetic, but films such as *The League of Gentlemen* allowed a wry acceptance that, in organisational terms at least, quality will out in those used to giving orders.

A different kettle of fish is *Blind Date* (1959), which demonstrates the rebel's desire to upset (and possibly even destroy) a calcified social order which keeps the iconoclast firmly in place. Joseph Losey's diamond-hard film has a thesis: those who rock the boat can expect to have doors closed against them. In this, of course, the director's sympathy with the underdog is forcefully demonstrated – although, to some degree by 1959, part of the establishment himself (a fact he might have vehemently denied, but no commercial products such as *Blind Date* could be made without the entire apparatus of the film studio, publicists, distributors, etc.), Losey was all too aware of his status as a celebrated rejector of the status quo – the very status which obliged him to live and work in the UK.

Blind Date focuses on a young Dutch painter (who is only intermittently successful) played by the German actor Hardy Kruger. While giving lessons in art to a well-heeled, confident woman played by Micheline Presle, the inevitable happens and the pair begin an affair. Their trysts take place in his functionally equipped studio, but when the artist visits his lover at her well-appointed home, her body is discovered – she has been murdered. Things are complicated by the fact that the wealthy woman is suspected by the police of having another affair – with an important political figure. It is expedient that the policeman assigned to the case, Inspector Morgan (played by Losey stalwart Stanley Baker), makes an arrest – and that expedience is pointing (with some pressure from above) to the arrest of the young painter. Needless to say, Morgan is reluctant to follow this all-too-convenient line of investigation and believes in the innocence of the young painter.

By this stage in his career, Joseph Losey had moved beyond the simple imperatives of the crime thriller format within which he had been obliged to work as a director-for-hire in the UK, and the characters in *Blind Date* are much more multi-dimensional than before, with a variety of disparate issues being tackled. What's more, those issues are tackled with a level of sophistication that anticipates the director's later British Pinter-scripted masterpieces such as *The Servant* and *Accident*. Almost certainly, had the film been made by a less ambitious director than Losey, there would have been some attempt to render the artist sympathetic in order to make his 'fitting up' for the crime (in order to protect an important foreign office figure) more onerous, but Losey is having none of this, stressing the slightly supercilious, fiercely proud nature of the Hardy Kruger character. Art, as the painter describes it, is about the pursuit of truth – and he instructs his students that (for instance) the rendering of the human figure must be an act that takes into account corporeal rather than spiritual values. In this way, perhaps, Losey is pointing out that the pursuit of a certain ideal (in which notions of truth are not for bartering) is part of a more organic approach to everyday life – this is, in fact, the agenda of the unbiddable policeman played by Stanley Baker, who is similarly resistant towards a manufactured truth that several *éminences grises* would impose upon him. As so often in films featuring Baker, class is a key issue, and the jaundiced eye that his copper casts of the life of the dead rich woman and her impoverished young lover is refracted through his lower middle-class background (to which he makes caustic reference). This pursuit of truth in relation to the murder case is tackled in the face of establishment collusion – and the artist's own difficult nature. *Blind Date* perhaps reserves its most cutting analysis for the revelation that Englishmen of a certain class behave with an utterly unsentimental ruthlessness, and the film suggests conclusions to be drawn about the emptiness (on anything but the most crass materialist level) of this denatured society and its moral vacuum.

Regarding *Blind Date*, Losey was acutely aware of a variety of improbabilities in the narrative and utilised a variety of schemata to draw attention towards the stronger elements of the scenario (one of these improbabilities is that the narrative hinges on the fact that the discoverer of the body doesn't take the trouble to examine it closely – an action not really justified in the screenplay). But, by creating fully three-dimensional characters in his *dramatis personae*, Losey drew the focus away from such infelicities by establishing a verisimilitude that was further finessed by the authentic settings (such as – perhaps for the first time in a feature film – a convincingly portrayed artist's studio; similarly, the truthfulness in the presentation of the workings of a police station may seem quotidian today when we are used to such texture in modern police procedurals, but it was groundbreaking in its day).

The cool and radical picture of the morality and ethos of police work in the film was similarly ahead of its time and was initially dismissed as unrealistic (though Losey was particularly pleased when real-life events began to mirror the scenario of the film and, essentially, life began to imitate art). The director was also criticised at the time for his unblinking treatment of violence, a recurrent theme in his films. Again, by twenty-first-century standards, such elements are hardly likely to raise an eyebrow, but any viewing of *Blind Date* or Losey's other key crime movie, *The Criminal*, today demonstrates how ahead of his time he was and the realistic treatment of such elements have ensured that these films have dated far less than most contemporaneous product. Regarding the vexed issue of violence, Losey was obliged to remark that he had a personal detestation for it, but felt the need to represent it unflinchingly on the screen.

Losey's films from this period are now universally well regarded, but (as was so often the case) it was the French who were the first to notice some very individual work being forged in a commercial genre in the UK (British critics were characteristically sniffy both of the 'sensational' subject matter and of Losey's treatment of it). If most thoughtful British film critics are more disposed to overpraise Losey these days, this is perhaps a kind of justice, given the ungenerous critical response that his films received when they were playing in British cinemas. Certainly, the director himself, a notoriously difficult man, had more than his fair share of *amour propre* and was as prepared to argue the merits of his work as were many of his admirers (not, in fact, a particularly British characteristic – his new colleagues were more disposed to effect a degree of modesty, whether simulated or not). But looked at today, Losey's achievement in the British crime film genre was exactly as accomplished as the director himself always said it was.

Given that auteur theory (with its primacy of director over screenwriter, actors, etc.) has being undergoing some revisionist attention in recent years, an affirmation of the creed may frequently be found within the neglected byways of the British 'B' film, in which a director of imagination and distinction can utilise precisely those elements available to his less talented colleagues (shopworn screenplay, efficient (if familiar) actors and the standard studio facilities available to all his peers) and produce work of a far more idiosyncratic quality. The director Wolf Rilla, though born in Germany, produced much well-crafted work in the British film industry, with an unquestionable career apogee being his adaptation of John Wyndham's *The Midwich Cuckoos* (as *Village of the Damned*) in 1960, which demonstrated a fierce intelligence and a mastery of the orchestration of film tension. If these qualities are more fitfully evident in his crime film *Piccadilly Third Stop* (made in the same year), a comparison with other films made by similar production companies instantly demonstrates the quantum leap in the quality achieved over product from other studios. The writer and journalist Leigh Vance had worked with *Piccadilly Third Stop*'s producer Norman Williams on a film set in the criminal world of Soho, *The Shakedown* (once again, made in 1960), which has its virtues – not least in the attempts to deal honestly with the milieu and denizens of this world. However, that film's director, John Lemont, was (at best) a journeyman technician, unlike Wolf Rilla, who was hired to work on another Vance/Williams project, and *Piccadilly Third Stop* was to be by far the more memorable piece of work, despite its obvious limitations.

While the thick-ear gangster types of Soho in the 1950s are represented here, the director and screenwriter are far more interested in the scrabbling for money by decayed upper-class figures living on their wits and sporting an easy amorality predicated on their unquestioned sense of superiority and contempt both for those lower down the social scale and (unusually) for the easy pickings to be found in their own class. The charming if morally bankrupt protagonist here is Dominic, alternating between an enjoyment of the sybaritic lifestyle involving a succession of sexually available women (all of whom are treated in a casually misogynist fashion and are used for whatever they can provide for Dominic's crooked schemes, such as the casually utilised lover played by Mai Zetterling – moving from Ingmar Bergman films to the sleazier world of the British 'B' picture – married to a violent and unstable smuggler, and the naive Chinese girl played by Yoko Tani who provides entrance, after a heartless seduction ('You won't respect me!'), to the safety of her father's embassy).

More than many other British films, Rilla and screenwriter Vance are prepared to present a character who has virtually no redeeming features – the audience scrutinises Dominic for one action which will redeem his strictly utilitarian view of other human beings, but Rilla is simply not interested in providing such banal excuses. However, it is not just Terence Morgan's ruthless performance as Dominic that fascinates, but the always excellent Dennis Price as the supercilious owner of a roulette club who is also an upper-class fence and who takes Dominic's upper-crust contempt for those he is taking to the cleaners to even more rarefied levels. If Morgan is granted at least a certain level of self-contempt for his unedifying lifestyle, the character played by Price is completely at ease with the venal lifestyle that he enjoys. The services he provides for his equally well-heeled colleagues are in the nature of a gentleman's agreement, but the protocol is clear: however criminal the enterprise, the officer class gloss is maintained by the threat of strong arm thuggery from his brutal enforcer.

The film builds towards a tensely staged robbery of an embassy which demonstrates that Rilla had been looking at a variety of American models, but his is as crisply directed and edited as the equally pulse-accelerating climax of *Village of the Damned*. What follows the robbery, however, is one of the bleakest endings in British crime film (circumventing the 'hell hath no fury like a woman scorned' resolution we have been led to expect) – the days when Old Testament morality was shaken loose from the crime film were some years in the future, but the film still carries a considerable force in its unsparingness. The success of *Piccadilly Third Stop* meant that Rilla was a given larger budget for his succeeding film, *The World Ten Times Over*, three years later, but the director did not produce work that was pleasing to either the audience or critics, and his last few films in the exploitation vein were sad shadows of his accomplished earlier work. However, on the strength of films such as *Piccadilly Third Stop*, he deserves a place in the pantheon of the most adroit directors of British crime films.

Apart from its considerable virtues as a tautly constructed heist movie, Quentin Lawrence's *Cash on Demand* (1961) also affords the viewer a masterclass in film acting from two of the most consummate professionals in British cinema history. As the film was made under the auspices of the Hammer studios (in a break from their more profitable Gothic horror fare), the company was able to call upon the services of two of its most reliable actors, Peter Cushing and André Morell (in another Hammer outing, *The Hound of the Baskervilles*, the duo were satisfyingly teamed as Sherlock Holmes and Dr Watson). The publicity material for *Cash on Demand* claimed that the film showed 'the most daring bank robbery ever', but a more appropriate adjective than 'daring' might be 'ingenious', and the working out of the mechanics of the screenplay by David T. Chantler and Lewis Greifer (from a play by Jacques Gillies) is handled with a Swiss watch-tooled precision. Despite the fact that the scenario bears strong evidence of its stage origins, filmgoers in the 1960s (and those who have managed to catch it on its infrequent appearances since) will have little cause for complaint about the invisible proscenium arch. Cushing is icily effective as the unsympathetic Fordyce, an impeccably middle-class bank manager, who is self-important, pompous and over-fastidious, with (as Cushing expertly delineates) a certain hint of cruelty in his nature as he humiliates and taunts his put-upon employees (notably the long-suffering assistant Pearson, played by another exemplary British character actor, Richard Vernon).

The bank is thrown into some confusion by a visit from an insurance company security inspector, Hepburn (Morell), who, it appears, can match Fordyce for fussiness and attention to detail. His military bearing and smooth regimental accoutrements soon have Fordyce keen to demonstrate that all is *comme il faut* in his bank – but alert viewers will have soon realised that Hepburn is a phoney: a highly intelligent bank robber who has formulated a near-perfect scheme for taking Fordyce and his bank to the cleaners. This ingenious method does not involve pulling guns on cashiers (Hepburn has a line on the subject: 'I want bank robberies to be smoother – more sociable'), but allows the now-terrified bank manager to hear his wife crying for mercy on the phone; she and Fordyce's son will be tortured if the alarm goes off.

The details of the robbery itself are somewhat mechanical and reviews of the day were relatively lacklustre, finding this particular sticking point insurmountable. Viewed today, a great deal of the film's pleasure is derived from the two actors at the centre, with the unspoken class assumptions as relevant in their interaction as the subtle shift in the various power plays (when the Morell character demonstrates the kind of cruelty towards Fordyce that we have seen the bank manager utilise, we are placed firmly on the side of the witty, clubbable criminal), and there are even levels of interest provided by a game that aficionados of impeccable screen acting might be tempted to perform: envisioning how the film would work if the casting were reversed, with Morell as the fussy bank manager and Cushing as the plausible officer-class robber. Vernon Sewell's economical and measured *Strongroom* (1961) treats similar material in intelligent (and bleak) fashion, with Derren Nesbitt as a thief with a conscience and Colin Gordon as the bank manager locked in an airtight strongroom with a cashier over a bank holiday.

Less successful films can be equally instructive concerning key issues such as class. Bryan Forbes' occasionally entertaining misfire from 1968, *Deadfall*, merits some attention, not least for its calculated clash between quintessential cockney Michael Caine and the impeccably upper middle-class character actor Eric Portman. The plot involves cat burglar Henry Clarke (Caine) and his accomplices, the married Moreaus (Portman and Giovanna Ralli), attempting to steal diamonds from the chateau of alcoholic millionaire Salinas. *Deadfall* plays each performer off against the other with some skill (though Portman, as ever, comprehensively steals the show) and, on balance, the film's virtues are marginally more evident than its lacklustre reputation might suggest. For a start, there's a balcony-scaling *Rififi*-style robbery (intercut with a performance of John Barry's striking Rodrigo-esque *Romance for Guitar and Orchestra*) that is a sequence everyone who has seen the film remembers. And there is the nonpareil Portman, the other principal reason for watching the film (as the film's nominal star, Michael Caine – always generous in such matters – would no doubt admit; Caine's turn melts away alongside Portman's insidiously compelling underplaying). With Caine settling for his line in caustic cockney charm (with a taste for the better life), *Deadfall* is further compromised by the fact that it is directed in list-less fashion by Bryan Forbes (quite some way after the far superior heist movie *The League of Gentlemen,* scripted by Forbes) and along-side the colourless Caine, there is (as mentioned above) Portman pro-viding the wattage missing from the above-the title stars (Giovanna Ralli is the underwhelming female star, with Forbes' wife Nanette Newman shoehorned into the narrative, *comme d'habitude* – the director never had problems with nepotism). Portman's tormented, gay, incestuous criminal planner is a fully developed character whose anguish in the later scenes (after some seismic self-revelation) has a dramatic force notably lacking elsewhere in the film.

The British crime movie, by this time, was moving into fresh terri-tory, as detailed in later chapters. But social division remained a key concern.

By the late 1990s, the gloves were off in terms of addressing the issues of proletarian crime. Gary Oldman's highly impressive 1997 directorial debut was a celebration of his East End roots. For most of its gruelling running time, it's hard to regard *Nil by Mouth* in any-thing but the most uncompromising terms, as the squalid picture of drunkenness, violent abuse and drug-taking presents a picture of working-class lives which are impoverished in every possible sense of the term. But then a moment happens – near the end of the film – a brief glimpse of the humanity and warmth possible among the dispossessed. Most of the time, though, the characters are totally given over to the relentless four-letter abuse that everyone – includ-ing the women – routinely converse in. Language here is as dead and meaningless as the lives of the protagonists, their swearword-laden inarticulacy a mirror of their blighted lives.

But if all of this makes the idea of watching the film sound dispir-iting, it is anything but that, so manifold is the artistry on display here, not least Ray Winstone as the violent, alcoholic wife-beating petty criminal Ray, a portrait of incoherent brutality to set beside De Niro's similar turn in *Raging Bull.* Winstone and his director-writer withhold our sympathy for the character for most of the film – a daring move, as Ray is so appalling – then a crucial speech about his unloving father makes us understand, if not forgive (and this is not handled in any facile, pop-psychology fashion). Kathy Burke is equally on-the-nail as Ray's brutalised, pregnant wife, abusing her own body (and that of her unborn child) with endless cigarettes almost as tirelessly as Ray, who spares himself no possible indulgence.

There are no epiphanies here and Oldman avoids a linear narrative (key moments happen off-screen), but a scene in a pub in which the women of the film enjoy the great popular songs of the golden era (*Can't Help Lovin' Dat Man* and *My Heart Belongs to Daddy*) encapsulates the indomitable human spirit that is Oldman's real concern. The actor's turns in Hollywood (and latterly returning to Britain for the 2011 version of le Carré's *Tinker, Tailor, Soldier, Spy*) have perhaps reduced the possibility of another directorial outing as muscular as *Nil by Mouth* (finance for the film came from such sources as Francis Ford Coppola, for whom Oldman played an over-mannered Dracula, and Coppola's *Apocalypse Now* gets a witty riff spun on it in Oldman's movie).

4
Between Left and Right: Politics and Individuals

The treatment of politics in the British crime film has varied over the years from the glancing to the full-on, firstly via the use of metaphor and analogy in more cautious times, and succeeded more recently by head-on attacks on the ethos of the right (as in the presentation of the ferocious Thatcherite protagonist of *The Long Good Friday*), but with similar cynicism for ameliorative left-wing solutions. And the cult of the individual has been thoroughly re-examined in the crime film, with iconoclastic or criminal egotists both celebrated and criticised by filmmakers (often in the same film). For the doomed, (momentarily) high-achieving protagonists of these bloody dramas, hubris is customarily identified as the fatal flaw, a trend often tied in with the now-standard notion of the gangster as tragic hero.

The British cinema has never had a precise equivalent for the political lines in the sand so carefully drawn in the literary arena. The early books of Kingsley Amis were generally construed as being left of centre in their anti-establishment stance (before the author's decisive move to the right as age transformed him into a classically blimpish figure), but with the benefit of hindsight, it is possible to see Amis' work as akin to that of the more clearly defined upper middle-class/patrician world of Anthony Powell's *A Dance to the Music of Time* sequence of novels, in which the philosophies of both left and right were similarly lacerated to precise satirical ends. The popular cinema of Britain occasionally indulged a similar contempt for fondly held notions – contempt spread across political divides (the classic case here is the Boulting Brothers' labour relations satire *I'm All Right Jack*, which directed machine-gun fire against both the intransigent idiocy of Marxist trade unions *and* the self-serving, corrupt grandees of the management class).

However, such clear lines of demarcation are more difficult to find in the arena of British crime cinema. Viewers of a conservative persuasion might have enjoyed the fact that the British working class (most often represented in the cinema as Cockney, rather than, say, Brummie or Geordie) was generally accorded a certain 'there but for the grace of God' complaisance regarding criminal activity – outside of the homilies to idealised working-class family units. But Tory viewers of the average British crime movie would have been similarly dismayed at the presentation of public school types as snobbish, effete and asexual, when they were not being characterised as white-collar criminals whose scams involved ambitious stock market frauds rather than the dynamiting of bank safes and the coshing of coppers – pursuits of the lower orders.

The skills the professional classes received at public schools were generally presented as slightly sinister – the institutionalised bullying a training programme for more subtle social control. But if such notions were simmering beneath the surface of crime cinema, they were to erupt with full visceral force in the work of such directors as Lindsay Anderson – ironically, filmmakers from the very class being excoriated by the films they made.

The landowning gentry, similarly, is generally presented in the cinema as utterly ruthless in their desire to hang on to the baubles handed down to them from robber baron ancestors, and their function in crime films is frequently to present a target for criminal enterprise from operators lower down the social scale (cf. Bryan Forbes' *Deadfall*, where the unpleasant aristocratic 'mark' is not only superciliously proud of his inherited wealth, but is also both alcoholic and licentious – vices carefully placed in order to allow the audience a smoother ride for their consciences; he deserves to be taken to the cleaners). Of course, certain films which only peripherally utilise crime as their plot engine (such as the Anthony Asquith film adaptations of Terence Rattigan's plays *The Winslow Boy* and *Carrington VC*) locate acts of criminality within specific individuals, with class not conspicuously an issue and corruption not class-endemic. Political issues would be more wont to appear in the work of such outsiders as Joseph Losey. His highly-thought-of *Blind Date*

(1959), as discussed earlier, bears his personal stamp in a plot strand where the maintenance of the political status quo is more pressing than the solving of a particular crime. The same director's *The Criminal* (1960), by contrast, broadens its attack to present a prison as the whole of society, with social strategies laid bare from top to bottom (those who reject consensus politics are given the mark of Cain).

Another strand, of course, is the slide into criminality by ineffectual members of the professional classes (such as the milquetoast schoolteacher lured into lawbreaking in *The Lavender Hill Mob* (1951) – and it's instructive that such comic essays in the crime movie genre can often be as allusive as more straight-faced entries). The dominant ethos in the genre was often implicitly Tory, as in such films as Basil Dearden's *The Blue Lamp* (1950), in which the ultra-cautious hand of producer Michael Balcon is clearly evident in the attempt to make the British policeman a figure of impeccable moral rectitude, quite some distance from the image of the force subsequently presented in such films as David Greene's *The Strange Affair* (1968), where endemic corruption is the norm, and there is a common currency between the police and the criminals; similar uncritical mythologising of *The Blue Lamp* variety is, of course, to be found in the USA, with such films as Mervyn LeRoy's complacent *The FBI Story* (1959), a film that in some ways is the apotheosis the self-mythologising that J. Edgar Hoover finessed throughout his career. Nevertheless, before an anti-establishment ethos kicked in during the 1960s, there are several different strands of political thought to be found in the humble genre movie – sometimes concealed, sometimes unconscious, but particularly fascinating when winkled out in the twenty-first century with eyes peeled for such provocative substrata.

In interviews, those British filmmakers involved in making genre product from the 1940s to the 1960s were rarely asked to give interviews (as compared with the twenty-first century, when every aspiring director is spendthrift with his opinions for the purposes of DVD commentaries and documentaries). But on the few occasions when these craftsmen discussed their craft, they usually echoed the modest ambitions of their American counterparts. Their principal job (at least insofar as they were prepared to characterise it) was to simply entertain or (putting it more crassly) to simply earn their pay cheques by delivering what the producers and much-feared owners of the circuits required for the omnivorous commercial maw. Certainly, ideology and particular social agendas were not a prerequisite – although it might be argued that the statements filmmakers from the 1940s to the 1960s made were rather disingenuous, it is possible to detect the sound of axes being ground. Inevitably, discretion was the order of the day for British commercial filmmakers in the 1940s; there was a suspicion in the industry of any particular ideological agenda being pursued. The deeply conservative Methodist leading lights of the British film industry saw their purpose as not so much bread and circuses for the diversion of the masses, but the presentation of an idealised British society, in which those who created instability in the social order were ruthlessly expunged. To some degree, the crime film could then serve the purposes of both the establishment figures and the more questioning artists and artisans who actually made the films: on the one hand, the Rank circuit could be reassured by the destruction of the criminal or the unfortunate fate of the honest man who takes the wrong path, while the filmmakers could invest a considerable amount of energy into the anti-establishment strivings of the doomed central characters, allowing the audience the frisson of taboo-busting before the chickens came home to roost.

In the final analysis, the foiling of the criminal enterprise at the centre of these films was both conservative (with both a small and large 'c') and at odds with the clear trajectory of the narrative, which was temperamentally on the side of the criminals (a classic case of this arbitrariness being the Basil Dearden film *The League of Gentlemen*, discussed earlier). But in the same fashion in which Hollywood directors had circumvented the false innocence imposed by the censors on their adult narratives by indirection and nuance, British directors were able to employ similar strategies and place emphasis on those elements of their films with which they were in sympathy. Audiences accepted the conventions of retribution and annihilation as par for the course; the challenging of these conventions was not to arrive in the British cinema for a decade or so.

Right-wing governments (or the left-wing equivalents that share the repressive philosophies most often associated with them) are perhaps as useful to the film industry – in reverse psychology terms – as stringent censorship; they inspire in the filmmakers a keen desire to chip away at the received opinions of the day and incorporate political and social commentary into otherwise straightforward genre product. The result is often a curious hybrid – but one in which the passion of the filmmakers creates an energy and direction. The politics of Thatcherism, in which the entrepreneurial spirit was celebrated (it was often felt) at the expense of the social fabric (Thatcher's famous dictum 'there is no such thing as society' seemed to be a failsafe provocation for filmmakers to demonstrate how wrongheaded they felt that assertion was). Certainly, the films that created riffs on (and rebuttals to) Thatcherite motifs were among the most vividly characterised and visceral experiences that the cinema of the 1980s had to offer, and when Margaret Thatcher was sidelined by her colleagues in November 1990, the various governments that succeeded her perhaps inspired less loathing (and concomitantly fewer confrontational responses).

Nevertheless, political themes have been a common currency in British crime films since that era, and it might be observed that a more nuanced approach is evident today, given that there is no longer a straightforward Manichaean view of good regarding such philosophies. Such man-the-barricades strategies now might seem reductive, and the new success of the Conservative Party in Britain at the beginning of the twenty-first century (albeit that the Party was obliged to share government in an uneasy coalition with the Liberal Democrats) is beginning to inspire (as response) several strikingly committed films, both within the crime genre and in other popular forms.

If the British crime film is to be considered (as it often is) as a repository of masculine values, it might be said that the nation is in trouble. Certainly, the heroes of many of these films show a single-minded tenaciousness in pursuit of a goal and a considerable amount of physical courage when taking on formidable odds. But if these protagonists were on the wrong side of the law (as they so often were in the crime film), it was inevitable that a certain dichotomy would be set up in the expectations of the (presumably) law-abiding members of the audience: would viewers feel comfortable identifying with these figures when their modus operandi often consisted of stealing from people very like those in the audience vicariously enjoying their criminal endeavours? Or even (in many cases) killing people who got in their way? This was a moral quandary explored by the uncompromising American Patricia Highsmith, a writer who set several of her books in the UK, but although Highsmith undoubtedly set up a series of morally queasy conundrums, it cannot be said that she really answered them, seemingly espousing the values of her ruthless, murderous heroes on several occasions. At least it might be said that Highsmith was being honest; the directors of many British crime films maintained an uneasy equilibrium vis-à-vis their attitudes towards their criminal characters.

Of course, such films demanded a particular kind of actor, and it was some time before the British cinema realised who were the most appropriate performers for the increasingly tough and uncompromising fare that audiences were being offered. Discussed later in this study are the several occasions in the 1950s on which the otherwise excellent actor Dirk Bogarde was miscast as a tough juvenile – but such ill-judged casting was perhaps inevitable as the new breed of actor who could tackle the ruthless protagonists of these films was yet to make his mark. Trevor Howard, while unquestionably suggesting the demeanour of the officer class, displayed a degree of taciturn toughness in such films as *They Made Me a Fugitive*, which suggested that his career in the field might have been more fruitful had the right parts been offered to him. One such part was located in *The Clouded Yellow* (1950), a film which, after years of neglect, has enjoyed considerable acclaim in recent times and has become something of a cult item. Journeyman director Ralph Thomas' mystery is now recognised as an intelligent and strikingly directed Hitchcockian thriller which surprises even jaded crime film aficionados, with narrative revelations that still carry a jolt. Ex-spy David Somers (subtly played by the always-reliable Howard, suggesting layers of complexity and bitterness) is obliged to take a low-profile job in the country cataloguing a butterfly collection, but finds that danger is still on the agenda for him. With strong support from Jean Simmons, this is a neglected gem, with Howard as authoritative as ever.

But it was with the rise of the working-class actor – most notably the Welshman Stanley Baker – that a new verisimilitude was introduced into the field. Actors such as Baker and the similarly rough-hewn, pre-007 Sean Connery (who played a small part in a seminal Baker film, Cy Endfield's *Hell Drivers*) were to display the kind of qualities that had made stars of such American actors as James Cagney and John Garfield – a rough sensitivity combined with a degree of blue-collar toughness which persuaded audiences that they were prepared to spend time in the company of these men, however ambivalent their actions.

Politics of a variety of shades were striated through the crime film genre consistently from the 1940s onwards, and issues in society concerning the place of men and women and the expectations of individuals within given social strata were treated in often sophisticated and ambiguous fashion. Many elements were to play a part in the changing perceptions of men and women in society (and the fashion in which such perceptions were reflected in films), such as ex-servicemen returning from the war to find a very changed society from the one that they had left; not just the new independence of women in this altered post-war world but the much-resented advantages enjoyed by those men who had stayed behind and had profiteered during the period. To some degree, the frequent identification of the place of women (the Madonna/whore syndrome) played into these expectations, and the British crime film was as ready as its American counterpart to present the femme fatale as a destabilising paradigm of female sexuality – female sexuality, that is, which was both threatening and dangerous. Set against this image was of course the faithful wife (usually in pinafore) maintaining the status quo at home, but many crime films, while trading in these *kinder/küche/kirche* images, were nevertheless prepared to deal with a wider range of experience, both male and female. It should also be pointed out that not all returning servicemen were presented as noble, wronged figures, and there was a degree of corruption demonstrated in a variety of films where such now-displaced individuals were concerned. The location of blame in such scenarios was often spread between the destabilising effects of war on both the human psyche and society, as well as an analysis of what was perceived to be specific evil in the human character; in other words, the behaviour of these individuals was usually located in a primeval, negative force rather than in the corrosive effect of warfare on individuals.

By the end of the 1940s, criminal enterprise was often presented in films as a way of establishing a new role or status for men (and, to some degree, women) within this newly transformed society. It would be at least a decade or so before films began to address the problems of rectitude and honesty (or otherwise) in the police (and by the 1960s, filmmakers were prepared to cast a cold eye on corruption and malfeasance within the force – a far less common feature in crime films of earlier eras). There is an interesting distinction to be drawn between the accoutrements of the male and female characters in these films. In men this physical presentation would be represented by an acquisition of weaponry for the commission of crime and in women by the application of make-up, stockings and so forth. With these impedimenta it was suggested that the protagonists were ready for action.

Moral choices were often central to 1950s British cinema. With *Orders to Kill* (1958), Anthony Asquith, the director of *Pygmalion* and *The Winslow Boy*, demonstrated his reach with an unblinking examination of the nature of politics and courage, both moral and physical. Young bomber pilot Gene Summers (Paul Massie) is sent to Nazi-occupied France to kill a man believed to be betraying his comrades in the French Resistance. Willing to do his duty and kill on command from the air, he finds it a very different proposition when having to murder with his own bare hands. The film's reputation as a minor classic is well won. Another (later) Asquith film has a far less lustrous reputation. At the time of its release, *Guns of Darkness* (1962) was a film that enjoyed no more than lukewarm reviews and vanished without causing much of a ripple. Nevertheless, the director was able to fashion an intriguing spin on Francis Clifford's political novel, *Act of Mercy*. Although little read today, Clifford was one of the most adroit of British novelists working within the genre of the crime/espionage field; his *métier* was fashioning situations of extreme danger for his protagonists and freighting in a *crise de conscience* that pushes them to the furthest limits of human resilience. *Act of Mercy* won the Crime Writers' Association Dagger Award in 1959. Clifford's protagonist, Tom Jordan, is a successful businessman in a volatile South American country, with a regime supported by corporate money. His wife has just told him she is pregnant when the country erupts into murderous revolution and the old regime is brutally exterminated in a totalitarian coup – all except Camara, the deposed president, who stumbles, bloody and weakened, into Jordan's garden. Almost as a reflex action, Jordan finds himself trying to spirit Camara out of the country – on foot, with Jordan's pregnant wife in tow and with brutal soldiers on their trail. And when Jordan is forced to kill to protect his charges, he is forced to ask himself (as his wife has continually done) why he has thrown away everything he owns and risked their lives to protect a man he barely knew. For his adaptation of the novel as *Guns of Darkness*, Asquith simplified the characterisation (the conflicted Jordan, played on autopilot by David Niven, the sympathetic, injured ex-president who sets the narrative in train, and Jordan's wife Susan, a fully developed protagonist in the novel, but much reduced for the film), but the director showed his usual skill at evoking landscape. However, what Asquith's otherwise compromised film makes clear is the novel's point about the tendrils of European big business having quite as negative an impact on the country enjoying such largesse as the brutal revolutionary liberators. This (for the time) unusual attitude to interests once considered sacrosanct looks forward to the later, post-war novels of John le Carré; in the latter, the pendulum has swung to such a degree that Anglo-American capitalists are invariably painted a darker-than-pitch hue, capable of everything from large-scale corruption to ruthless murder. Asquith, in many ways a director of his time, nevertheless demonstrates a similar readiness to criticise supposedly benign business interests (le Carré *avant la lettre*, in fact), with a reluctance to toe any particular party line that distinguished him from his contemporaries, allowing his work to look relatively fresh in the twenty-first century when so much else now looks dated and retrograde in its thinking. The film may also be read as an understated parable for the unwanted and unpredictable consequences of British interference in foreign affairs, however well meaning – a reading all too apposite in the early twenty-first century if Middle Eastern countries are swapped for Asquith's Latin locales.

The establishment – and judges in particular – were a central concern for the pugnacious, contrarian British-born filmmaker Pete Walker working in the 1970s and 1980s. And his view of such institutions – as promulgated in his lively, dark, violent and ambitious films – was dyspeptic to say the least; this is surprising, given his oft-repeated support in person (apparently without irony) for the pillars of the establishment who would have been guaranteed to dislike his films intensely. The English director/producer was something of an exotic plant in the field of British genre cinema – a Shires-style Tory cheerfully utilising all the apparatus of the despised liberal left. Making his mark in low-budget sexploitation movies, Walker grew tired of the limitations of this restrictive genre (not to mention his burgeoning taste for 'added value' social commentary) and moved into the area that proved to be his true *métier*: films crammed with grim and remorseless crimes committed behind the drawn blinds of British bourgeois society. His main area of attack was hypocrisy, particularly that committed by the establishment, of which no sanctimonious area is spared, from state to church. Surrounding himself with a reliable group of colleagues, his all-too-brief moment in the sun as a filmmaker produced some eye-opening (if frequently misfiring) work, his finest moments involving the character actress who was to be his muse, the remarkable Sheila Keith. Keith had been a reliable (if unexceptional) performer in British TV comedy, but Walker was the first to realise just how terrifying she could be as one of his establishment figures with dark secrets or suburban housewives with homicidal tendencies. Her *Grand Guignol* talents were given free rein in Walker's movies, and then she disappointingly sank back into far less demanding work when Walker gave up cinema for the less creative field of real estate. Walker's remarkable exploitation movies include the workaday *Die Screaming Marianne* (1971), which is basically him finding his feet as a director, but has flashes of the inspiration that was to come later. *House of Whipcord* (1974) has a full measure of Walker's unique mix of hysteria and stiff-upper-lip rectitude on the part of its hypocritical institutional villains. Here, the director has the British judiciary handing out grim and summary justice, and *House of Whipcord* remains one of the most subversive movies in popular British cinema (not least for its tongue-in-cheek dedication to the self-styled guardians of morality – a dedication taken seriously both when the film was issued and even on its reissue). *House of Mortal Sin* (1975) has a Roman Catholic priest dealing with his repressed sexuality by murdering unbelievers and seems topical today as the Religious Right gains ever more ascendancy in both the USA and (to a much lesser extent) the UK. But the director's masterpiece remains *Frightmare* (1974), in which Sheila Keith is the murderous and corrupt centre of an outwardly respectable bourgeois family. In conversation, Walker frequently came across as the most unbending breed of Thatcherite; fused with this, his violently iconoclastic streak may have been the sand in the oyster that produced the director's lacerating tales of twisted morality.

5
Heritage Britain

Who created the cosy, reassuring cinematic (and televisual) image of Britain fondly held by many foreigners throughout the world – even in the twenty-first century? One woman might be said to be the *locus classicus* here. Agatha Christie is indirectly the progenitor of a certain heritage view of Britain, in which the upper classes hold the reins of power (however much they may be distracted by murdering each other in ingenious ways – without rupturing social protocol), while the lower orders know their place (usually as forelock-tugging domestics). The middle class has its function in the Christie universe: doctors and other facilitators for the famously ingenious plots.

Many films have been made of the bestselling novels of this most successful crime writer in the history of the genre, but very few of any lasting merit. Is the fact that *Murder on the Orient Express, Death on the Nile, The Mirror Crack'd* and *Evil Under the Sun* remain such journeyman efforts due to the workmanlike (and rarely inspired) directors? (One of few auteur filmmakers to tackle Christie was René Clair in his classic 1945 Hollywood adaption of *And Then There Were None* – and, unsurprisingly, it remains one of the most impressive Christie adaptations.)

However, all of the adaptations above enjoyed successful (and remunerative) cinema releases – for all their pitching of the novels at (largely speaking) a parodic pitch, guying the material fairly mercilessly, they caught the public's taste for Christie, with the sumptuous production design (to be replicated in the various TV adaptations) that supplied the necessary gloss. Christie's two signature characters, the amateur Jane Marple and ex-professional Hercule Poirot, were taken through their increasingly familiar paces in a series of sedate mysteries (usually involving the expeditious murders of deeply unpleasant characters). Holiday resorts, grand stately homes, small villages and (en voyage) boats and trains offered challenges to a variety of location managers – but money was prodigiously spent in these areas, and dividends accordingly paid. Of course, despite the generous budgets, the films are hit-and-miss affairs (with all elements of social observation ruthlessly expunged), but there are a sampling of diverting elements on offer, with a consistent level of cinematic professionalism that compensates for the lack of directorial vision or any attempt to find a modern objective correlative for the material: the ever-reliable Angela Lansbury takes a creditable stab at the sharp-minded Jane Marple (but vanishes under the weight of the obligatory star-studded cast), while Albert Finney and Peter Ustinov propel their broad-brush Poirot characterisations in the direction of caricature and comedy (Ustinov allows fleeting glimpses of real character to emerge from the one-dimensional caricature, making the constant comic emphasis all the more dispiriting). Needless to say, the now much-discussed notion of Miss Marple as a proto-feminist is no more in evidence in these latter-day adaptations than in the unashamedly lampoons of the earlier efforts with Margaret Rutherford as a comic Marple some distance from Christie's original.

Was Agatha Christie a feminist writer? How much did her elderly protagonist, the English spinster Jane Marple, incorporate elements of the author's own veiled personality?

There are, of course, two diametrically opposed schools of thought about Christie, principally concerning social attitudes. If you hate the patronising attitude to the working classes and the never-never land Britain she nostalgically creates, then nothing will persuade you to open a Christie novel – or watch one of the film adaptations. But Christie was able to take on board social change (albeit peripherally). And it might be argued that the position of women (and clever women at that) in the society of her day is a key theme – one that is craftily (and invisibly) freighted into page-turning crime narratives, though such undercurrents tend to have vanished in the cinema versions.

Despite her place in the pantheon as Britain's premier queen of crime, there are those who will simply never read an Agatha Christie novel. The endless TV and film adaptations have created a series of ineluctable images in the public mind of unrealistic picture-postcard

English villages. Christie's two principal heroes, the Belgian detective Hercule Poirot and the rural, genteel Jane Marple, feature in around half of her novels. The spinster-cum-amateur detective Marple's laser-like observational skills help her nail hidden criminality with far more rigour than the police. Unlike the masculine Sherlock Holmes, ever the Great Detective, Marple (except to those with sufficient perception) is not to be taken very seriously by those around her – and her genius can work its forensic marvels under the tweeds. The bird watching and knitted sweaters are perfectly calculated to give her murderous prey a false sense of security, even as she closes in. But it might be argued that Christie was herself a clever woman whose real life was more eventful beneath the surface her public saw (apart from her famous disappearance at a hotel in Harrogate, now felt to be part of an ill-conceived act of revenge on her straying husband). And Marple – as with so many women through the ages – concealed her intimidating intellect behind a non-threatening appearance. It is enough for her that a select group of people – principally those she aids – see the coruscating mental brilliance beneath the tea-sipping. Modern female sleuths struggle against male condescension – but make damn sure everyone knows their feelings. Christie's Marple achieves results (and a certain *amour propre*) with more subtle means. And the understated feminist agenda makes its mark – even if Christie herself might have dismissed such notions. Certainly, the films have little truck with such tricky agendas.

The other pillar of British crime fiction – with a massive influence on cinema (which is still discernible in the twenty-first century) – is, of course, the creator of the Great Detective. Sir Arthur Conan Doyle's own life was often as strange as anything to be found in his more outlandish fiction. A famous Punch cartoon of the day showed the author shackled to his celebrated pipe-smoking creation, and Doyle often voiced his exasperated desire to be remembered for something other than his cocaine-using protagonist (who he unsuccessfully tried to kill off with a plunge down the Reichenbach Falls). But it was Sherlock Holmes rather than the author's own preferred historical fiction that made Conan Doyle (along with H.G. Wells) the most celebrated popular writer of his age – even though he seemed to lack the rigorous deductive reasoning of his hero. The most famous incident in the author's non-literary life – dramatised in a both a film and a television play – involved Conan Doyle's credulous belief in doctored pictures of fairies produced by two schoolgirls. To modern eyes, Doyle's acceptance of this ludicrous hoax seems astonishing, but the author's personal losses (as is so often the case) predisposed him towards a passionate desire to believe in the supernatural (surprisingly, not reflected in his fiction) and he famously espoused several very suspect causes – he was, in fact, something of a target for charlatans.

But his finest hour probably came when he emulated his detective by taking up unpopular causes in attempts to prove the innocence of men accused of crimes, an echo of the many occasions on which Holmes refused to accept the conclusions of the police. A famous example of the author taking up the cudgels was on behalf of George Edalji, a half-Indian barrister who had been convicted in 1903 of mutilating cattle, but who (Conan Doyle maintained) was in reality the victim of racial harassment by his neighbours and the malicious collusion of the police. Similarly, Conan Doyle fought quite as hard as Sherlock Holmes ever did in the *Strand* magazine to prove the innocence of Oscar Slater, who was convicted of murder in Glasgow in 1906. Yet again, the case had a racial element: Slater was known to the police as a pimp, but it was his status as a German Jew that marked him out as a logical suspect for the killing in Glasgow of Marion Gilchrist. All the gullibility that Conan Doyle demonstrated in dealing with the supernatural vanished as he brought a cool intellect to bear in attacking what he saw as miscarriages of justice, and he was never afraid to confront the entrenched prejudices of his day to right what he saw as cruel legal wrongs. In many ways, Conan Doyle's embracing of these controversial cases echoed Emile Zola's similar stance across the Channel, when the great French author took on prejudices quite as entrenched as those to be found in London to defend Dreyfus, another victim of racial injustice.

Conan Doyle would probably regard with a cold eye the financial farces that have dogged the disposal of his legacy – despite his ill-advised embrace of spiritualism (and the great deal of money his folly cost him), he was a man who liked to see justice done.

It is interesting to note that the most famous (if not the best) of all Conan Doyle's Sherlock Holmes stories, *The Hound of the Baskervilles*, received perhaps its most imaginative staging in 1959 from a production company most celebrated for its Gothic horror outings, Hammer Films. To some degree, the studio's adaptation was subsumed into the generic category of horror which was Hammer's *métier* – not, in itself, a particularly challenging task, as the macabre elements to be found throughout Conan Doyle's work are most prominent in his most famous novel. The director of the film was the veteran Terence Fisher, Hammer's signature director, who had re-energised the Frankenstein and Dracula franchises earlier for the company (and launched its world-conquering success). Fisher was an unpretentious craftsman who was clearly at home with the period grotesqueries of Conan Doyle's novel. The casting of *The Hound of the Baskervilles* too was particularly auspicious, with the saturnine Peter Cushing, an actor whose precise, intelligent tones and energetic, charismatic acting style was perfectly suited to Holmes (Cushing was subsequently to incarnate the detective again in various television series). His Watson was to be the nonpareil André Morell, who so impeccably partnered Cushing in a duel of wits between bank manager and thief in Hammer's *Cash on Demand* – and, moreover, who thankfully opted to play Watson as the intelligent man presented in the stories as opposed to the buffoon that was the default portrayal of many films. Writers Peter Bryan and Anthony Hinds performed some deft surgery on the novel (a task previously carried out for the company's adaptation of Bram Stoker's *Dracula*, which conflated several locales for the purposes of economy) and, with the aid of Fisher's superbly crafted direction, set up an intriguing antithesis between the cool ratiocinations of Holmes and the apparently irrational supernatural events represented by the Baskerville curse and the monstrous throat-ripping hound. As played by the impeccable Cushing, Holmes combines the scholarly virtues of the unsentimental, asexual ascetic with the astonishingly intuitive party tricks which are the detective's stock-in-trade. As so often in the films that Terence Fisher made for Hammer, the rational and thorough methodology of the Cushing character is presented as the most apposite way to deal with events that defy logical explanation, an effect perhaps reflected in the hard-headed non-intellectual approach of the director.

If the film (the first of a projected series that regrettably never materialised) sometimes suffers from its budgetary constraints, compensations are to be had in the sumptuous-appearing production design and art direction which (as is customary for this company) renders a handsome and impressive look for the film (although, famously, the unimpressive hound itself is a massive disappointment and its ultimate 'reveal' is, sadly, one of the things that viewers of the film most remember, to the detriment of the whole experience). But Cushing and Morell have rarely been equalled (except perhaps by Jeremy Brett and David Burke/Edward Hardwicke in the Granada television series) and sterling support is provided by Christopher Lee as one of the Hound's potential victims.

If Terence Fisher's film was not particularly concerned with the wider political dimensions of Victorian society, such aspects were to be supplied by subsequent films, notably Bob Clark's *Murder by Decree* (1978), a British/Canadian co-production which boasted a distinguished cast and strong writing credentials (the screenplay was by the playwright John Hopkins, based on the contentious *The Ripper File* by Elwyn Jones and John Lloyd). As with Fisher's film, the principal strength here lies in the casting of Holmes, with Christopher Plummer giving one of the most understated and effective incarnations of the role. Hopes were raised by the participation of James Mason, an actor of immense skill, as Watson, but while largely successful, Mason is occasionally encouraged by the director to play up the Nigel Bruce-like buffoon quality (fortunately, not sufficiently to upset the balance of the dynamic between the two men).

Bob Clark's film is one of many literary and filmic attempts to pit the denizen of 221b Baker Street against the most famous (and contemporaneous) serial killer of all time, Jack the Ripper, and is surprisingly successful in juggling the disparate elements. Beginning in 1888, with Holmes and Watson running into the Prince of Wales arriving late at the opera, we are (in short order) shown the grisly dispatch of the third prostitute to die at the Ripper's hands, 'Long Liz' Stride. Here, Holmes' involvement comes about when Whitechapel shopkeepers request the detective's assistance in tracking down the eviscerating (and bad for business) monster. Utilising elements from the outrageous but intriguing source book by Jones and Lloyd, Clark's film has Holmes discovering the involvement of the Prime Minister, the Home Secretary and the Freemasons (a key meeting takes place at an impressive Masonic Temple). It's a trenchant picture of corruption in the upper echelons.

Of the various (often outlandish) theories involving the Royal House of Saxe-Coburg-Gotha in the Ripper killings, the unlikely thesis posited here is given an intriguing airing (an earlier film, James Hill's *A Study In Terror* in 1965 – see below – had traded in similar territory).

But the vision of Victorian society shown here, striated with corruption and conspiracy from top to bottom, is handled with genuine intelligence, and there is even a suggestion that documentary-style elements were being grafted onto a popular entertainment, though the director is clearly more concerned with raising the pulse of the audience than giving play to a variety of conspiracy theories (except as grist to the mill of the narrative). But if *Murder by Decree* deals in largely discredited theories about the identity of the Ripper, it still offers a picture of British society at a particular time which manages to freight some verisimilitude into its distinctly unlikely scenario.

Far less celebratory of a fondly remembered vision of England was another Holmes film with Saucy Jack once again the murderous quarry. While variously marketed as a violent and sexually graphic exploitation movie in the UK and (bizarrely) as a camp TV-Batman-style comic-book movie in the USA, James Hill's *A Study in Terror* is actually one of the most ingenious and intelligent entries in the Sherlock Holmes versus Jack the Ripper subgenre, with what now looks like a remarkable cast (Judi Dench and Anthony Quayle in small parts), while John Neville makes a solid, unnuanced, energetic Holmes (regrettably, Donald Sinden has made Nigel Bruce his model for Watson – only Bruce can get away with this level of dimwitted bluster). It is the late 1800s: Jack the Ripper is terrorising London's East End and murdering prostitutes. The only clue Sherlock Holmes has to work with is a mysterious box sent to 221b Baker Street. The box contains a selection of surgical instruments and bears the crest of a well-placed family ... only the scalpel is missing. The smorgasbord of graphic 1960s violence, a revisionist take on Holmes and some ingenious plotting more than make up for the missteps here.

The heritage Britain of the Holmes films was Victoriana in aspic. *The List of Adrian Messenger* (1963) presents a stylised picture of England which nevertheless has a ring of truth: it is set in stuffy cabinet rooms in Whitehall; ancient offices in the City with antediluvian lifts (easily rigged for purposes of murder); noisome Thameside pubs where the punters wear flat caps and drop their aitches while an organ grinder plays outside; palatial county piles where bluebloods sip brandy and port, legs astride, buttocks positioned for warming in front of massive fireplaces; and liveried hunts where the 'blooding' of a new hunt member is an important ritual. The picturesque vision is that of an American director who is a confirmed Anglophile and who has chosen an estate in Ireland as his home: John Huston. The film, something of a guilty pleasure (it has accrued quite as many detractors as supporters), owes some of its virtues to Philip MacDonald's commanding original novel, with its canny sleuth Anthony Gethryn tracking down a highly ingenious and utterly ruthless murderer – a murderer who, in fact, is prepared to kill a great many innocent people to conceal the death of his one individual target.

Philip MacDonald (1899–1981, who also wrote as Oliver Fleming, Anthony Lawless, Martin Porlock and Warren Stuart) is now a neglected name in the crime field, but enjoyed some popularity for his ability to create an entirely different style of narrative and subject matter for each novel. In 1931, a year in which he wrote some eight novels (one under the Coleridgean pseudonym Martin Porlock), MacDonald took a significant trip to Hollywood where he wrote several screenplays (perhaps making the cinematic potential of his most famous novel no surprise). He worked with Alfred Hitchcock and also toiled on the long-running Charlie Chan and Mr Moto series. His most frequently used protagonist was the intuitive Colonel Anthony Gethryn, who advised Scotland Yard and first appeared in *The Rasp* (1924), an undistinguished novel with a country-house setting. The much later *The List of Adrian Messenger* (1959) was nominated for the prestigious US Edgar Award.

John Huston's film of the novel (made some four years after its publication) was generally dismissed on release as a lightweight, gimmicky *jeu d'esprit*, but under the diverting surface, it is actually something more. However, the pleasures that the film affords today are precisely those which brought down much critical wrath on the head of its director when the film was released in 1963: that is to say, its extremely contrived nature (now perhaps a touch post-modern), whereby a slew of major Hollywood stars (Kirk Douglas, Burt Lancaster, Frank Sinatra, Robert Mitchum and Tony Curtis) masquerade under several pounds of latex as a variety of suspects (or murder victims) in an investigation that wends its way from gloomy pubs to hunt meets for supercilious aristos. Ironically, although the information was kept rigorously secret at the time, it has subsequently been revealed that several of the Hollywood stars we think we are seeing – all (apparently) looking stunningly grotesque in their make-up – are often not the performers themselves, but are played by the journeyman actor Jan Merlin – except for Kirk

Douglas, an unmistakable Robert Mitchum and the final sequence in which the actors strip off their make-up (a sequence as eerie and grotesque as that of a horror film). What makes the film deeply pleasurable is the pitch-perfect performance as the English sleuth Gethryn by the American actor George C. Scott, who most audiences would have been happy to have seen in a whole series of Gethryn films, so winning was this understated performance. Similarly, Kirk Douglas as the only one of the big-name American stars given something substantial to do proves yet again that he is an actor prepared to play fast and loose with his heroic image. At the time, some literary quarters applauded the return of the English detective to the big-budget feature film, with all the accoutrements of country houses and familiarity with the less intelligent detectives at Scotland Yard, and even a French Watson (played by Jacques Roux) who is actually a survivor of one of the murderer's more outlandish acts of carnage. But the critical response of the time was marked by dismay at what was felt to be a tongue-in-cheek disregard for the hallmarks of the genre by Huston, who (most felt) had left his glory days in the past. What is clear, however, is that the director is enjoying himself, appearing in a cameo as a red-coated foxhunting type – exactly the sort of role the director chose for himself in his Irish mansion (hence the film's largely uncritical stance towards some of its blueblooded hunting/shooting/fishing characters) – and the sheer filmmaking acumen never deserts the director; apart from the impeccable casting, including such actors as Clive Brook and Gladys Cooper, there is the finessing provided by a highly atmospheric Kurt Weill-esque score by Jerry Goldsmith, one of the many incidental pleasures that this unfairly dismissed movie now affords the viewer.

British 'heritage' – in terms of history and crime – also has its less salubrious side. Long a difficult-to-see movie, Robert Lynn's sombre *Dr Crippen* (1962) is a somewhat too-understated drama which features Donald Pleasence, who is impeccably cast as the henpecked murderer who found his transatlantic nemesis in (then) modern technology, with Samantha Eggar as his mistress. Inevitably, Coral Browne as Crippen's blowsy, drunken wife (who exists in the film as an obstacle to be removed with the full approval of the viewer) delivers a scene-stealing turn that makes all else appear as if rendered in pastel shades. The film reflects the fact that public opinion regarding Crippen has undergone something of a sea change over the years.

Up until the late 1950s, his name was something of a synonym for the act of murder, and he had joined the list of such notorious killers as Christie and Haigh in the lexicon of criminals who painstakingly remove all evidence of their crimes. The notion that Crippen was somehow (as an adulterer) a victim of the moral imperatives of Edwardian society is a relatively recent one, and Lynn's film echoes this shift of feeling. As sensitively played by Pleasence, Crippen is a weak and vacillating figure, utterly in thrall to his bullying, dominating spouse played entertainingly (but without much nuance) by Browne, utilising the stentorian character of her voice which she was able to call upon to great effect in many parts. Belle Crippen's drunkenness and open dalliances with other men quickly put the viewer on the side of the not unlikable Crippen, and his wife's suggestion that he is not performing his marital duties with her is perfectly understandable to the audience in light of the character's repellent qualities – and the idea of sexual congress between the two is presented as unfeasible. As played by the attractive ingénue Samantha Eggar, the young typist Ethel le Neve, Crippen's mistress, is a far more attractive figure, and the attraction between the couple is clearly designed to create sympathy for their subsequent liaison. The film's treatment of the fashion in which the unpleasant Belle died (was the tranquillising drug administered by Crippen designed as a fatal overdose or was it an accident?) tends towards the latter inasmuch as Crippen is distracted by his wife's loud shouting when administering the drug, though he is not let off the hook. Crippen's famous nemesis (courtesy of the telegraph on a transatlantic cruise) has no sense of an evildoer brought to justice, but rather an open-ended happenstance in the real world, a world in which many situations do not lend themselves to simple moral equations.

Of course, this cinematic image of heritage Britain has (to a large extent) moved from film to television, now the default home of sumptuous Golden Age crime adaptations; a phenomenon to be discussed in a later chapter.

6
Shame of a Nation: Juvenile Delinquents and Exploitation

British crime cinema's sensational, censor-baiting treatment of delinquency in the 1950s and 1960s was catnip to the self-styled guardians of morality (in both the popular and serious press, prissily condemning such shock tactics while simultaneously exploiting sensationalism to massage sales). But this manufactured outrage did little harm to the filmmakers' bottom lines; to some degree, it acted as a useful promotional tool. Such condemnation was read by cinema audiences as a promise of tempting sex and violence; it became, in fact, a key exploitation element which helped in targeting a crucial cinema-going demographic in terms of age. Such films, in fact, were often aimed at young adult audiences looking for taboo-busting fare. There was a synergistic crossover with the equally disreputable pop music of the day (finessed by the use of popular singers in British crime films, usually as alienated teenagers, though this was also the era of squeaky-clean pop from the distinctly unthreatening Cliff Richard, subsequently famous for his Christian proselytising). The intimations of teenage moral torpor helped stoke new levels of alarm among politicians and the press. Intriguingly, the more perceptive viewer might have spotted a corollary between the shock tactics of the filmmakers and other elements freighted into the edgy, confrontational scenarios; for instance, more committed, sensitive treatment of such themes as homosexuality.

The latter theme had particular application for one major British star. A certain exercise of memory is perhaps required these days to remember quite how massive a box-office star Dirk Bogarde was in his matinee idol days and how audacious a move it was for the actor (who never actually came out as gay, despite his unapologetic lifestyle) to tackle the gay-oriented parts that caused such a stir – the bisexual solicitor in the brave (if compromised) *Victim* (discussed below) and the doomed composer in Luchino Visconti's film of Thomas Mann's *Death in Venice*. Of course, viewed today, certain of the actor's films now appear irredeemably camp, such as his louche, soigné bandit in Roy Ward Baker's *The Singer Not the Song*, dressed in form-fitting black leather trousers and wanly lusting after the priest played by John Mills. Audiences today would not be fooled by the presence of the French actress Mylene Demongeot, clearly a 'beard' in what is fairly obviously a homosexual love story. By the same token, Bogarde's performance in *The Blue Lamp* now looks similarly quaint: the beautiful, impeccably mannered actor as a violent teenage thug? Bogarde does his best with the part, but it remains an egregious piece of miscasting. Teenage thugs were also to be found in the meretricious but watchable *Cosh Boy* (1952), although this film has (initially at least) a tougher edge than Michael Relph and Basil Dearden's homage to the British bobby, with a particularly jaundiced view of society's attitude towards rehabilitation.

Bogarde also appears in *The Sleeping Tiger* (1954), a salutary example of the director Joseph Losey's skill at investing the tired clichés of the crime film with something new and innovative – and doing this with a dynamism that make the clichés of the genre come shaking out like loose nails. Bogarde (whose teenage thug in *The Blue Lamp* had signally lacked any sense of verisimilitude) is much more effective in the hands of the director with whom he was to do some of his best work (when both men had moved firmly beyond the genre requirements of a project such as this). Here, Bogarde is a young thug who is being treated as something of experiment by the supercilious psychologist played by a frosty Alexander Knox, who is locked in an unsatisfactory marriage. Canny viewers will have realised that the psychologist's initially unsympathetic wife, for all her caustic right-wing views and impatience with notions of rehabilitation, is destined to end up as mere fodder for the attractive but dangerous young man. Alexis Smith is able to invest the clichéd character of the sexually frustrated wife with a fair degree of smouldering, suppressed eroticism beneath the carefully preserved image of rectitude, and Losey skilfully conveys the fact that what slender passions the psychologist played by Knox nurtures are for his profession and the youthful charge he hopes to save rather than his neglected wife.

Keeping firmly on the right side of melodrama, Losey is particularly adroit at playing with audience expectations regarding the inevitable destruction which will result from this volatile clash of personalities. It might be argued that the wife played by Alexis Smith is the victim of a strong will to destruction, a textbook case of a certain kind of fatalistic determinism not a million miles away from the novels of Thomas Hardy. In this area, the American Losey mostly proves himself – not for the last time – as a very English artist.

Juvenile delinquency is a central theme of Leslie Norman's *Spare the Rod* (1961), and if the film is largely forgotten today, so are the bitter censorship battles that plagued this now-innocuous piece. What slender virtues the film possesses are largely eradicated by the generally overwrought style (leaving aside the non-performance of singer Max Bygraves struggling in the role of a liberal teacher) and the filmmakers are largely content to deal in stereotypes, so that all the teachers (liberal or illiberal) and the pupils (well behaved or delinquent) largely exist to further the film's thesis (summed up in the film's title, though there are shades to the argument). The victimised pupil Harkness, for instance, is an unreal figure created simply to function as a focus for the film's by-the numbers narrative, and eruptions of violence and threat presented by the barely-civilised pupils in the teacher's class have, accordingly, little force.

Loamier fare was to be found in another juvenile delinquent-related outing a year earlier. Any cinema showing in the twenty-first century for Edmond T. Gréville's *Beat Girl* (1960) would probably be met with a certain degree of derision from a modern audience – this once-sensational exploitation movie (with its famous poster showing Gillian Hills pouting provocatively in black bra, suspender and stockings) now looks quaint ('Dynamic drama of youth – mad about "beat" – living for KICKS!'), even though there are a few interesting harbingers of highly successful careers inaugurated here: Christopher Lee is at the beginning of a lengthy career in screen villainy, though his one-dimensional spivvy nightclub owner here gives little indication of his talents, while the late John Barry's distinguished career as a composer for the cinema began with *Beat Girl* (Barry came to the film as part of a package with its singing star, Adam Faith, as the composer had arranged Faith's pop hits). But for all this incidental obscura, there are elements that (viewed today) comprehensively torpedo the film's credibility. As in the same year's *Never Let Go* (discussed below), the inexpressive Faith (present more for marquee value than any conspicuous histrionic skills) is the inarticulate voice of youth, but here accoutred with a guitar and sporting other 1950s characteristics of the 'creative musician' (filmgoers of the day would have been prepared to go along with this credulity-stretching notion, such was Faith's celebrity – perhaps a more difficult reach for the modern viewer). Nevertheless, in this pre-Beatles era, popular music is posited by Gréville as an avenue of escape for teenagers who might wish to avoid the easy lure of criminality as represented by the not-too-convincing sleazy nightclub, with its petty crooks and the sexual availability of the cleavage-flashing female employees. In the early twenty-first century, audiences might be indulgent towards this hilariously dated vision of adult lowlife and teen rebellion, but such indulgence would be unlikely to be extended to the architect (and disapproving parent) played by the stolid David Farrar.

In fact, there was only one director in Britain who saw the possibilities of this intriguing actor – Michael Powell, who in the deliciously overheated *Black Narcissus* presented him as a virile symbol of male sexuality, creating hormonal disturbances among a group of sexually repressed nuns. In the very different *The Small Back Room*, Powell undercut the weary professionalism of the character played by Farrar with a tragic character flaw based on alcoholism. No such interesting directorial nuances are to be found in *Beat Girl* for a cut-adrift Farrar, and it is remarkable to note just how dull this charismatic actor's performance is. The contrast between the two characters (teen rebel Faith and stuffy parent Farrar) goes for nothing, and it is only the erotic rebelliousness of the Gillian Hills character that offers some suggestion of the film's once vaguely unsettling charge. Nevertheless, for all its infelicities, *Beat Girl* offers an intriguing snapshot – not so much of the late 1950s Soho nightclub scene, but of the image of the same that 1950s audiences in the provinces fondly nurtured, with entry into the benighted portals leading naive young girls into the (similar) iniquities of stripping or prostitution.

In the more socially committed British crime movies, there is a suggestion that certain jobs involve a sense of morality which had less time for niceties than the better paid professions – and, accordingly, were more open to an insidious slide into less-than-legal activity by the protagonists. The salesman played by Richard Todd in John Guillermin's *Never Let Go* (also 1960) certainly seems to owe a little to Arthur Miller's Willy Loman in *Death of a Salesman*; the quotidian commercial life displayed here is not so much one of quiet desperation but of a headlong rush into the Last Chance Saloon. Todd's character simply has to maintain his job or the little that he has left to him (including his under-strain marriage to a generally supportive Elizabeth Sellars) is likely to slip away. And the theft of his all-important car (stolen by a surly teenage coffee bar thug played once again by the modestly-talented pop singer of the era, Adam Faith) is the final straw. The Todd character simply has to recover it, whatever the cost. Viewers of a cinéaste bent will spot the other key influence on the scenario here, of course: the necessity of recovering a stolen mode of transport in order to keep a job (cf. the increasingly desperate father in Vittorio De Sica's *Bicycle Thieves*). But John Guillermin, whose imperatives are less lofty than his distinguished Italian predecessor, allows the violence that is beneath the surface in that neorealist model to erupt in *Never Let Go* more quickly. Alfred Hitchcock often remarked that it was important to answer early in a film the question that the audience always asks concerning the desperate hero: why doesn't he go to the police? That question is answered very swiftly in Guillermin's film: the palpable lack of interest by the police in the stolen car is made crystal clear, and Todd (ignoring the concerns of his cautious, frightened wife) screws his courage to the sticking place and decides to tackle the local juvenile delinquents (who are clearly behind the theft) in their jukebox-throbbing haunt – notably the Adam Faith character.

At a distance of many decades, it is perhaps hard now to understand how an audience in the 1960s would have reacted to the casting of an ephemeral pop star such as Faith in this crucial part; Teddy Boys and petty criminals were basically the singer's lot throughout his acting career, and though contemporary audiences would have accepted this typecasting (inevitable, given Faith's pronounced adenoidal Cockney accent – much mocked at the time, as it was so evident in his pop hits), such audiences would have expected a basic decency to show through, despite the petty criminality. Which, of course, it does. The real villain of the film is the crooked (and sexually sadistic) garage owner played (in a rare 'straight', non-comedic role) by Peter Sellers, and this unorthodox casting is one that needs no retrospective adjustment on the part of viewers in the twenty-first century. The verdict on the late Sellers is that he was one of the great comic actors, his occasional straight performances (as, for instance, Humbert Humbert's rival in Stanley Kubrick's *Lolita*) being highly regarded. The eccentric, neurotic actor's first venture into such territory was as the violent, bullying garage proprietor here (complete with a convincing Birmingham accent; accents were the actor's speciality). Although Sellers makes a valiant stab at the part, there is a pronounced sense of him trying too hard to distance himself from the comic roles he was best known for.

At some point in *Never Let Go*, it's inevitable that the vulnerable but tenacious Todd will get past the intermediaries and come face-to-face with the deeply unpleasant dealer in stolen cars who is the film's principal heavy (the violent fight in a garage was strong stuff in its day). And any consideration of the film (beyond its outward accoutrements as a tough, American-style drama) will note a possible political strand here, in which the honest commercial salesman protagonist is taken advantage of by a corrupt example of management – to whom people like him are beneath consideration. Though there is a moral force in the final savage confrontation (with the Sellers character letting out a high-pitched scream when his hand is caught in a car door that has been slammed shut – a scene cut in some television showings), it is basically on the level of good versus evil rather than a nuanced consideration of the honest working man versus the bent capitalist figure. A reason for this reductiveness is not simply the unambitious, too-linear screenplay, but the studio-bound shooting ethos, which keeps any sense of veracity at bay. If anything, the real saving grace of the film is Todd's truthful performance. As an actor, Todd was happy to frequently slip into undemanding officer-class mode, but like his contemporary, John Mills, he could bring a pithy verisimilitude to his creation of characters further down the social scale – which is very much the case here. *Never Let Go* is actually not critical of a certain acquisitiveness and is fully aware of the value of objects and accoutrements to survive in a milieu which is not a million miles away from the cold-eyed criticism of the commercial ethos to be found in Miller's *Death of a Salesman*. However, the hero's stolen car is not a luxury item but an essential concomitant of Todd's commercial survival. And set against this is the top-of-the-range hi-fi equipment conspicuously demonstrated by Sellers'

villainous garage owner (this much-prized gramophone also provides a rationale for apoplectic anger when Sellers' reluctant young
mistress deposits lighted cigarettes on the machine), Sellers' character is nothing if not aware of the value of expensive objects, and
his dismissive judgement on those work for him (and on those
whom he pays for sex) is predicated on their appreciation – or lack
of it – for material objects. If the film's picture of Teddy Boys happy
to be employed by an outwardly bourgeois figure such as the garage
proprietor seems a little unreal, this striation of different levels of
criminality was probably dictated by dramatic imperatives. The film
itself offers no solution to the questions about class and aspiration
that it raises, but that is hardly a criticism, as it is sufficient that
such thoughts are prompted by what is essentially an unchallenging piece of entertainment.

Appearing a year later, *The Boys* (1961) was an early film for the
director Sidney J. Furie, and this pre-*Ipcress File* drama bristles with a
young man's energy and ambition. This is a social melodrama – very
much of its time – that avoids worthiness in its picture of four youths
who are all implicated in the murder of a night watchman. The
acting abilities of the eponymous 'boys' are on a sliding scale from
top-notch (Ronald Lacey, at the start of lengthy career as a reliable
character actor) to rudimentary (the pop star Jess Conrad, of limited
singing and acting ability), and the courtroom scenes are not helped
by Robert Morley's phoned-in performance as the defence attorney
attempting to inspire generosity towards his youthful charges, while
prosecuting attorney Richard Todd is not to be persuaded. Furie's
sympathy for his young protagonists (and impatience with his older
cast) gives many of the scenes featuring the former a nervous energy,
and it's not surprising that the film led to larger budget efforts for a
clearly talented director.

Public disquiet about the 'juvenile delinquency' phenomenon
underwent a radical change in the 1970s and 1980s, with a more
general disenchantment with under-motivated youth taking hold,
divorced from a neatly locatable social problem and morphing into
a panoply of related concerns, such as feckless youths with 'slacker'
lifestyles. The typical adult perception of the Timothy Leary-style
'turn on, tune in, drop out' hippie generation of the late 1960s/early
1970s was that teenage violence had been replaced by an alienated
generation mired in inertia (apart from copious sexual activity).

There was also the stereotype of the barely-educated, drug-dealing, largely unemployable council estate youth. But the notion of the menacing knife-wielding teenager, the new incarnation of the Teddy Boy, was to return with a vengeance by the end of the 1990s, when cinema once again caught up with popular perceptions.

By the twenty-first century, the view of juvenile delinquency had undergone radical changes. *Goodbye Charlie Bright* (2001) was the debut film for Nick Love, serving as both writer and director, and it demonstrated a willingness to invest shopworn material with some innovative touches. Love's chosen locale is a south London housing estate and his picture of the dispiriting lifestyle of his protagonists is matched by the concomitant vision of a rundown, depressed capital, where once-bright visions of a new living model for the city have collapsed into what is virtually a prison for the inhabitants, who are unable to escape (either for reasons of poverty or inertia) the crumbling, graffiti-covered brick prisons they inhabit. Love focuses on a band of teenagers (played by Paul Nicholls and the ubiquitous Cockney actor Danny Dyer, among others) whose lives are inscribed in a downward spiral of alcohol, robbery and general anti-social behaviour. While the director shows the occasional moments of exhilaration captured in these blighted lives, he makes it clear that the final life tally for the group is zero, with jail or extinction the only abiding certainties. Despite this, the effect of *Goodbye Charlie Bright* is not entirely dispiriting, given that Love is able to contextualise his work in a variety of fashions. For one thing, there is the casting process, which draws on the history of the crime genre to make a variety of comments. The actor Phil Daniels had in his youth played the kind of violent rebels represented here by Paul Nicholls and co. (with Danny Dyer as the go-to actor of choice for directors seeking a modern-day equivalent), but Daniels, approaching middle age, is cast as a cast-adrift veteran of the Falklands conflict, living in a spartan flat accoutred in the fashion of his time in the services. The unhinged quality that Daniels brings to the role (something of a speciality of the actor) allows Love to make several points: by the use of the iconic Daniels to suggest that the future for the young protagonists may (in different ways) perhaps be as sobering as that of the ex-soldier and (in a broader context) that the escape from social deprivation presented to young men by the army may be illusory, leaving them with the kind of bleak legacy inherited by the Daniels character. Similarly, other professions offer hardly less attractive escape routes: the estate agent played by Richard Driscoll is used to demonstrate the less salubrious aspects of this fast-money-based career in which (essentially) anything goes in order to make the sale. But perhaps Love's most confrontational tactic as writer-director is to avoid any romanticising of his youthful anti-heroes – there is nothing here of the mock nobility that (for instance) the director Walter Hill gave to his street gang in *The Warriors* (who are similarly left with a hopeless future at the end of the film). Love presents his character with an unsparing honesty, suggesting that they simply aren't clever enough to reject the kind of pointless lifestyle they are locked into. And while suggesting that (regarding the scenario of the film) there is a suggestion that something should be done for these youngsters, it is not at all clear what that something is. Love would appear to regard such suggestions – even if he had them – as tendentious.

7
The New Violence: The Loss of Innocence

The changing representation of violent criminal psychology in British film over the years has resulted in a sea change in the genre, with previously marginalised psychopathic killers moving from periphery to centre stage. Needless to say, the threat (or promise) of violence has long been an integral element of the genre, but its filmic representation has often been circumspect – even in the era when the Kray Twins ruled London's East End with extreme retribution for those who crossed them. The fact that the actual crimes of the duo can now be represented unblinkingly (no discreetly averted camera is necessary) is something of an index of the new, franker orthodoxy in such matters. This move to full-on confrontation with the reality of East End gangsters is suggestive of a new honesty and a readiness to confront once-taboo themes, such as police corruption – which also became standard in modern cinema from the late 1960s onwards.

Standing apart from the great majority of people who conform to the expectations of society, the anti-heroes of the crime film – British and otherwise – seem (for a time) to be invulnerable as their stories unspool, taking chances that the rest of us dare not take, and surviving violence from both the forces of law and their equally violent colleagues in crime (if there is one recurrent theme of the genre, it is that there is little honour among thieves). The degree to which a biblical notion of evil is *de rigueur* for the protagonists varies from film to film, but even today (with a more nuanced approach to the psychology of character), it is still expedient for filmmakers to incorporate notions of evil – as a pure, primeval, malignant force. Of course, dealing in such primaries has often resulted in the crime genre being sidelined by critics as reductionist, and for many years the crime film was a despised genre (at least until the French coining of the term 'film noir' gave it a new and added respectability; a similar accession of respectability has been attained by the literary versions of the genre). Though the best British and American crime films constantly demonstrated prodigal invention and a muscular approach to the techniques of film often lacking in other fields, it was felt at the time that such films lacked poetry – a cliché of much mainstream criticism that is particularly ironic when the bleak, rain-washed visual poetry of the crime film is now almost a *sine qua non.*

The elemental hero/villain of such films may be something of a throwback to the earliest notions of storytelling, and these generic protagonists display a variety of qualities that in a more heroic figure would be considered as virtues: courage, single-mindedness, willpower and an admiral readiness to disregard the expectations of those around him. All of this, of course, is compounded by the other side of the coin: selfishness, callousness, a strong strain of misogyny and – displayed more comprehensively than even these qualities – a total, unyielding egocentricity.

In the world of the crime film, the protagonist is often presented in a simple antithesis between good and evil. In order for the narrative to function at its most primal level, there is often no subtle distinction in terms of shading of character. Malevolence reigns and is *sui generis* in this world. The world of the crime film is often in itself as codified as a medieval mystery play in which characters perform their allotted actions and are permitted little deviation from such codification. Frequently, of course, the more ambitious directors granted their anti-heroes a degree of nobility (usually at war with the baser, more venal aspects of the characters' personalities), but the fate of such protagonists is almost invariably a lonely destruction.

By the 1960s, however, the straightforward evil of a film villain had been shaded into something that allowed for a degree of psychological complexity, utilising literary notions of the anti-hero (such as Meursault, the casual murderer of Albert Camus' *The Outsider*), but the more ambitious film directors and writers have enjoyed second-guessing the expectations of audiences (and critics) and have performed complex and dexterous surgery on our responses – to the degree that it is often impossible to know how far one is colluding with the actions of these anti-heroes. We live in an age of violence, disillusionment and cynicism, so that the defeat of the anti-hero in the crime film perhaps lacks the tragic dimension of, say, a Shakespearean over-achiever such as Macbeth. But the canvas can be as sprawling and vividly coloured (at least in terms of emotional response) as that of grand opera, and the working out of these sanguinary scenarios is endlessly fascinating.

To some degree it has been difficult to actually see a great many of the important (and less important) British crime films, even in the era of availability that followed the VHS revolution and (subsequently) the DVD and Blu-ray reissues of many films. Even such seminal British films as *Performance* and the original *Brighton Rock* were slow to make their way onto the silver disc medium, and some important British crime films remain unavailable to this day, such as David Greene's unusual *The Strange Affair*, which (at the time of writing) can be tracked down only in a dismal pan-and-scan grey market edition. The attitudes displayed in many of the crime films from the UK (both past and present) have come into their own in terms of the new culture of magazines aimed at younger men, so that the dismissive attitudes towards women of many of the protagonists of these films may be seen in both a post-modern light (look at how these men behaved in previous eras!) but with a guilty, vicarious enjoyment of the pre-feminist attitudes on display.

The psychopath is the harbinger of the new dimension of violence in British crime film – even when the more extreme violence is perpetrated off-screen. *Night Must Fall*, Emlyn Williams' famous (and once-shocking) drama of crime and psychopathic behaviour had already been memorably filmed in 1937, with Robert Montgomery as the murderous psychopath Danny (the playwright himself had acted the part on stage) and had provided an image which had passed into popular mythology: the severed head in a hat box. So before a remake appeared in 1964, the news that the director was to be Karel Reisz – with the youthful killer played by Albert Finney – created something of a stir. This was, of course, the duo who between them created the memorable film adaptation of Alan Sillitoe's *Saturday Night and Sunday Morning* in 1960, so expectations were high: the new version of Williams' drama had everything to play for. If director and star brought something new to the material and re-energised its slightly jaded melodramatic thrills, all to the good; and if the team were to strip down and reconfigure the material to create something entirely new (with, it might be expected, added layers of psychological realism), this would have chimed with more complex approaches to such fare in the mid-1960s. Either way, it was felt that Reisz and Finney would certainly do as much justice to the material as might be possible.

In the event, neither set of expectations was fulfilled, but the film remains an interesting failure. Danny is the charming monster who transports the heads of his victims in a hatbox and inveigles his way into the favour of an elderly woman and her lonely daughter in a secluded cottage. Acute social and psychological observation was clearly not on the agenda here, but although the mechanics of Williams' expertly-turned play were relatively sure-fire, the feeling of disappointment devolved from the fact that Reisz and Finney had taken an approach to the material that was bereft of radical rethinking. The script by Clive Exton updated the more antediluvian elements of the play and was able to bring the sexual elements (perforce underplayed in the earlier version) centre stage; this was 1964, after all, and a new sexual freedom was being explored in cinema. *Night Must Fall*, for all its faults, was full of intriguing incidental detail, such as the antic, child-like behaviour of Danny, including his bizarre reactions to (and even conversations with) the macabre souvenir he carried around with him. But Finney's playfulness vitiated the menace of the terrifying Danny; Robert Montgomery – a far less interesting actor than Finney – had rendered him a much more disquieting figure in the 1937 film version. Typically colourful playing by Mona Washbourne (as the older woman charmed by Danny) and carefully judged underplaying by Susan Hampshire as her suspicious daughter Olivia add some texture. The bucolic locales are evoked with some sensitivity by Reisz and demonstrate that he was keen to get away from the grim urban locales that had been his previous stamping ground in the British new wave. But an attempt to impose an art film sensibility of what is essentially a *Grand Guignol* thriller finally demonstrated an incompatible interface between the two sensibilities, with neither establishing itself for long before a lack of focus is visible. Perhaps, finally, what compromised Reisz's version of *Night Must Fall* is its accretion of atmosphere at the expense of carefully modulated, building tension.

Physical mutilation is the hallmark of one largely forgotten film of the 1960s. The fact that a film has become extremely difficult to see frequently has the effect of burnishing its cult credentials beyond its actual merits, and it is undeniable that there is an element of this situation in any consideration of David Greene's elusive *The Strange Affair* (1968). The director, who had made his mark in television, had already demonstrated a sure-footed way with genre cinema in the unusual and inventive *The Shuttered Room* a year earlier (a film inspired by, but some distance from, H.P. Lovecraft), and even the slight but modish *Sebastian* (1968) has its virtues. *The Strange Affair*, however, was a more highly-spiced brew, an interesting, genre-bending mix of ultraviolence, sexual experimentation, drug-dabbling and (most significantly for this study) utterly endemic police corruption woven into a scenario that stretched credulity but was never less than forceful. The police services of the late 1960s were offended by the film and pointed out that this level of corruption simply did not exist (subsequent scandals over the years would make such protestations even less plausible today), while there was the usual flurry of outrage from the customary moral guardians concerning the film's graphic treatment of violence (famously, an electric drill being driven through young copper Michael York's cheek by thugs wearing nylons over their faces). The notion of naivety coming into collision with the grimness of the real world (as represented by the initially unworldly York character's ever-deeper involvement in some very nefarious activities) seems less persuasive today, though it chimed with notions of innocence and experience held at the beginning of the 1970s. What does aid the film is the director's assurance at conveying the tactility of surfaces. His acute visual style (already comprehensively demonstrated in the earlier *The Shuttered Room*) is copiously in evidence here, with a succession of visual coups evident throughout, but not formulated as a simple series of striking images for their own sake. And throughout there is incorporated a telling picture of British society of the day, with images of conspicuous wealth in the leafy lanes of Hampstead set against dispiriting high-rise blocks surrounded by rubbish and decay. Other details, too, register strongly concerning the world that the youthful policeman moves in: the over-fussy sergeant at his station and the quotidian life of a copper in the late 1960s (with all its temptations to stray from the straight and narrow), the flotsam and jetsam being pulled into the busy police station on Saturday night. And if Susan George's hippie temptress is a figure cut from conventional cloth (in fact, the actress – whose very British identity marked her out as decisively different from better known American peers – was routinely used as an image of feckless erotic abandon throughout the decade), she serves a dramatic function, largely existing to draw the Michael York character into a destabilising new world. And there is real grit in several other pieces of casting, notably the always-reliable Jeremy Kemp as a menacing copper who has a psychopathic dislike of his corrupt colleagues; similarly, another solid British character actor, Jack Watson, makes a strong impression, his drug-peddling criminal drawing uncomfortable parallels between those on either side of the law. The growing disillusionment of the young policeman is well found by the actor. York was one of the most frequently used (if underrated) talents of the era (with the film of the musical *Cabaret* a career high), and the expectations for David Greene's future career – much discussed at the time – were greatly finessed by the cult success of the film. Regrettably, neither York nor Greene has sustained this promise, but *The Strange Affair* remains a significant British crime film.

One film was key in bringing about a new visceral approach to screen violence. The trials and tribulations of the censor-enraging *Performance* (1970) are now well documented. But this illegitimate filmic offspring of cult British directors Nicolas Roeg and Donald Cammell is a surrealistic and graphic phantasmagoria that extended the parameters of screen violence and sexuality so radically in its day that its parent company, Warners, was famously at a loss to know what to do with the film. In fact, only a change of management at the top of the company finally facilitated its belated release. That release, of course, was in large part due to the iconic presence of the louche Mick Jagger as the washed-up, substance-abusing rock star Turner (considered prescient at the time, the dissolute Turner figure was, in fact, something that the singer never actually became, cleaning up his act and cutting down on the prodigious drug taking).

Living in his substance-using never-never land of an untidy London stucco mansion, engaging in a none-too-enthusiastic but versatile sexual ménage with two women, the listless Turner clearly has Blake's invisible worm burrowing away at his soul. Jagger, then riding high as the lead singer of the Rolling Stones, was felt to be a marketable presence, and there is no question that for all the barely-visible acting skills he demonstrates in this film, the duo of iconoclastic filmmakers Roeg and Cammell utilise Jagger's presence intelligently (Roeg was to pull off the same legerdemain with the similarly-limited singer David Bowie in *The Man Who Fell to Earth*) and forged something of a new type of film, infused with the anti-establishment ethos of the day (in which sexual experimentation and drug use were almost obligatory).

Of course, *Performance* is a patchwork, hybrid work: as well as an immersion in the hippie lifestyle, it is also an abrasive gangster film (violently propelled into that territory by the presence of Chaz, a vicious East End criminal who takes refuge from his enemies in Turner's house, at considerable cost to both the gangster and the ex-rock star as the very basis of their identities begin to shift). At the time, the actor James Fox was hardly as well known as he is today, becoming most celebrated for his incarnations of upper middle-class characters (reflecting, in fact, the actor's own background). In fact, the film nearly ended his career; the draining experience of making *Performance* (not to mention its hallucinogenic accoutrements, sampled by the actor) drove the troubled Fox into a period of evangelical Christianity and a forced cessation of his acting career, which was subsequently resumed. As the psychopathic Chaz, however, Fox is truly terrifying, and the film's eruption of bloody violence (notably a sadistic homoerotic beating of the gangster in which his exposed buttocks are whipped) caused almost as much of a furore as the then-graphic sexual couplings in the film.

The latter were rendered even more incendiary by an interesting strategy: the difficulty created for audiences by Roeg and Cammell of identifying precisely which actors or actresses the intertwining naked bodies belonged to. In an era of polymorphous sexuality, it is no accident that the androgynous-looking actress Michele Breton is used to deceive the audience into thinking that she and Jagger are engaged in what appears to be a homosexual clinch (the directors would have been well aware that the actress's flat-chested appearance would have this confusing effect on audiences).

The dislocated time schedule, the mystifying questioning of identity and the sheer visceral impact of the film combined to quickly grant it cult status, but perhaps its lasting legacy are the political points (and the vision of a divided contemporary society) presented by the two directors: the East End gangsters in the film complacently (and self-servingly) regard themselves as representatives of secure, older values (honourable, in their own terms) and disapprove of the sexual licence of the drug-taking hippie generation, while the latter are presented (via Turner's inchoate ménage) as irresponsible, vaguely middle-class dropouts (audiences would have been expected to read Jagger's own hedonistic background into the character he plays here) and consequently less industrious or goal-oriented than the criminal subculture that they are set against, however corrupt this may be. But unlike most films made in Britain before *Performance*, the directors (themselves anti-establishment figures, though in a markedly different fashion from Turner) eschew any notion of taking sides in this class and cultural conflict; yes, the gangsters display a work ethic, but their version of a traditional East End ethos is self-deluding and their dislike of society's rebels is hypocritical in the extreme (as evinced by the readiness of the gangster Chaz to plunge into the sexual excesses of his host); similarly, the Turner character, rejecting all society's debased and commercial values (as he sees them), has nothing to offer in its place other than a plunge into soulless excess and inertia.

The film's jarring, violent ending with a bullet burrowing into a human brain is the logical conclusion to one of the most nihilistic pieces of filmmaking that British cinema has ever given birth to; what's more, the nigh-subliminal image of the writer Jorge Luis Borges that appears at the end of this sequence is a further indicator of the nebulous quality of reality that is the theme of the film (along with, perhaps, a demolition of conventional notions of narrative structure – a Borges trademark). But the logic here is the stripping away of illusion, and the idea of offering something to fill the void thus created is not on the agenda of the two directors.

What seemed so revolutionary in its day (when considered in the context of a crime movie) is the pithy verisimilitude of the gangster scenes (real-life villains were used in supporting roles), notably the hilariously caustic dialogue traded by the violent thugs. The screenplay, though, with its repetitions and non sequiturs, was clearly indebted to the writing of Harold Pinter, who had similarly rendered demotic East End dialogue traded by criminal characters in his groundbreaking plays. These aspects of the film, when viewed in the twenty-first century, render its picture of crime undated, as proved by its congruence with such later films as *Lock, Stock and Two Smoking Barrels* (1998).

As for the drug culture accoutrements with which the film is liberally dusted, it is something of an achievement that what coherence

Performance possesses registers on the screen at all, given that the cast (and many of those behind the camera) were heavily immersed in this very culture. No doubt that aspect would have been less shocking to contemporary audiences than the violence (Warners famously registered metaphorical alarm bells ringing when members of preview audiences apparently vomited after the scene in which the James Fox character is stripped and brutally flogged by the fellow criminals he has crossed).

Interestingly, the film's attitude to music (given the fact that a rock star is cast in a central role) is surprisingly dismissive, and even Jagger's one song in the film ('Memo to Turner') is delivered in a deeply unsympathetic fashion. In many ways, *Performance* can retrospectively be seen as a snapshot of the well-heeled Chelsea 'rebels' of the day, with its mix of middle-class types smoking grass, a variety of sexually available young women (up for whatever diversion was on offer) and ill-focused (and ill-fated) creative types, uncertain of the best avenue through which to express their incoherent vision (one of the directors, Donald Cammell – who embodied certain of these aspects – was to prove ill-fated, dying young with very little of the promise of this film subsequently utilised). Co-director Nicolas Roeg has had a long and interesting (if chequered) subsequent career. Looked at today, the mystification of the Warners executives in Hollywood was an indicator of how much society was (and is) split between the money men and the teenage rebels, a bifurcation which is at the centre of the narrative in the film. And for British viewers in particular, the elements of class conflict remain instructive (the film is largely set in Lowndes Square, which, as Donald Cammell pointed out, boasted more titled residents than any other square in London apart from Eaton Square). Cammell's own fascination with suicide forms a cogent element here and his subsequent fixation on guns had its ultimate expression when he placed a .38 revolver against his forehead and pulled the trigger in his Hollywood apartment. It was a violent end prefigured in the suicide sequence in this most cultish and unorthodox of 1960s British films.

Directors of arthouse films have long enjoyed loving flirtations with genre cinema, notably the durable crime film. In the heyday of the French *Nouvelle Vague*, such genre-literate directors as Jean-Luc Godard, François Truffaut and Claude Chabrol made memorable ventures into the field, although both Godard and Truffaut attempted to maintain a distance by affectionately parodying the form while utilising its devices. British arthouse directors (a club with fewer members) were less attracted (though Chris Petit showed an interest in the form), but one of the most striking syntheses of ambitious personal cinema and the crime fiction genre is Peter Greenaway's *The Cook, The Thief, His Wife and Her Lover* (1989), which utilises a more linear narrative than the director was wont to do in his more esoteric, less audience-friendly work. The casual misogyny of the crime genre (no doubt a reflection of genuine attitudes held within the criminal fraternity, *pace* such British female crime writers as Martina Cole) is examined and deconstructed in the Greenaway film via the treatment of the Helen Mirren character. At this point, the actress was yet to acquire the 'national treasure/nonpareil actress/ mature sex symbol' sobriquet which is now ineluctably her due (a relatively unique combination of copper-bottomed acting creden tials as a Shakespearean of note and a proudly displayed voluptuous sex appeal, latterly finessed by her maintaining of the latter into her sixties). Greenaway was well aware that the hideously brutal, sadistic treatment afforded to her (sophisticated) gangster's moll character by her psychopathic criminal husband (Michael Gambon in a characteristically treble *fff* performance as a vulgarian gang boss who nevertheless prides himself on his appreciation of haute cuisine) is constructed with the knowledge that the audience will be reading the Mirren character closely for her reaction to the violent abuse (including the gruesome murder – and cannibalism directed towards – her bookish lover, played by Alan Howard); certainly, the nuanced reading of the female character here is quite some distance after James Cagney pushing a grapefruit in the face of Mae Clarke in *The Public Enemy*. In other respects, the film is harder to read, except as a critique of the consumerist society which was in full flood in the wake of the celebration of acquisitiveness by the Conservative government (though the fetishisation of food in all its colour and beauty is uncritical, in the usual fashion of the director's customary synthesis of sensual and visual indulgence). Visually, the film has all the rococo flourishes and painterly consciousness that are the hallmarks of Greenaway's work.

The violence of *The Cook, The Thief, His Wife and Her Lover* was kindergarten fare compared to one of its successors. At the time of its initial release in 1990, Peter Medak's *The Krays* caused something of a stir with its unflinching and bloody presentation of the mayhem committed by its ruthless protagonists, but by this stage, the criminal duo's murderous antics were common knowledge, along with their blithe disdain for police interference (the twins had good reason to suppose that the police were turning a blind eye to their score-settling activities). And there was their dubious celebrity status, with such American stars as Judy Garland being introduced to them as part of a lowlife grand tour for visiting showbiz types, not to mention politicians such as Lord Boothby, for whom the homosexual Ronnie Kray arranged sexual favours.

The casting of popular singers Gary and Martin Kemp of Spandau Ballet in Medak's *The Krays* was considered a something of brave move on the part of the director, but it was a decision that paid off, with the insouciant Cockney bravado cleverly captured on film, along with multiple acts of extreme violence, including murder and mutilation with a sharp blade (the so-called 'Chelsea smile', a vicious cut from ear to ear through the victim's cheeks). Another canny casting decision was to employ the respected stage and film actress Billie Whitelaw as the duo's formidable and much-adored mother. The much-mocked retrospective sentimentality indulged in by East End residents who knew (or claimed to know) the Krays devolves upon two morally dubious characteristics, always advanced in defence of the malevolent twins: one, they only murdered their own kind, and two, they were always good to their mother (who, in turn, worshipped them and turned a blind eye to their bloody professional activities). It was important for Medak to confront this special pleading head on, without making the Krays' mother a monstrous harridan in the vein of America's Ma Barker and her brutal offspring; the supremely talented Whitelaw manages to find a humanity in the character while still chilling viewers' spines with her disingenuous acceptance of her sons' behaviour.

In terms of a picture of an efficiently functioning economic unit (as the criminal underworld run by the Krays undoubtedly had to be), Medak cleverly conveys the destabilising effect of the brothers' increasingly erratic behaviour, first undermining the family unit and ultimately leading to their final downfall (the many campaigns to have the surviving Kray brother Reggie released from a long jail sentence, which were successful shortly before his death, are not covered by the film; perhaps Medak felt that he had made his point about the readiness of those in thrall to the Kray legend to forgive two boys who loved their mother).

Knife-wielding mayhem, graphically rendered, was a signature motif of the late 1960s British crime film that found expression throughout most of the 1970s. Based on the autobiography of former criminal Jimmy Boyle, 1979's uncompromising *A Sense of Freedom* was one of the most influential dramas of its time, a film that generated much media attention (not least for its unflinching treatment of bloody and extreme violence). Directed by John Mackenzie (best known for *The Long Good Friday*) and featuring the adroit cinematography camerawork of Oscar-winner Chris Menges, it was justifiably hailed by critics and the public alike for its unflinching depiction of prison life and criminal rehabilitation. But the treatment of violence on film had long been a controversial topic – with the seismic effect of a 1948 film causing a sea change in public attitudes to the subject, as we shall see in the next chapter.

8
Scourging the Unacceptable: Censorship Battles

In the 1930s, American society (inspired by an *avant-la-lettre* Religious Right quite as vociferous as the resurgent movement to be found in the US Republican Party in the twenty-first century) worked itself into something of a lather about the perceived immorality of Hollywood, notably concerning the destabilising influence of such crime films as William Wellman's *The Public Enemy* (1931) and Howard Hawks' *Scarface* (1932). Hollywood, under attack from such organisations as the Catholic Legion of Decency (founded by the Archbishop of Cincinnati in 1933), elected to form its own self-censorship mechanisms to protect itself against pending legislation. The notoriously censorious Hays Code quickly began to enforce ludicrous mealy-mouthed notions of adult behaviour for many years (Michael Curtiz's *Casablanca* prompted the stern edict 'There must be no suggestion of a sexual relationship between Humphrey Bogart and Ingrid Bergman'), until iconoclastic filmmakers such as Otto Preminger began to challenge such censorship in the 1950s with films that treated their audiences as adults.

As is so often the case, a sneeze in the USA resulted in a cold being caught in the UK. A similar readiness was demonstrated by British politicos and journalists to blame the ills of society on the scourge of 'immoral' crime films, and parliamentary questions over a variety of crime films were to follow from the 1940s onwards. Major battles over (and the banning of) such films ensued, notably a furore over a maladroit adaption of James Hadley Chase's then-scandalous *No Orchids for Miss Blandish* (1948). The new liberalism of modern cinema (in which uncut versions of films raise no eyebrows) was decades away.

It has long been the principal rallying call (and not just of those on the right of the political spectrum) that a sure-fire way to unite both the party and public opinion is to pick a soft target for vilification – and what better than the 'noxious influence' of the crime film? The issue as to whether or not crime is the result of a combination of the venal aspects of human behaviour and social deprivation (along with dozens of other factors) is more simply dealt with by subsuming it in an attack on such popular entertainments as the crime film. Popular entertainments have been subjected to moral disapproval since Victorian diatribes against Penny Dreadfuls, and such things remain sure-fire material for conjuring public indignation. Censorship battles have been rife over the years, and the same scenario tends to reappear, transmogrified into different battles with different enemies (crime and horror comics in the USA were the target in the 1950s, while videos were the target in the UK in the 1980s). There is also a certain paternalistic assumption that the working classes – presumed to be the principal consumers of popular entertainment – need protecting from malign influences, otherwise there will be an inevitable slide into lives of criminality (the implication being that other factors are less pressing – or less straightforward to tackle). It remains a modern-day preoccupation along the lines of the famous prosecuting counsel's blithe remark in the trial of D.H. Lawrence's *Lady Chatterley's Lover* in 1960: 'Is it a book you would wish your wife or servants to read?'

The fears concerning such issues stretch back to the early days of the British and American sound cinema, inspired by the brutal and astringently made crime films of the era, which engendered new censorship regulations on both sides of the Atlantic. In the 1930s, the British Board of Film Censors, after an initial over-reaction to the more violent aspects of American cinema, began to assume a slightly more liberal line, possible due to the transatlantic 'distancing' effect; this was, after all, a picture of another society and it was felt that Britons regarded America as a more lawless place in any case. Such perceptions were to change when it came to home-grown product. In this period, there was in any case considerable self-censorship, with many proposed scenarios not getting beyond even the script stage (this pre-censorship operated well into the 1960s; Hammer Films, which had made its mark with crime movies before its profitable move into the gothic, regularly submitted scripts to the then-censor

John Trevelyan, who made suggestions as to precisely how the films should be filmed – to some degree the censor had become a film-maker, as Trevelyan himself somewhat immodestly stated, perhaps hoping to give his decidedly uncreative calling a creative finessing). Some of the objections raised by Trevelyan and his easily-shocked colleagues now seem quite hilariously naive to modern viewers, but resulted in a certain neutering of many films, similar to the American pre-censorship of such films as *Casablanca* (as mentioned earlier) and Hitchcock's *Suspicion*.

The popularity of the pulp writer Edgar Wallace in Britain worried moral guardians. The crime author's output was prodigious in the 1930s (that popularity has since waned considerably and most of his books are out of print, although he still posthumously maintains a strong German readership); it was adaptations of Wallace, who specialised in tough gangster scenarios along with his myriad other preoccupations, that to some degree was the literary voice behind British gangster films of the day and their (now phoney-seeming) toughness. However, the most celebrated censorship clash of the 1930s and 1940s in the UK was probably the faux-American British film of James Hadley Chase's *No Orchids for Miss Blandish*, discussed below. But there were other examples of acrimonious censorship battles – and the 1970s were to prove equally contentious as representations of murder and the carnal became more explicit.

The more straightened circumstances of British residents after the end of the Second World War created a black market, and black marketeering was certainly an issue in many of the British crime films of the 1940s. But this type of misdemeanour worried potential censors far less than issues of sex and violence, always the most hot-button issues when it came to the potential cutting of films. The response to the brief period of liberalism under Stephen Murphy in the 1970s was another one of the periodic cracking downs by the establishment against the crime film and, in 1971, the film *Villain*, directed by Michael Tuchner, was subject to much tampering, with both dialogue and action treated to careful amendments, although by now there were no issues with the homosexuality of the central character played by Richard Burton and clearly based on the gangster Ronnie Kray. A similar furore greeted John Mackenzie's *The Long Good Friday* (1980), which at one point was to be both a cinema and/or a television release; because the British Board of Film Censors allowed the film to be shown uncut (notably with its blood-gushing throat killing with a piece of broken glass), it was released in the cinema rather than on television (which would have required cuts) and thus began its progression to becoming one of the most influential of British crime films.

Societal attitudes to prostitution were affected by the Street Offences Act of 1959 and the subsequent Betting and Gaming Act of 1960, with its revaluation of attitudes to gambling. At the same time, reverential attitudes to the police were beginning to be revised downwards in light of a variety of scandals affecting the Metropolitan Police. But it was in the 1940s that one of the most influential of filmic challenges to the status quo occurred, resulting in a radical rethink on censorship and a much more frequent use of the censor's scissors.

The astonishing furore that greeted the 1948 British film of *No Orchids for Miss Blandish* now seems absurd. The direct replication of the screams of outrage that greeted the source novel was, perhaps, to be expected, given the fact that the director St John Legh Clowes (whose sole film credit this is) clearly set himself the task of producing the strongest and gamiest material (within the censorship limitations of the day) that he could get away with in order to match his source material. In fact, the very fact that Legh Clowes did (initially at least) get away with it sent out a false signal: a new dark age of censorship was to follow the film, and the consensus between critics and moral guardians quickly coalesced along the lines of 'how was this depraved drama allowed to be passed uncut?'. In fact, the stricter censorship of sexual scenes and violence that followed the lenient treatment of this film was to be echoed in the 1970s after the then-head of the British Board of Film Censors, Stephen Murphy, took the decision to allow adult audiences to make up their own minds about such contentious films as Stanley Kubrick's *A Clockwork Orange* and Sam Peckinpah's *Straw Dogs*. Murphy's liberal decisions had the consequence of creating battle lines between those who argued for the freedom of filmmakers to follow their vision without fear of upsetting the squeamish or the prudish and those who would only be happy with films designed for a family audience. As with the 1948 brouhaha over the Legh Clowes film, there were those in positions of authority who felt that mass-market films (along with other forms of popular entertainment) offered a serious challenge to established morality if they moved into certain taboo territory.

James Hadley Chase's original plot details how a wealthy young heiress is kidnapped by a depraved gang led by a monstrous mother figure. The latter was patterned after several influences: the real-life Ma Barker gang (with its rebellious alpha male son who wrests control of the gang from his suddenly weaker Mother – a motif maintained both here and in several films based on the real-life Ma Barker gang, Roger Corman's hyperkinetic version with Shelley Winters) and also the classic American novelist William Faulkner, whose shocking 1931 novel *Sanctuary* similarly featured the brutal rape of a kidnapped young woman. Interestingly, the American actor Jack La Rue, who was to be hired for the British film of *No Orchids* (after such actors as George Raft and Franchot Tone passed on the project), had already played the similar part of the kidnapper in a 1933 film of Faulkner's novel, retitled *The Story of Temple Drake*. Ironically, given the uproar that the British film created, it still represented a considerable softening and neutering of the original novel, in which the brutal psychopathic rapist Slim Grissom is presented as a loathsome figure as opposed to the more sympathetic Bogart-like characteristics he is granted by the British writer-director and American actor here. Similarly, the aspect of the novel that so outraged George Orwell in his famous essay 'Raffles and Miss Blandish' written four years before this film (such as Slim's orgasms when knifing a victim to death) were nowhere to be seen, but such elements were also removed by the author himself in the heavily censored version of the novel he himself prepared, perhaps smarting from Orwell's attack as much as the more general moral outrage that the book generated. Having said this, it should be noted that the violence and sexuality in the film are unquestionably more unbuttoned and graphic than in most British product of the day and is much closer to the pre-Hays Code mayhem of early James Cagney crime movies. But that very violence – not least because of its maladroit handling – is more likely to promote laughter than revulsion in modern audiences for several reasons: the barman bloodily hit across the face by a bottle is played by the comic character actor Sidney James, sporting one of the film's many unconvincing American accents – and even when the actor reappears with his face bandaged (and having suffered the apparent loss of an eye), there is no real sense of violent injury. Similarly, the Foley track of the film – before sound designs were referred to as such – presents an unconvincing sound picture, with the many gunshots sounding like cap pistols.

In terms of sexuality, however, the film remains more intriguing. The producers may have been unable to secure the services of their first choice for Miss Blandish, the handsomely equipped Jane Russell, from a recalcitrant Howard Hughes, but the British actress Linden Travers (who had played the part of the heiress on stage) nevertheless conveys a strong sexual allure until the deeply unconvincing romantic scenes when she falls in love with the murderous Slim Grissom (these scenes are not helped by the lugubrious string writing by the film's composer George Melachrino, who seems unaware that he is scoring a carnal *amour fou* rather than a straightforward romantic tryst). Nevertheless, the sexual elements that so upset Christian groups of the day are still provocative: the frequent presentation of the threat of rape (which, in the event, does not happen – despite received thinking on the subject, all the sex in the film is consensual) and Jack La Rue's sliding of his hand beneath Linden Travers' dressing down onto her breast are certainly things that would not be seen again in films for over 25 years. But the sexual politics of the film cannot really be addressed on any serious level; nor, for that matter, can the unreal picture of America so assiduously created (to little avail) by the British filmmakers and actors.

By the time the film was shown in the USA, it was in a heavily censored form and suffered a limited shelf life in the UK despite its considerable commercial success (as usual, all the attempts to censor the film had a healthy impact on its box-office returns); it was to be decades before *No Orchids for Miss Blandish* was made available in an uncensored cut (facilitated by its original US distributor, the producer Richard Gordon, who has proved to be an illuminating commentator on the film's history and notoriety). Its reappearance after many years of obscurity in the UK was courtesy of its showing in a 'banned' season on Channel 4. The novel itself was remade in 1971 by Robert Aldrich – this time in the USA – as *The Grissom Gang*, but created no hysterical reaction to echo that which greeted the St John Legh Clowes version.

The principal target for the censor is sex – and sex (of a twisted and repressed variety) is central to the innovative psychological study of murder, *Peeping Tom* (Michael Powell, 1960), a film which was loathed and reviled by the popular press when it was released and its director publicly pilloried for his perceived dereliction of good taste as a result. The ultimate censorship for Powell was his neutralisation as a filmmaker – the sidelining of his career. Though he made few films of note in the intervening years, Powell is today highly regarded by contemporary filmmakers such as Francis Ford Coppola and Martin Scorsese, and attitudes to the film have been radically revised.

It is particularly sad when the critical or commercial failure of a film ends a director's career (the most famous example being Charles Laughton's beautiful and poetic *Night of the Hunter*; the lack of success of Laughton's sole film as a director precluding further attempts – although, of course, he could return to his considerable talents as an actor). Not so, however, for Michael Powell – a man who, after years in the wilderness, was gradually recognised (along with the expatriate Alfred Hitchcock) as Britain's greatest director. The crushing critical barbs hurled at his masterpiece *Peeping Tom*, together with its relative commercial failure, virtually crippled his directing career, followed only by sporadic and unsatisfactory efforts like *Age of Consent* (sporting a young, nubile and mostly nude Helen Mirren).

Powell enjoyed an Indian summer as friend and adviser to such younger American directors as Scorsese and Coppola, both of whom acknowledged him as an influence on their own films, notably in his remarkable use of colour. But this late appreciation has hardly com-pensated cinéastes for the potentially brilliant work that might have followed a film on which the establishment and press vented their accumulated self-righteous fury – much as the video industry was to be used as a scapegoat for reasons of political expediency (with several undistinguished MPs enjoying a brief moment in the sun by decrying the moral turpitude of the film industry).

Powell's earlier films (with Emeric Pressburger as collaborator) were ahead of their time in the full-blooded, startlingly un-English romanticism of their visions: surrealism, Celtic mysticism and deliri-ous colour schemes jostled with an astonishing feeling for the English countryside. Elements of the horrific and the supernatural surfaced in *The Thief of Bagdad* and *Black Narcissus*, as well as the two films which may be respectively the most imaginatively cinematic opera and ballet films ever made (*Tales of Hoffmann* and *The Red Shoes*). But British film critics of the day respected only the realistic approach and had little time for these astonishing films, which have only recently achieved their rightful status. Politically, the tone is a bizarre mélange of Conservatism and romantic libertarianism: an unsettling mix.

However, critical coolness erupted into spluttering fury with the release of Powell's small-scale film about a disturbed young photographer who films his victims while murdering them. Any comprehension that Powell had made one of the most rich and complex films to explore the very relationship between the viewer and the work of art in the most rigorous terms was not evident in the furore. '*Peeping Tom* stinks more than anything else in British films since *The Stranglers of Bombay*' (*New Statesman*); 'It wallows in the diseased urges of a homicidal pervert ... from its lumbering, mildly salacious beginning to its appallingly masochistic and depraved climax, it is wholly evil' (*Daily Worker*); and, most famously: 'The only really satisfactory way to dispose of *Peeping Tom* would be to shovel it up and flush it swiftly down the nearest sewer. Even then the stench would remain' (*Tribune*).

This nigh-operatic vituperation might now seem all too familiar when one thinks of the vilification subsequently hurled at videotapes during the aforementioned 'video nasties' hysteria. But whereas many films seek only to shock (admittedly a laudable intention, with a lengthy and respectable pedigree), Powell quickly makes apparent to the viewer that he is initiating a dialogue with our expectations and preconditioning when experiencing any work of fiction. It is, like those of his countryman Alfred Hitchcock, a dialogue concerning our own voyeurism – the deepest logic of the cinema experience. In *Peeping Tom*, our gaze becomes a metaphor for the psychopathic hero's murderous impulses.

Clearly, what disturbed moral guardians of the day more than the violence (mild and oblique by today's standards) was the accompanying overlay of sympathy and understanding for the emotionally and psychologically crippled hero, Mark, subtly played by Carl Boehm, whose understated Germanic quality plays against the quintessential Englishness of the film. The latter is most resonantly represented in the corner shops selling pornographic magazines and sleazy camera-for-hire photoshoots of nearly-nude models; the British attitude to sex is cannily anatomised and the presence in the film of the premier nude model of the day, Pamela Green, is emblematic.

In fact, the issues regarding the ambiguous gaze by Powell in the film are embodied in Mark's appalling father, seen only in the protagonist's own home movies – the father's treatment of his son represents a repression and controlling of instinct by 'organising' forces, which results in massive damage to the psyche.

It now seems clear that what really upset the pundits was Powell's clear accusation – as mentioned above – that all our personalities incorporate elements of voyeurism: the very act of watching a film is a gazing at private, behind-closed-doors experiences (an element also to be found in that other once-maligned, now-celebrated masterpiece of 1960, Hitchcock's *Psycho*).

This theme of 'looking' is rigorously examined throughout the film, as is the constant reminder that we are viewers watching a film. The very first sequence, seen through the gate of Mark's camera, is his pursuit and murder of a streetwalker played by Brenda Bruce. And it is the radical daring of the film's technique – first demonstrated in this sequence – that has sustained appreciation of Powell's boundless inventiveness over the years.

Mark's job, as 'focus-puller' in a film studio, is supplemented by his part-time 'girlie' photography (the late-1950s world of corner shop pin-up magazines of photographer Harrison Marks and his contemporaries is cleverly evoked, with the avuncular Miles Malleson (of all people), that cosiest of British character actors, giving a delightful cameo as a prospective buyer of 'artistic views'). But Mark's obsession is murdering girls while simultaneously photographing their terror – and the full symbolism of twisted sexuality is expressed in the phallicism of Mark's camera tripod – the instrument that sublimates the function Mark cannot perform by terminating the objects of his desire.

The house Mark lives in, along with lodgers Helen (Anna Massey) and her blind mother (Maxine Audley), is an inheritance from his father, a psychologist who studied the effects of fear by submitting his own son to vicious experiments – resulting, of course, in his traumatised adult personality. And here we find one of the many references in the film that become relevant when we *know* about them – Mark's father is played by Michael Powell himself, with his own son as the tormented youthful Mark seen in the 8 mm movies. Not essential knowledge for the viewer, of course, and there's no way that most people would pick up on this, but as Powell is controlling our responses (much as Mark's father does his son's), it's a fascinating side issue, more suggestive since the rise of semiotics. The same is true of the screenwriter Leo Marks giving his protagonist a kind of 'mirror image' of his own name, Mark Lewis, or clever touches such as Mark's reply as to which newspaper he works for (*The Observer*) or as to whether or not he knew a murdered starlet (Moira Shearer, of Powell's *The Red Shoes*): 'Only by sight.' And a film director is played by Powell regular Esmond Knight – himself partially blinded during the Second World War. We're clearly dealing with rich textual density here.

But the 'vision' motif is also integrated on a deeper basis. The mother of Mark's naive girlfriend Helen is played by Maxine Audley, and this character, though blind, *sees* in a kind of psychic way the dangerous depths beneath Mark's outwardly shy persona – and is accordingly the victim of a murder attempt by Mark fraught with Oedipal overtones. And Mark is unable to 'see' the potential salvation in a sexual relationship with Helen – rather like Anthony Perkins' blind-alley meeting with Janet Leigh in *Psycho* – a character deformed by parental insensitivity is unable to respond to 'normal' relationships.

Of course, the deaths we witness in the film are orchestrated unlike any other filmic violence. The impersonal, unseen assassin of the first 8 mm assault forces us to become a camera – as well as the client of the prostitute (the client actually being Mark). Later scenes, in which we know that Mark is psyching himself up to kill the actress and photographer's model he is alone with, have a quality that disturbs on two levels – the tension and suspense engendered for the soon-to-be victim (Moira Shearer, making a screen test in an empty film studio), as well as Powell forcing us to identify with Mark's attractive vulnerability despite our full knowledge of his psychotic character (i.e. in the delicious scene where Helen discovers that Mark is her landlord rather than a shy fellow lodger: 'But you creep around as if you haven't paid the rent!' 'I haven't.').

The effect of the threatened violence in the film is generally gripping and compulsive, while its actual expression (a cut to a red spotlight at Shearer's death, for instance) would hardly satisfy the tastes of today's audience for more specifically graphic effects. Powell's own disingenuous statements about the film, however, are presumably to be taken with the proverbial pinch of salt: '*Peeping Tom* is a very tender film, a very nice one. Almost a romantic film. I felt very close to the hero who is an "absolute" director, someone who approaches life like a director, who is conscious of and suffers from it. He is a technician of emotion.' While Powell is right about the sympathy extended to, and engendered by, his hero, we are never allowed to forget what lies beneath his nervous surface – after a conversation with Helen, he 'frames' her just-absent face with his hands, and we wonder if she is next for the lethal tripod.

The scene that stays with the viewer the longest is Mark's suicide – as the police approach the house, he sets up his camera to film the moment of his death and impales himself in the throat on his own tripod. Apart from the double voyeuristic charge of the scene (Mark watching his own death in a mirror even as we watch), we are allowed to feel both a sense of release – there is, we realise, no hope for Mark – and a dramatic 'rightness', an organised conclusion to an organised series of events. The final frames leave us looking at ourselves – innocent but involved voyeurs.

Direct censorship issues involved a film made some five years later. Guy Hamilton's *The Party's Over* (1965) had accrued a considerable reputation over the years as a butchered *film maudit*, despite the fact that few people had seen it in the form which its director intended. After all, how many mainstream films had utilised necrophilia as a theme? But the British Film Institute came to the rescue by restoring Hamilton's censorship-truncated film to its original state for a Blu-ray release, and it was now possible to see what had whipped the moral custodians of the day into one of their periodic panics. Needless to say, the once-controversial material would hardly be likely to shock modern audiences, but in its unneutered form, the film still carries a certain subversive charge.

The opening sequence is striking. A group of wasted-looking (but chic) young people wander in desultory fashion over London's Albert Bridge at dawn to the sound of Annie Ross' plaintive theme song, and what follows is a picture of ill-focused lives seeking direction but finding distraction in increasingly dispiriting ways. The actor Oliver Reed (then at the height of his self-destructive Byronic period as an actor) plays a charismatic young man who treats his pliable acolytes with contempt, but utilises his sexuality to keep a variety of sexually biddable women in their places (his character is reminiscent of – though not as vicious as – America's Charles Manson, taking weak-willed followers into the realms of depravity). The film's eponymous party is to feature both a death as well as inadvertent necrophiliac situations – and it is this last element which landed Hamilton and co. in such hot water. An American businessman (played – in one of his best performances – by Eddie Albert) is traversing London, looking for his daughter, unaware that she has died accidentally at a party given by the Reed character's group, 'The Pack', and has undergone a posthumous sexual attack. The fact that her attacker subsequently commits suicide was one incendiary element too many for the British Board of Film Censors, along with one element that always appeared to foster concern: rebellious youth groups unshackled by the restraints of convention, and indulging in carnal activity. The brouhaha created in the offices of the BBFC resulted in a delay of nearly two years before the film was released in a heavily cut form. But director Guy Hamilton and producer Anthony Perry removed their credits from the film, feeling that the truncated piece that remained was not the work they had committed themselves to. Interestingly, the film is a touch reminiscent of Edmond T. Gréville's *Beat Girl* in its picture of dissolute youth, though Hamilton's moral commentary on his protagonists is more nuanced. Much of the film's power is communicated in Oliver Reed's hypnotic performance, and it is salutary to remind oneself how much presence and dark sexual menace the young actor had before he put on weight and allowed his own hedonistic lifestyle to affect his performances for the worse. He is partnered in *The Party's Over* by the always-impressive Ann Lynn, an actress who never quite achieved the stardom she deserved but who turned in a series of truthful and sharply etched performances; she is particularly notable here as Reed's despairing, much-abused girlfriend. The Reed character's contemptuous use of all those around him may be read as an expression of self-loathing, but perhaps the filmmakers (despite their non-judgemental stance) are indulging in some of the moral disapproval which was (ironically) to come down heavily on the film when it was submitted to the BBFC. That organisation saw a way out of the problems created by the depravity practised by the youthful anti-heroes; much in the fashion of Hollywood films of the 1940s, it was felt that moral order might be restored by the wholesale death of the characters – a solution, needless to say, that found no favour with the director. Ultimately, 18 minutes were removed from the film, to ruinous effect, and it is hardly surprising that the reviews of the day were unenthusiastic – not least because a wholly redundant narration was spatchcocked onto the beginning of the film. The element that particularly upset the censors was the disturbing scene in which members of 'The Pack' take off the underwear of the comatose young girl, and the variety of reactions from the group (not least the leader's reluctance to stop the outrage, along with his apparent nervousness concerning the juggernaut he himself has set in motion). The excision of this scene made a nonsense of the points that Hamilton was trying to make about the complaisance (or otherwise) of his characters' participation in this violation. Perhaps Hamilton's real sin in the eyes of the censor was to detail his ignoble protagonists' rejection of society, but not to allow them to find a new direction for their lives. Where was the moral uplift? Clearly, the cinema of the day was not ready for such a nihilistic vision as that on offer here, but at least in the early twenty-first century, audiences can judge for themselves what cinema-goers had to be protected from several decades earlier.

9
Metropolitan Murder: London

A particularly idiosyncratic view of the capital may be perceived through the British crime film over the years: kaleidoscopic, ugly, full of quirky character and colour, as authentic in its vision as it is deceptive. And there is no gainsaying the value of such films as snapshots of a vanished London (such as the two gasometers at the back of King's Cross station – one remains – or the railway bridges, corpses-for-the-disposal-of, for instance, in *The Ladykillers*, or the busy, pre-re-development docks of innumerable films, perhaps most notably *Pool of London*). Other cultural artefacts abound along with such pictorial elements: certain non-heritage (and less respectable) facets of the capital were utilised only in the crime genre (such as the seedy subculture of pornographic photo studios and bookshops in Michael Powell's *Peeping Tom*, as discussed above). More specifically, the genre has afforded a vision of the compact district of Soho as a microcosm of Britain.

For audiences (from whatever class background), the crime film afforded an opportunity to move into locales which may or may not have been familiar – areas some considerable distance from the well-appointed Curzon Street or Park Lane. The world shown in such films as Arthur Woods' *They Drive by Night* (1938) evokes everyday settings presented with a real sense of verisimilitude, and the cafés and dance pavilions against which the drama is played out have a liveliness which is absent from the artificially conceived drawing rooms of more respectable film product (or West End theatre, the natural home for such milieux from the 1930s to the 1950s). Later films such as Roy Ward Baker's *Flame in the Streets* (1961), which dealt with racial prejudice rather than crime, demonstrate a similarly acute feel for the well-chosen downmarket location (often the public house, before the latter setting was hijacked for endlessly repetitive dramatic confrontations in TV soap operas). As with the classic American private eye drama, movement across social divides in films such as these was granted to two groups: the coppers licensed to ask unacceptable questions of anyone (from whatever background) involved in a crime and the viewers of the film themselves, taken on an odyssey which may lead from restored Georgian houses in Kensington to the insalubrious backstreets of Whitechapel.

London's East End and its inhabitants are frequently traduced, both on the printed page and on film. Whether judgements have issued from Victorian writers, contemporary sociologists or the *soi-disant* neo-Georgians who have canonised Cockney London, the image is frequently of an under-threat tribe, studied as if they were anthropological subjects to whom a key exists – if it could just be identified. Working-class Londoners, of course, are as much the result of socioeconomic influences as the proletarian inhabitants of Manchester or Leeds, but enjoyed more cinematic anatomising – London, after all, was where most films were set; the city is an exportable commodity. Crime films (and television) have found fecund territory in London-set generational clashes, drug crime, the creation of Docklands from disused wharfs and warehouses, and the concomitant property crime that followed.

Patrick Hamilton's *Twenty Thousand Streets Under the Sky* is a book that supplied many readers with defining images of London, and the celebrated 1935 trilogy (which was, until recently, relatively undervalued) is particularly trenchant when dealing with those lower down the social scale. The novelist's influence on films has been peripheral, but his influence on other writers was considerably stronger; it might be said, therefore, that some of the crime writers he influenced – and whose work was subsequently filmed – have carried the shadow of the Hamilton influence into the cinema, albeit indirectly.

The capital has long been a place of criminous associations, dating back to the eighteenth-century Newgate Calendar recording illegality. And many modern writers on the city (notably the prolific Peter Ackroyd) have spent as much time lovingly detailing London's criminal past as its literary glories and architectural splendours. Moreover, the filmic possibilities of London's most notorious criminals – from Jack the Ripper to the Kray Twins – have been thoroughly exploited (although the latter duo have made their way into films principally in disguised form, and even conflated into one character, as in the psychopathic Vic Dakin in Michael Tuchner's *Villain*). As for the locales, the disadvantaged and impoverished of Victorian London were, of course, denizens of slums which were a breeding ground for crime, but wartime racketeering and post-war spiv activity in the terraced houses of the East End have presented just a handful of the useful settings so thoroughly utilised in British crime films. Writers such as Arthur La Bern have creatively drawn on this malign topography in such novels as *It Always Rains on Sunday* (a book which was filmed with distinction by Robert Hamer).

Murder apart (and statistically over half the murders in Britain have for several decades taken place in the metropolis), in the twenty-first century, drug-related crime and people trafficking (including that of young Eastern European women for prostitution) have been the mainspring of many a contemporary crime narrative. Actually, some filmmakers have not been slow to recognise how fruitful the novel is as a source for adaptation, a tradition that continues to this day with such writers as Jake Arnott providing the source for the distinctive gangster epic *The Long Firm*. Interestingly, the preoccupations of modern crime writers remain essentially those of the city's greatest chronicler Charles Dickens, who brought to life with maximum vividness every social strata of the city itself from its loamiest crime-ridden slums to its exclusive gentlemen's clubs. Some important novelists appear to have resisted the filming process, notably (so far) the remarkable Robin Cook, not the late British politician or the American medical thriller writer but the louche old Etonian who wrote as Derek Raymond and produced a series of scarifying and utterly uncompromising novels such as *He Died with His Eyes Open* and *I Was Dora Suarez* – books whose jet-black vision has permeated modern crime films without direct adaptations. But from whatever time period and from whatever social background, the infinitely rich and varied possibilities of London continue to be a rich source of inspiration for both novelists and filmmakers.

It is interesting to note that two of the most striking films in terms of presenting an image of London (now frozen in aspic, as development has swept away many of the locations utilised) are two comedies from the otherwise staid Ealing Studios: Alexander Mackendrick's *The Ladykillers* and Charles Crichton's *The Lavender Hill Mob*. Both films show a remarkably detailed (if geographically inexact) picture of London, and Mackendrick's film in particular may be studied for its images of the King's Cross and St Pancras area (the site of the film's robbery and now the city's gateway to Paris), although it is interesting to note that considerable liberties were taken with the topography of the area. The innocent old lady's house from which St Pancras station may be seen did not in fact exist (except as a matte shot) and the bridge behind her house – from which various murder victims are unceremoniously dropped onto passing trains – was, in fact, a couple of miles away. Cinéastes have been known to track down these particular areas, which had until recently remaining fragments that ensured they might still be recognised, despite a flourish of industrial development. What is equally significant about these Ealing films, though, is their sub-versive charge: the fact that a director with as bleak and cynical a vision as Alexander Mackendrick could make a film such as the remarkably bleak (if hilarious) *The Ladykillers* within the unbend-ingly tidy Calvinist universe of Michael Balcon is remarkable, and even more so when viewed today. The film is as black a comedy as one could wish, with the deaths of virtually its entire male cast still shocking even in an era when wholesale carnage is hardly novel. The fact that it is an Ealing film in which such things take place is particularly piquant – but less so when one realises that the director was to go on to film one of the most abrasive visions of America in *Sweet Smell of Success*. Watching *The Ladykillers* in the twenty-first century is a truly salutary experience: Mackendrick's marvellous 1950s black comedy dates only in the best possible way, and apart from being a showcase for some of the best of British comic acting talent (not least Alec Guinness' sinister mastermind, always on the verge of losing his fragile sanity), this is now something of a 1950s social document, and the picture of London's pre-Eurostar King's Cross and St Pancras stations (with the dual gas rings and endlessly rushing steam trains) as a setting for the skulduggery is particularly serendipitous today. It is a shame, though, that a ludicrous censor-ship cut of the day has not been restored for subsequent showings of the film: an underlit shot of Guinness' basilisk face when his madness is ill-advisedly touched upon. Mackendrick's *The Man in the*

White Suit (with Guinness in a very different role) remains a sharp satire on consumerism, while T.E.B. Clarke's bristling and witty screenplay for *Kind Hearts and Coronets* has a lustre that simply cannot be found today, but William Rose's jet-black screenplay for *The Ladykillers* is *sui generis*.

However, London – imaginatively utilised as part of the fabric of a film – could function as a metaphor as much as a canvas, as in the integral use of the city in a 1956 film directed by Roy Ward Baker.

Tiger in the Smoke – from the Margery Allingham novel – is a significant film in many ways for the British film industry at the time. Films of celebrated crime novels have an intrinsic interest (depending on the level of expertise employed) in how much justice they do to the source material. Allingham is well served. Director Roy Ward Baker's version of Allingham's most influential novel freights in several extra layers of rewarding material for the informed viewer: a picture of British filmmaking conventions in the mid-1950s; a striking visual record of London not available for a novelist; the compromises forced on any filmmaker in adapting a difficult novel. Firstly, it appropriates the police procedural form (as it existed in the UK at the time) and treats it in an unorthodox fashion, with a far greater stress on the psychology of the criminal than was customary in the 1950s. *Tiger in the Smoke* focuses on the activities of a group of ex-servicemen in London and the swathe a murderous criminal cuts through his opponents. Several crooked Second World War veterans track down their former sergeant, Jack Havoc, who appears to have absconded with loot from a wartime commando raid. Havoc has, in fact, broken out of Wormwood Scrubs and is similarly tracking down the missing loot, but is ruthlessly eliminating anyone who gets in his way (including a luckless caretaker). Taking its cue from Allingham's novel, Baker (who – once underrated – is now seen as one of the more interesting genre directors who worked in the UK and abroad) offers an intriguing study in criminal psychosis rather than simply accepting the reductive notion of evil for his malefactor. The director has already shown his skill in the crime film format with the unusual *The October Man* (written by Eric Ambler) in 1947, but *Tiger in the Smoke* was an altogether more ambitious piece of work. Despite Alec Clunes' straightforward incarnation of detective Charlie Luke (which makes only a cursory impression), the film is a relatively sophisticated treatment of the mind of a murderer (located in the homicidal figure of Jack Havoc – the name, of course, possessing a Dickensian utilitarian quality), and it is a measure of the director's skill that he is able to make the character so grimly convincing, given that the actor Tony Wright does not really have the measure of Havoc's homicidal charisma. (It's interesting to speculate what Laurence Harvey, another actor of widely disparate achievement – from the exemplary to the truly bathetic – might have made of the figure.) Havoc makes life miserable for a clergyman and his daughter who he threatens (Laurence Naismith and Muriel Pavlow both respond intelligently to Baker's direction), and the pursuit of the film's Maguffin (an object of desire and wealth) is given an almost metaphysical direction, particularly as Havoc's success in his quest turns out to be a pyrrhic victory.

Perhaps the film's real achievement is an evocation of the city of London at a transitional period in its history (with ex-soldiers struggling to come to terms with a post-war world and the traditional moral values once held so dear now up for grabs), while never forgetting the imperatives of a carefully orchestrated suspense narrative. The film of *Tiger in the Smoke*, when set against other contemporary British crime movies such as *Blind Date* and *Sapphire*, demonstrates that the cinema of the day was attempting to engage with various social issues (such as racism in *Sapphire*) and it addresses the issue of servicemen cast adrift after the war and moving into criminality (other examples of this trend include *They Made Me a Fugitive* and *The Flamingo Affair*). The moral issues here are ambiguous: what is the responsibility of society to the men who have fought for it? Answers are not forthcoming. The film, like most other entries in this subgenre, ends with the death of the crooked servicemen. However, the most memorable aspect of *Tiger in the Smoke* today is its prescient picture of affectless evil as embodied in the ruthless Havoc menacing a variety of victims. Tony Wright, while patently not plumbing the depths of psychopathic menace that both earlier and later actors had strip-mined (notably James Cagney and Robert De Niro), is still a disturbing presence, and the film transcends the genteel qualities of many British crime films to convey an authentic, lean minatory quality. In addition, Baker is able to present an all-encompassing picture of the city and its benighted inhabitants – the eponymous 'Smoke', London itself, as evoked here, is as vividly realised a locale as anything in British crime cinema.

Gerald Kersh had long been written off as something of a hack writer and his subsequent reputation as a cult novelist was some distance away when a film was made of his most celebrated novel *Night and the City*, originally published in 1938. To some degree, the film reflected British cinema's eternal problem in selling its product to an America that took such efforts under sufferance (in the 1960s, Harry Saltzman and Albert R. Broccoli had some difficulties persuading American distributors that James Bond, Fleming's super-agent, would be accepted by American audiences, who (it was felt) were reluctant to be persuaded that a British hero could be so ruthless and sexually voracious – a situation that seems quaint today). Certainly, the selling of the 1950 film adaptation of *Night and the City* was finessed by the presence in the film of the charismatic American star Richard Widmark, who had made such a mark as the giggling psychopathic killer pushing a woman in a wheelchair downstairs in *Kiss of Death*. Other elements were incorporated to make the film of *Night and the City* more palatable for its American sales. There was, of course, the fact that a vivid and phantasmagorical picture of a seedy London was very much part of the package, and that had never been a difficult element for American audiences to accept, who had long regarded the city as gloomily atmospheric and the perfect setting for crime (a reputation stretching back to Sherlock Holmes – both Arthur Conan Doyle's stories and the famous series of Basil Rathbone films made in Hollywood). The film was further rendered palatable by the use of a striking symphonic score by Franz Waxman, who (despite being German) was one of the crucial elements in creating the synthesis of nineteenth-century symphonic writing, American jazz and other elements that became the signature sound of the American film. (The film was re-scored in the UK by the craftsmanlike Benjamin Frankel.) The final element in making the soufflé rise for American audiences, of course, was the presence of another bankable American star, Gene Tierney, who is somewhat underused in the film but provided marquee value with her name.

Harry Fabian is one of the great spiv figures of the age, and the film presents a picture of his destruction aided both by the strong direction of the varied cast and the production design, such as the vividly rendered nightclub owned by the sinister Nosseross (played in splendidly repulsive fashion by the corpulent Francis L. Sullivan). The club's vocalist Mary (Tierney) is in love with the charming but feckless Harry Fabian, even though she is well aware that the possibilities of a settled life for the couple are remote indeed. Her realism is partly due to the fact that the untrustworthy Harry has attempted to make off with the nest egg she has been collecting for the future that the couple are ostensibly planning. Needless to say, Harry (along with the various other criminal activities we see him take part in) does indeed steal this money, and his moral restitution at the end of the film lies in his trying to persuade the villainous promoter Kristo (memorably played by Herbert Lom in one of his many telling criminal roles of the day) that Mary is responsible for pointing his enemies to him and is worthy of the reward that Kristo has put on his capture.

The film itself is a remarkable polyglot mix of American and British elements, and the dialogue has a non-naturalistic, mannered feel (not to everyone's taste) which to some degree reflects the original Gerald Kersh novel, but adds a poetic resonance of its own. There are elements here, too, of German Expressionism and even the fatalism of Shakespearean tragedy, with the steady orchestration to a terminal climax for the doomed hero. For audiences of the day, the film would have presented a transatlantic synthesis that chimed with an appreciation of all things American in Britain (American films were, in fact, the most popular product in cinemas at the time), but also painted enough local colour in the milieu and mores of the characters to resonate with British viewers. If the film's modus operandi today seems a touch overwrought, it is none the worse for that and still offers (not least in its picture of austerity Britain) a vivid snapshot of a post-war country struggling to survive in the face of shortages and privations.

A film made ten years later shows a similarly idiosyncratic view of the capital. Looked at retrospectively, *The Day They Robbed the Bank of England* (1960) is interesting – among other things – for its memorable (if not quite star-making) turn by Peter O'Toole in a small part. But the film's cultural interest as a cunningly constructed, intelligently textured heist movie has granted it a certain longevity. Irish nationalists led by the (Welsh) Hugh Griffiths searching for a chink in the layout of the Bank of England is the mainspring of the narrative (a search by such individuals in real life was the source of the original novel by John Brophy) and director John Guillermin does full justice to Howard Clewes' cleverly constructed screenplay. American marquee value is provided by middle-ranking star Aldo Ray as an Irish-American mining engineer who is the brains of the operation, but the actor's gruff-voiced blue-collar appeal is not utilised to any great effect here, and the under-writing of his character dulls any social edge the film may have possessed. In fact, the movie belongs to its nicely shot period London setting and Peter O'Toole, as the none-too-bright guardee Captain Fitch whose attempts to exercise his under-used mental facilities prove only marginally successful in validating his military career.

What works splendidly in *The Day They Robbed the Bank of England* is the cumulative tension of the film's climax, in which the tunnelling criminals and the out-of-his-depth soldier arrive swiftly at a conclusion which actually goes for rather less than it should. But incidental pleasures are to be found in the small-part playing, with some of the most reliable old stagers of the day delivering the goods: the always bibulous-appearing Albert Sharpe as an alcoholic wreck with a sentimental attachment to the sewers he knows so well and the ever-eccentric Miles Malleson as a fussy curator in Sir John Soane's Museum. Any slackening of tension in the narrative is compensated for by the value-for-money character playing here.

In 1963, when *The Small World of Sammy Lee* appeared, there was something of a fashion for British films which opened up a variety of subcultures of metropolitan life to cinema audiences. And certainly the unvarnished (if stagey) image of Soho presented here was considered to be an accurate one by many who did not live in the capital. Director Ken Hughes' screenplay has the pithy ring of authenticity and a grasp of idiom of which a talented cast (the unconventional Anthony Newley, of course, as the beleaguered Sammy, and such reliable British characters actors as Wilfred Brambell, Kenneth J. Warren and Warren Mitchell) take full advantage. Sammy is a fast-talking, ducking-and-diving compère in a strip club, faced with the nigh-impossible task of coming up with the £300 cash that he owes his bookie before he is viciously worked over by the latter's heavies. As the five brief hours which Sammy is granted to find the money ebb away ever more swiftly, we are presented with the picture of a hermetically sealed, cloistered community outside of 'respectable' society which lives by its own peculiar rules, as codified as those of a religious institution (and of which it is something of a reverse image). Crucially, in Sammy, we are shown a man possessing very little less self-respect but obliged (in the time we spend with him) to divest himself of what little remains. His naive but nubile girlfriend, played by Julia Foster (a specialist in such roles), becomes part of a strip act in order to help him, and Sammy is even reduced to trying to sell reefers – all to no avail. The sharply observed dialogue is a considerable plus point and is one of the signal achievements of the film – notably with Sammy's caustic onstage diatribe to strip club punters, who are impatient for the next minimally-dressed girl to appear ('I don't know what you come here for. The girls here, they hate you, you make 'em sick. There's no love here, mate – there isn't even any sex. If it's sex you want, you won't get it here'). Ironically, this contemptuous outburst is treated amiably by the customers on the receiving end of it, and the suggestion registers that such moral niceties are unimportant to them – who cares what the girls think?

The sleazy characters that Sammy encounters as the clock ticks (notably the lascivious and calculating club owner played by Robert Stephens, an actor perfectly able to move across the social spectrum whenever required) ensure that identification with the luckless Sammy, however compromised, survives intact, and Ken Hughes' dramatic instincts rarely desert him, except, crucially, in the inevitable final beating of Sammy, which is desperately anticlimactic. The audience has been led to expect that Sammy will be beaten (and perhaps knife-slashed) to within an inch of his life, but he seems to finally be on the receiving end of a fairly cursory roughing up, from which he recovers with surprising speed. Given that this beating has been the Damoclean sword hanging over him throughout the film, what was clearly required (for dramatic purposes) was the kind of bloody, realistic working over that Marlon Brando endured at the end of Elia Kazan's *On the Waterfront* – or, for that matter, in many of Brando's films of the period. Nevertheless, muffled conclusion (and some less-than-convincing Soho sets) aside, *The Small World of Sammy Lee* is a strikingly individual piece of work, as much a study in loneliness and self-destruction as it is a snapshot of one of the less respectable corners of British society. Even the notion of family is presented as offering no amelioration in this bleak world (a desperate visit to Sammy's initially sympathetic brother to ask for money is cut short by the latter's unsympathetic wife) and Hughes' knowledge of then-recent developments in French *Nouvelle Vague* are put to intelligent use. Interestingly, the now-neglected film itself was to influence much successive work, including, indirectly, Mike Hodges' very different *Get Carter*. It was of course regrettable that the film has been unseeable so many years, but it has recently been made available again and time has, in general, been kind to it.

A London boarding house may be a microcosm of a city – or of a whole country. *The Man Upstairs* (1958) was virtually buried after a brief and unheralded showing in London's West End and has become virtually impossible to see since (the DVD industry may, hopefully, come to the rescue). This is a shame, as this low-budget effort is something of a neglected gem, not least for its original story and screenplay by Alun Falconer, which marshals its limited resources both intelligently and creatively. A crisply edited opening sequence introduces the audience to a conflicted young scientist who draws the attention of his neighbours in a rundown London apartment building. The police appear, and one of them is endangered. It becomes necessary, they believe, to eject the troubled scientist violently from his flat, but by now his concerned neighbours are beginning to believe that there are other ways to deal with a potentially explosive situation. Other films have dealt creatively with the siege concept (notably the tense *Fourteen Hours*, directed by Henry Hathaway), but here both the script and (equally importantly) Don Chaffey's adroit direction succeed in incorporating other elements into the film: limits on individual responsibility, society's attitudes to its outcasts and even the viability of modern police methods. If the presence of Richard Attenborough in the central role guarantees a solid performance, his presence nevertheless produces an 'actorliness' that is at odds with the modest dimensions of the subject. However, it remains an overlooked film which deserves attention.

By the time Otto Preminger filmed *Bunny Lake is Missing* on location in London in 1965, he had famously established the careful jettisoning of an identifiable directorial vision which was, intriguingly, the hallmark of his cinematic style. Each new film established itself in its own terms, and the milieu and concept were always at the service of the subject, whether epic or intimate. This London-set psychological thriller was undoubtedly in the latter category, although the large cast perform the necessary sleight of hand to give what is essentially a chamber piece with walk-on parts a larger dimension. It is intriguing that the two leading characters, played by the Americans Keir Dullea and Carol Lynley, are used for the blankness and inexpressivity that both actors customarily brought to their performances (Stanley Kubrick utilised Dullea in a similarly low-key, blank fashion in *2001: A Space Odyssey*) and set against the keenly observed upscale London settings, the performers' doll-like qualities are particularly effective. And Preminger is no fool, surrounding the principals' almost-not-there performances with much more characterised playing from such old pros as Laurence Olivier (as a persistent police inspector looking into the disappearance of Lynley's daughter) and (entertainingly) Noel Coward stealing scenes outrageously as a camp landlord.

The fact that the basic material here concerns twisted psychopathology within upper middle-class settings is obfuscated by the necessity of withholding information from the audience for the mechanics of the plot to work – and it is to Preminger's credit that even today, audiences are not always able to second-guess the revelations. Given that other small parts are equally well cast (such as the late Anna Massey as an under-pressure kindergarten teacher and Martita Hunt as an officious headmistress), another level of success is assured, particularly in the way in which Preminger is able to play upon the alienness of the central characters as Americans adrift in London (there are echoes of Henry James' naive American innocents set against more worldly Europeans in the narrative here). If, finally, *Bunny Lake is Missing* is a lesser piece from Otto Preminger, the director's skilfulness with the material is never in doubt.

London is central to another, more recent film. There is a growing (if fitful) cult interest in *Empire State*, an intelligent, flawed, colourful and over-ambitious 1987 effort (shot through with a distinct homoerotic strain) from director Ron Peck. The film is an attempt to synthesise elements of *The Long Good Friday* (notably the latter's scabrous political commentary on the voracious acquisitiveness of Thatcherism) and *Mona Lisa* in a stylised and vivid 1980s clubland thriller which is finally compromised by its stretched resources; Peck (who made an impact with the gay-themed *Nighthawks* in 1978) simply doesn't have the cadre of acting talent to meet his narrative ambitions; pros such as Martin Landau (at his most smoothly repellent) and a choleric Ray McAnally hold their own, but throw into stark relief the struggling, lesser-known principals who simply lack the acting chops for the demands that Peck makes of them. The film utilised the resources of a British Screen Film Finance/Film Four production budget and sets its gangster action and bare-knuckle fighting in the sexually-charged 'camp' of the 1980s East End club scene (as represented by the eponymous Empire State nightclub, which, despite its elaborate trappings, has a distinctly pop-up night-club air in the film). Peck is at his most trenchant on the complaisance of Dockland entrepreneurs, focused on sweeping away the seediness of the rundown East End that is clogging up potentially remunerative real estate, even though there is little nuance in his picture of yuppie venality (the speculators – to a man and a woman – are an unappetising bunch).

London's then-to-be-developed Docklands is the focus for the strip-mining of Britain's colliding social strata, in a setting where disparate lives uneasily intersect. The Thameside area has possibilities for both social groups (playground of the rich and an escape from poverty and squalor for the impoverished working-class inhabitants, although it's the latter who are shown getting screwed). This is also the battleground for a primeval conflict between the hard men who have ruled the East End for decades and – set against them – the ruthless new breed of racketeers. The interaction between these groups and the moneyed incomers is encapsulated in the smooth, viperous Chuck (Landau), an American with £3 billion to spend (and a taste for rough stuff with Cockney rent boys). Chuck manipulates his eager business colleagues with promises of potential investments, while the young, blond, heavily accented and none-too-bright Pete has arrived from the regions in London (anywhere beyond the Watford Gap is seen here as hinterlands to be fled from as quickly as possible). Pete has come to find a friend who has disappeared in the glossy corridors of the Empire State. Chuck and Pete, though, are only two of the film's large ensemble cast, none of whom are concentrated on at the expense of others. The film's problem is encapsulated in the performances here: Landau is supremely understated and fastidious as the gay American money man, while the non-acting Jason Hoganson is totally unable to create any kind of character for the bottle-blond young visitor from the sticks. Hoganson is cast for his looks – though, strangely, despite the clearly gay-oriented agenda of the director, the erotic effect of the film is negligible. Peck is at least 'equal opportunity' in his erotic gaze – although there are close-ups of the hairy crotches of male strippers, the director's use of nudity incorporates buxom female breasts and buttocks, which are shown being enthusiastically soaped in showers.

There is also the problem of the presentation of the nightclub itself, which, while being accoutred by the production designer with the perfectly plausible trappings of a trendy nightclub, never really convinces as being the real thing. But the key preoccupations of Peck and his co-writer Mark Ayres are the challenges thrown up by the re-development of the Docklands area (an astringent metaphor for 1980s Britain), with the director being remarkably even-handed in his criticism of the various groups squabbling over the spoils: the corrupt East End gangsters (with their bloody bare-knuckle bouts – another of the film's metaphors) and the soigné property developers – a judicious mix of races and sexes, but all presented as venal and superficial. Ironically, given the director's sympathies, it is interesting that the Martin Landau character is encapsulated in his unpleasant treatment of a spivvy East End male prostitute; homosexuality in this film might be said to have the same connotation of moral corruption as it did in such films as Hitchcock's *Strangers on a Train*, except that Peck casts plagues on every house in this film, whatever the sexual predilections of the characters.

10
The Regions

The treatment of non-metropolitan Britain may be mapped out in the cinema via a shift to the regions over the years, often (in the process) taking in aspects of British life marginalised by more mainstream British movies: such aspects included the contrast of Southern privilege with Northern joblessness, the breeding grounds of crime-ridden housing estates, a committed treatment of racism and the ideological distance of regional coppers from the London establishment. Needless to say, all of these elements were to be discerned in non-genre fare, but the presence of such themes was assured in crime cinema by one simple expedient: the need to provide a useful plot engine. This is not to say that such elements were mere narrative imperatives; the filmmakers who addressed such issues frequently took on board their more serious aspects along with any usefulness they presented in terms of in generating conflict. In fact, the level of sophistication in addressing these areas was more often to be found in genre product than in more overtly socially conscious fare. And filmic crime in British society was illuminated by a marked movement away from the most favoured location, London, to the provinces; the cinema's picaresque journeys around the island proved fruitful indeed, with the specific characteristic of individual cities used in creative fashion.

The great port cities such as Liverpool were to prove stimulating backdrops for a variety of criminous scenarios. Stanley Baker – perhaps the most iconic actor in British crime films – has his hands full in dealing with juvenile delinquents in the Michael Relph and Basil Dearden 'problem' production *Violent Playground* (1958), where the chosen urban setting is Liverpool, many years before that city's celebrated regeneration. Liverpool's Scotland Road district had become (rightly or wrongly) a byword for criminality and juvenile delinquency, and the city's middle-class inhabitants stayed close to the Georgian terraces, steering clear of the district's rundown streets at night (the area is now thoroughly transformed with an impressive array of green spaces). Baker's uncompromising copper in the film has conflicted views about the possibilities of saving his teenage charges from lives of crime, but the film posits a more ameliorative view than the less responsible *Cosh Boy*, with the possibility of redemption being tentatively held out for the young miscreants of the film. Having said that, the authority figures here are seen through rose-tinted glasses and the platitudinous good sense they dispense seems to belong to another kind of film altogether – these figures once haunted proscenium-arch-style drawing rooms (the kind to be glimpsed in every West End theatre throughout the 1930s and 1940s), not in the *cinéma verité*-style location photography that is one of the successful aspects of the film. David McCallum's not-too-convincing juvenile delinquent is something of a straw tiger; his rehabilitation is a foregone conclusion, given the slightly surrealistic middle-class trappings of this working-class Liverpool boy's home life. And Merseyside accents are conspicuous by their absence. But, as ever, Baker brings a trenchant truthfulness to the material that finally lifts it above those elements which have been insufficiently thought through. As with so many other films of this period, it is perhaps necessary to look beyond those things which have dated to winkle out the little felicities that a film such as *Violent Playground* has to offer. And a genuine sense of the zeitgeist of the historical city of Liverpool – at a particular point in its turbulent history – is encapsulated.

Such creative use of locale is crucial to the success of many a British crime film, and in few more so than J. Lee Thompson's Cardiff-set thriller *Tiger Bay* (1959). The director's inspired use of his port town locations has all the intelligence of his later American work such as *Cape Fear* (far superior to the Martin Scorsese remake).

The tale of a tomboyish young girl's pursuit by – and subsequent friendship with – a young sailor forced into committing manslaughter wears remarkably well, although the film's total avoidance of any paedophile associations (which will immediately spring to a modern viewer's mind in most of the situations where the young girl is menaced) either bespeaks a more innocent age or a realisation by Thompson that this is a story about trust and loyalty, not sexuality. While Horst Buchholz's desperate young Pole (guilty of the manslaughter of the bitter ex-mistress who has humiliated him) is constantly alone with latchkey kid Gilly in threatening situations, her most pressing danger is presented as one of murder rather than rape; it is self-evident that any remake of the film would have to take our more jaundiced modern sensibilities on board.

Of course, *Tiger Bay* is best remembered for its star-making debut turn by a very young Hayley Mills. Her performance has a still-astonishing naturalness, but the support from a sensitive Horst Buchholz and John Mills as the pursuing copper is impeccable. As an aside, it's interesting to note how much more convincing is Hayley Mills' transformation of her Home Counties vowels into Cockney glottal stops than she ever was at assuming an American accent in her subsequent career for Walt Disney.

Among the regions of Great Britain – if one is to include Wales – there are certain areas that remain under-utilised as movie locales. But one film that utilises the striking bucolic landscapes of the region (albeit economically) is the under-appreciated *Nowhere to Go* (1958).

Within the constraints of commercial cinema, the crime film has always afforded a range of possibilities for the filmmaker with challenging aspirations. As long as directors fulfil the general expectations of the target audience, a variety of personal and individual touches can be worked into the interstices of the plot. Of course, it is probably essential to keep the commercial imperatives (that is, continually ensuring the audience's total involvement) as a primary concern, and the fact that such American craftsmen as Don Siegel and Anthony Mann always bore such things in mind ensured their commercial longevity. As for physical longevity, the British director Seth Holt died before he had really fulfilled his promise, and there is always a sense of something unfulfilled when watching his slim body of work (a classic case of the same syndrome in another genre might be the early death of the young and talented Michael Reeves after the astonishing achievement of his *Witchfinder General*).

It is an undeniable fact that Seth Holt died before all the immense promise of his career achieved its final fruition, but he nevertheless left behind a slender film oeuvre which is more than worthy of excavation. A good place to start is the 1958 crime movie *Nowhere to Go*. Directed by Holt (who had worked as an editor and associate producer at Ealing) and written by the late Kenneth Tynan (whose celebrated theatre criticism was preceded by work as a script editor at the same studio), the film demonstrates considerable intelligence, and if it misses as many marks as it hits, it is nevertheless something of an undervalued achievement. The film is based on an efficiently written novel by Donald MacKenzie and concerns an escaped prisoner – a tough career criminal – on the run from jail. George Nader (an American actor giving US credentials to a British film, as was standard at the time) plays Paul Gregory, dumped by his ex-colleagues and cast adrift after an accidental murder. His escape from his past consists of a new life with a fashionable young woman (played by a young Maggie Smith) with whom he takes refuge in a sylvan hideout, but betrayal (or at least what Gregory believes is betrayal) and a grim fate await him.

If Holt and Tynan display some uncertainty in their attitude towards their benighted protagonists (is Gregory a victim of society or is society a victim of his?), in almost every other respect, the film is consummately handled with impeccable editing, always a Holt speciality (a prison break is handled with cool authority) and a marvellous use of London and Welsh locales. The dialogue too has a real edge, while the plotting delivers the requisite measure of bitter disillusionment. If the bleak ending in the strikingly shot Welsh countryside fails to achieve the tragic dimension that director and screenwriter appeared to be striving for, there is nevertheless enough here to suggest that the film is at least a harbinger of more interesting work to come from both men (which was, of course, to prove the case). *Nowhere to Go* is almost a textbook demonstration of Holt's astonishing eye as a director – the visuals here have a precision that complements their utilitarian nature, while simultaneously suggesting a cool European sensibility; Holt, for all his Englishness, was one of the most European of directors.

Val Guest's *Hell is a City* (1960) is set in Manchester, though Shelley (the source of the title) was referring to London – but let that pass. Guest's impressive film testifies to its Hammer Films origins inasmuch as it sports a notably tougher demeanour (and less pussyfooting attitude to violence) than many similar crime films – presumably as studio head Michael Carreras considered that it might be profitable to utilise the studio's unblushing approach to confrontational material in some other genre than horror. Stanley Baker's flinty Inspector Martineau might be described as one of his signature roles, except that the actor's consistency of achievement in the field renders the singling out of any one part as invidious, but there are details here which are particularly sharply etched, such as the portrait of the detective's unhappy marriage (his wife is played by Maxine Audley) – a character detail which is used specifically to define Martineau rather than simply as fleshing-out by rote as demanded by the genre. On the trail of brutal American criminal Don Starling (played by the actor John Crawford, routinely called in for such performances), the film's real achievement (apart from its screwed-down narrative drive and pithy characterisation) is the location shooting in Manchester – a city now familiar as a film location, but then something new in the cinema. And it's not just the suburban streets (prosperous or rundown) and imposing Victorian buildings that Guest evokes with particular skill, but even an unusual scene on the moors where illegal gambling (involving, of all things, shove ha'penny) is subject to a raid by the police. As in other regional films from this period (such as the Liverpool-set *Violent Playground* discussed earlier), the local accents utilised here will, to modern ears, sound inauthentic, but the film was made at a time when the sales of English films to foreign territories were sometimes predicated on the comprehensibility (or otherwise) of the English spoken in them. Famously, it was suggested that director Joan Littlewood's uncompromising Cockney voices in *Sparrows Can't Sing* needed to be subtitled for the USA, and director Ken Loach's refusal to modify the broad regional accents of the working-class characters in his films is almost a mission statement in terms of his refusal to be shown in multiplexes as much as a marker set against his middle-class characters (characters using received pronunciation in Loach films are not to be trusted). But while the accents are an element of *Hell is a City* which may ring false today (as with *Violent Playground*), the details of the relentless manhunt and Baker's conflicted, unhappy copper have dated not a whit, and the film still offers a comprehensive, unglossy snapshot of social attitudes of the late 1950s and early 1960s.

Decades later, Newcastle was to prove similarly atmospheric for the British crime narrative. Mike Figgis' ambitious first feature *Stormy Monday* (1988) is a deftly constructed crime thriller on the perils of sex (familiar territory, yes, but given a certain shaking up). Adroitly mixing gangsters, femme fatales and jazz, and relocated piquantly to Figgis' native Northeast (perhaps the film's most successful strategy), *Stormy Monday* cannily balances innovation and social commentary with a loving homage to film noir. The singer Sting (coaxed, for once, into something that actually resembles a performance) stars as Finney, a laconic Newcastle jazz-club owner who crosses the path of crass American gangster Cosmo (the ever-reliable Tommy Lee Jones). Cosmo wants to involve Finney in a land development deal – if only he'll give up his club. Entering into this increasingly dangerous game of brinkmanship is Kate (Melanie Griffith), a former gangster's moll trying to put her past behind her. Could a relationship with the club's innocent young apprentice (Sean Bean) offer a shot at redemption? With striking cinematography by Roger Deakins and an evocative score composed by former jazz musician Figgis and performed by the Krakow Jazz Ensemble, *Stormy Monday* makes one willingly forgive its frequent missteps.

Newcastle relocated to the USA? When the news broke that there would be a second American remake of Mike Hodges' gangster film *Get Carter* (the most seminal crime film ever made in the UK), there was a response along the lines of 'How can they do this?' (a lacklustre US remake with a black cast, George Armitage's *Hit Man*, had already sunk without trace). But the second remake was more high profile and provoked much disbelief, particularly as the star of the new version was to be none other than Sylvester Stallone, hardly likely to provide a substitute for the career-defining ice-cold incarnation from Michael Caine in the original. What was particularly strange was the royal seal of approval given to this ill-advised re-jigging by Caine himself, who played a cameo in the film. Needless to say, however, everyone's low expectations were fulfilled in the most dispiriting of fashions, and the film was generally regarded as a disaster. One of its most egregious errors was to relocate the action from the North of England to Los Angeles, and it is the sense of place (along with its acute observations about society and criminality) that made the original film so distinctive.

Ted Lewis' caustic original novel was the saga of brutal London criminal Jack Carter who returns to the Northern town of his birth (to arrange his brother's funeral), and its unvarnished picture of a bleak industrial setting seething with bent politicos and businessmen quickly acquired a devoted following. The novel laboured under the awkward title of *Jack's Return Home*, and the title change made for Mike Hodges' 1971 film adaptation was one of several improvements made to the original. Reading the novel today, it is hard not to see it retrospectively through the prism of Michael Caine's remarkable reading of the vengeful gangster Jack Carter and there is no doubt that the multi-faceted layers of the film afford a richer experience than that of the original novel (which still, nevertheless, contains much to applaud – most notably the vividly evoked Doncaster locales, which were, of course, to be famously changed for the film).

We begin by seeing Jack Carter watching a porn film with his smooth and reptilian employers (strongly reminiscent of the Krays) in London, then leaving for his home town of Newcastle to arrange the burial of a brother he has not seen in some considerable time. Jack quickly becomes aware that the circumstances of his brother's death are not as they appear to be, and it isn't long before he is cutting a bloody swathe through the criminal underworld of his home town, a home town which with its various criminal activities (prostitution, gambling and endemic corporate malfeasance) is a microcosm of the London he has left behind, but with a harder, more resentful Northern edge. Ironically, the Northern ambience so vividly conveyed by Hodges' film is reminiscent of the influential novels of John Braine, which similarly show the area to be quite as cut-throat and dangerous as the capital. It might also be pointed out that Jack Carter is vaguely related to John Braine's shark-in-a-suit arriviste Joe Lampton in the sense that the achievements that we see both men ruthlessly carving out for themselves are torn away by the end of the narrative (the difference being, of course, that Jack Carter has virtually no moral compass, so there is no fall from grace; Joe Lampton is unable to fully cauterise the core of humanity underneath his take-no-prisoners exterior, but ends up unhappy and dissatisfied rather than dead; in the original novel, Carter's fate is not so clear-cut).

In its day, *Get Carter* was a qualified, modest commercial hit, but few were able to predict its long-standing cult status – a status that is maintained to this day – and the film's influence remains prodigious (it should also be pointed out that Mike Hodges, despite directing several impressive films since, such as *Croupier* (1998), has not been able to surpass his magnum opus). Relocating the action to

Newcastle helped the director produce the most acclaimed gangster film ever made in the UK and it might also be said to be the best work of both its director and star. Hodges' screenplay for the novel showed a total understanding of the mechanics of the genre, such as betrayal by the hero's associates in London – which proves to be his undoing. A secondary plot device involves Jack trying to track down the makers of a pornographic film that features his own niece (the orphaned daughter of his dead brother Frank). The narrative itself is remarkably dense and the plotting might be said to owe something to Raymond Chandler, who similarly produced labyrinthine narratives. However, it is the pithiness of the dialogue and the panoramic, grimly urban evocation of the Newcastle setting that gives the film its real distinction. The film's picture of the criminal underworld suggests a distant inspiration via the milieu of Ken Hughes' influential Soho-set *The Small World of Sammy Lee*.

In the same year that Hodges made *Get Carter*, Don Siegel was filming his Clint Eastwood crime drama *Dirty Harry*, which similarly utilises an utterly ruthless avenger, one who was obliged to step outside the law – despite his police badge – to achieve results. (Stepping outside the law, of course, was hardly a problem for the equally misogynistic Jack Carter.) There are also elements here of the Paul Schrader film *Hardcore*, made some eight years later, in which a father attempts to discover the facts behind the making of a pornographic film featuring his own lost daughter. In fact, *Get Carter* begins (as mentioned above) by showing Jack and his associates in London desultorily watching a blue movie (some of the briefly glimpsed images were at the time the strongest ever to be seen in a British film). And their discussion as to whether or not Jack should return to Newcastle to find out whether or not the death of his brother was an accident are handled in the same fashion as any important corporate decision. Jack, it is suggested, is a middle-ranking executive who has a job to do, and the most important thing is whether or not the organisation will be able to thrive in his absence. It is interesting that among Jack's bosses is the actor-turned-playwright John Osborne, giving a chillingly sinister (and understated) performance. Osborne, of course, had created the most distinctive anti-hero of modern times in Jimmy Porter, but the violence in *Look Back in Anger* is mainly of the verbal kind; Jack Carter is equally good at that ('You're a big man, but you're in bad shape. With me it's a full time job. Now behave yourself'), but is perfectly happy to dispense physical punishment when he feels it is necessary.

When Jack arrives in Newcastle, we are shown a town in decline. There is still a sense of industry and commerce, but the suggestion is that anything successful in the town owes its success to corrupt elements (Hodges was clearly not in the business of wooing the Newcastle tourist board). Certainly, the director's choice of locales – rundown terraced houses, boisterous working-class watering holes and seedy wharves – is nonpareil, and as much as anything else grants the film the visual identity that marks it out from most of its predecessors (and successors). The class distinctions delineated here are based on the American model; success is not predicated by the blueness of one's blood but by the conspicuous consumption shown in the accoutrements of one's lifestyle, such as the country homes and well-appointed flats of the corrupt criminal chiefs of Newcastle. In this respect, the influence of the novelist John Braine may be noted again; Northern writers had forged a picture of unsentimental, unforgiving Northern males set against effete, overpaid and over-privileged Southerners, a contrast maintained (by suggestion) throughout *Get Carter*. This distinction between London and the regions is as acute (despite not being stressed) in Hodges' film as in anything made before or since, and to some degree Jack Carter is our conduit into this milieu; whether the viewer is a Northerner or a Southerner, it is still necessary to be shown the rules and regulations which shape life in this unforgiving world, and Carter provides this function.

Carter is, of course, quite as much a blunt instrument as many of the men he meets, and his various ways of dealing with people who he feels are implicated in his brother's death are as brutal as one might expect (men are thrown from high buildings, there is a fatality caused by a drug overdose and even an unintentional killing when a woman is left in the boot of a car which is subsequently pushed into the river). And given the actor Michael Caine's wry and avuncular nature, his truly grim and unforgiving portrayal here is an acting performance of immense skill and charisma – even more so in that, despite his brutality, Carter never manages to alienate the audience from his behaviour, even though that behaviour often has clear overtones of the sadistic.

Viewing the film in the twenty-first century, it remains instructive that Hodges is not tempted to offer an easy moral resolution for his bleak, diamond-hard story, maintaining an existential distance. The explosive central character and those who he encounters are largely speaking without redeeming features, and we are invited to view them *sub specie aeternitatis*, making our own minds up about the amoral behaviour we see. In many ways, the film's moral universe is reminiscent of the novels of Elmore Leonard, which similarly refuse to make a judgement on the characters – although there is far more sardonic humour in Leonard's novels than is to be found in Hodges' film. *Get Carter's* violence is, of course, extreme, and it appeared at a particularly significant period, when long-standing censor John Trevelyan had retired and the more liberal Stephen Murphy took over in 1971, beginning a short but much-applauded regime (applauded, that is, by those who felt that films should not be rendered anodyne by the self-styled morality police) in allowing such work to be shown (largely speaking uncut). The sexuality in the film is also uncharacteristically frank for its day. The scene that made a considerable impression is that in which Jack's under-appreciated girlfriend (played by Britt Ekland) in her underwear is instructed to masturbate long distance by an ice-cold Carter on the phone. Again, one has to remark on the centrality of Caine's performance to the film's success, which ruthlessly removed the good humour freighted in by the actor in such films as *Alfie* and *The Ipcress File*. The scene in which he frightens off a pair of Geordie thugs, while standing nude outside the house in which he is staying and armed with just a shotgun, is as famous as anything in the Caine canon (and his is a career which has had more than its share of iconic moments).

At the beginning of this discussion, it was pointed out how ill-advised any attempt at a remake of *Get Carter* was. Needless to say, apart from the two mentioned above, uncredited remakes (and riffs on the basic theme) have appeared by the dozen and are proliferating to this day. But the cool, glittering, utterly ruthless crime masterpiece that Hodges produced is *sui generis*.

Newcastle has had its fair share of solid crime films shot in the city. For most of its length, *Payroll* (1961) effortlessly maintains a considerable level of finely-tuned suspense with the Newcastle locations intelligently chosen and the pared-down dialogue completely at the service of the basic heist scenario. If the concatenation of coincidence and unlikely events compromises the otherwise adroit construction of the film, the treatment remains essentially truthful – and the pulse-raising first half of the film in particular demonstrates the skills that director Sidney Hayers was to exercise over the years (in such films as the intelligent supernatural drama *Night of the Eagle*, based on a Fritz Leiber novel) before American television claimed him and vitiated his talent.

To some degree, *Payroll* is something of a summary – or, in fact, a definition and reconstruction of the genre itself – a summary, that is, of both themes and stylistic traits in the field. Apart from the odd excrescence (dictated by box office considerations), everything has been pared away from the narrative except the most crucial elements, and the sense of economy is striking. Even the most rigorous examination of the film displays not a camera set-up or cinematic stylistic flourish that does not do the most basic service to the demands of the narrative. If the central characters can sometimes seem like specimens laid out on a table for forensic examination, the sheer single-mindedness of the technique makes such a caveat seem unimportant. Ironically, the director who most readily comes to mind in comparison with Sidney Hayers here is far richer in critical approval and cult status: Don Siegel, who was wont to remove everything that might be considered decoration to leave something existentially clean and lacking any other filigrees that would distract from the central preoccupation of the narrative.

Liverpool remained useful territory for the crime film, as evidenced by Stephen Frears' *Gumshoe* (1971), inspired by Neville Smith's novel. Albert Finney gave a characteristically minutely-detailed portrayal of a Liverpudlian bingo caller who nourishes a hopeful fantasy of a life as private dick in the hardboiled Bogart mode. If the film failed to have it both ways – i.e. to function as both an affectionate parody of the private eye genre and simultaneously to ask the audience to take the plot semi-seriously, *Gumshoe*'s pawky charm won it many friends, not least for Finney's winningly deluded protagonist. But a darker approach to the regions was some years away.

Hell, audiences were to learn, was Yorkshire. Television broadcasts emphasised the dark visuals of the *Red Riding* trilogy (2009), the much-acclaimed series of adaptations of David Peace's scarifying Yorkshire-set crime novels; recent DVD issues render detail far more clear and accessible. Scripted by Tony Grisoni and directed by Julian Jarrold, James Marsh and Anand Tucker, *Red Riding* is a grim but authoritative trilogy of films built around the six-year police investigation of the Yorkshire Ripper, folded in with other fictitious crimes. The reworkings of the novels by David Peace (*Nineteen Seventy Four, Nineteen Eighty* and *Nineteen Eighty Three*) are handled with immense assurance, though this is deeply uncomfortable viewing. It is perhaps a legitimate point to make that the treatment of the West Yorkshire Police – while consummately acted and directed – has something in common with Mel Gibson's treatment of the British in such movies as *The Patriot*: they are presented as brutal Nazi storm-troopers, utterly corrupt and beyond any law. But there is no gainsaying the skilfulness of the realisation here. The resolutely unconsoling dramas are bolstered with remarkable performances from a stellar cast including Sean Bean, Andrew Garfield, Paddy Considine, Warren Clarke, Peter Mullan, David Morrissey, Maxine Peake, Rebecca Hall and Mark Addy.

11
Breaking Taboos: Sex and the Crime Film

Sex, not violence, is the last taboo. The British crime film – with its less-than-respectable artistic pedigree – has (throughout its history) been unofficially licensed to undertake groundbreaking treatments of previously undiscussed sexual themes: paedophilia, miscegenation, homosexuality and sexual obsession. And inevitably, given its recurrent illegality, the oldest profession has been incorporated into many a crime narrative – with astonishingly varied takes on the subject, both in terms of frankness and sympathy.

The treatment of prostitution in British films is often fatally compromised by the perceived necessity of taking a dual view of the profession – even attempts to be sympathetic to the women involved inevitably carry a vaguely (or explicitly) condemnatory charge, almost invariably coloured (pre-1960) by something like religious disapproval. Ironically, this attitude was to find a modern correlative in Tony Garnett's *Prostitute* (1980), where the once standard disapproval of the prostitute's lifestyle – a disapproval which once would have been of a religious nature – is transmuted into something avoiding explicit condemnation; acknowledging the humanity and humour of the women, but suggestive of the inevitable toll of their bleak, pressured existence, ever the target of police harassment.

An earlier treatment of the theme, *The Flesh is Weak* (Don Chaffey, 1957), was something of a minor *cause célèbre* in its day, particularly as it tacitly sanctioned the viewing of such sensational material by more mainstream audiences (i.e. not those who would flock to taboo cinema club sex films in the next decade). Milly Vitale plays a girl who finds herself in the oldest profession after the blandishments of a seductive pimp (played by John Derek) lead her astray. We are shown the girl's dealings with her clients, which initially follow the classic 'look but don't touch' ethos of 1950s cinema in such situations (a young man is forced into an encounter with the girl by peer pressure from friends in the office where he works; unsurprisingly, there is no actual sexual encounter in this first experience); such unlikely moral equivocation was long gone by the time of Tony Garnett's uncompromising film, which in its uncut version even includes erections. But as with Garnett decades later, Don Chaffey allows some sympathy for the heroine who finds herself on the game and avoids the simple J. Arthur Rank party line of moral condemnation, while allowing the sadness of her basic situation to register at every opportunity. Chaffey is still obliged to move into the realms of violent melodrama to resolve the drama, a move that vitiates the more nuanced points he has been making earlier. Nevertheless, the film is of great interest as a picture of British society's view of prostitution in the late 1950s, refracted through the vision of a filmmaker who is not prepared to accept the shibboleths of the religiously-minded. Garnett's more frank *Prostitute* has finally been released uncut in 2011 (and it's easy to see why this wasn't possible before, given the film's unsimulated sex scenes, even under the then-liberal regime of Stephen Murphy at the British Board of Film Censors). Garnett's uncompromising 1980 piece about the lives of a group of Birmingham sex workers (largely pre-drug addiction) is dated but riveting – though his tendentious conclusions are (perhaps deliberately) confusing.

In terms of challenges to accepted notions of morality, the cinema (both in the UK and the USA) has preferred to sidle up to its battles rather than adopt an all-guns-blazing approach. A film such as Ken Hughes' *The Trials of Oscar Wilde* (1960), for instance, may be packaged as a drama with the emphasis on entertainment rather than a particular engagement with issues of homosexuality, but the mindset of the film chimes with then-contemporary thinking on such issues by presenting a sympathetic and attractive leading man (Peter Finch) in the title role, thereby guaranteeing a degree of audience compliance. Perhaps that same audience of the day was more sophisticated than it was generally given credit for, but there is no question that a more liberal stance on contentious issues was finessed by the success of such films.

A variety of different issues relating to sexuality were being addressed in popular entertainment films. Perhaps the sensational, come-hither advertising (with its concomitant promise of forbidden fruit) appealed more to the carnal instincts than the intellectual responses of the audience, but this sweetening of the medicine was hardly to be dismissed; the more subversive character of the variety of issues tackled (after the members of the audience were securely in their seats, having been tempted by the blandishments of the advertising) could accordingly be more radical than if such issues have been addressed baldly. In the early 1960s, the permissive society was just around the corner and was already beginning to inspire a moral panic in those authorities concerned with the rigorous maintenance of the status quo (when the loosening up of censorship and sexual mores occurred, the easygoing philosophy of the lotus eaters seemed to have set in for the long haul), but by the 1990s, conservative commentators were blaming the moral decline of society on the tolerance of the 1960s; as the word 'liberal' had become a term of abuse and disdain among Republicans in the USA, the *locus classicus* for almost every major ill of society could be located in the new freedoms that followed the more restrictive, reined-in 1950s. This attitude had its passionate adherents in the UK (the National Viewers' and Listeners' Association, led by the zealous moral reformer Mary Whitehouse, initiated endless attempts to ban TV and film drama utilising precisely this backwards-looking mindset). Interestingly, earlier protests against perceived injustices (such as the campaign by the suffragettes) were not, largely speaking, regarded as the progenitors of these new trends; sexuality was the hot-button issue in terms of rebellion against society's strictures.

British filmmakers in general held a different view of rebels or those outside society. The subtle distinction between the transgressiveness of criminals (as represented in the cinema) as against fifth columnists or spies lay in the fact that a certain honest criminality was to be understood (but not tolerated), whereas political dissent expressed in acts of espionage was totally beyond the pale. The same attitude, once again, was to be found in American crime films; in *Pickup on South Street* by the American 'primitive' Samuel Fuller, the sympathetic criminals who are the protagonists regard communists as being utterly beneath contempt, rather in the same fashion as prisoners in British jails regard one particular group of criminals as justifiable targets for violent retribution: the 'nonces' or paedophiles.

Sex and race have always been an incendiary combination for the cinema – and markedly so in the days before a new liberalism (in both cinema and society) drew the sting from such problematic areas. If the British cinema's treatment of the theme in the 1960s erred on the side of exploitation, that was an inevitable corollary of commercial imperatives: if treated in suitably shocking fashion, such subjects would be made – and shown to cinema-filling success.

Michael Relph and Basil Dearden produced one of their most talked-about 'social problem' films in 1959 with the then-controversial *Sapphire*, and it's interesting to note how often Dearden's name justifies its appearance in this study. Certainly, the director's films were considered to be strikingly well made in their day and enjoyed commercial success, but the encomium is a double-edged one, rather in the fashion that the traditional 'well-made' play in the British theatre prior to the appearance of such writers as Harold Pinter and John Osborne was considered to be the gold standard, only to become regarded as fusty and outmoded – a product rightly to be swept away by the more iconoclastic new breed of playwright (ironically, such is the cyclical nature of art that many of these discarded plays are enjoying a slew of new productions and favourable reappraisals in the early twenty-first century).

There was a fall from critical grace for Dearden, who (while tackling controversial subjects) was criticised for doing so in a conventional, unadventurous fashion while less respectable directors took a more radical approach to the 'problem' film (similar criticism was levelled at the producer/director Stanley Kramer in the USA). The criticism is, to some degree, unfair, and perhaps there is a parallel with feminist criticism of Freud's approach to female sexuality: Freud may have got it wrong, but at least he was prepared to talk about the subject when others wouldn't – and, to some degree, Dearden also tackled such issues as miscegenation and homosexuality long before such themes were accepted as part of the mainstream. The other principal criticism of Dearden concerns his perceived aesthetic limitations: that his well-made films lacked the cinematic intelligence of such unorthodox craftsmen as Seth Holt, whose all-too-brief career resulted in several truly adventurous films (discussed elsewhere in this book), mostly infused with the kind of vigour and filmic inventiveness that were not part of Dearden's otherwise craftsmanlike professional skills. Nevertheless, leaving such reservations aside, films such as *Sapphire* (while of less significance today) are still fascinating as a time capsule of society's attitudes – particularly within the context that (at the time of their releases) the Dearden films were regarded as provocative and shocking.

Although *Sapphire* is principally about race, it is built around a classic murder investigation which allows the coppers involved to encounter something of a straw poll of attitudes and outlooks across a wide section of British society of the late 1950s. The eponymous Sapphire is a young black student (who does not appear in the film bearing her name) and her death propels a police inspector (capably played by the authoritative Nigel Patrick) into an investigation that is as much concerned with attitudes towards colour as it is with sexual freedom and interracial relationships. Inevitably, white racism is a key factor here, but Relph and Dearden are sufficiently sophisticated to allow black-against-white prejudice, as represented by a black prince with a barely concealed loathing of white people. Given the relatively recent furore about so-called 'institutional racism' within the ranks of the British police, viewing of this film made half a century ago demonstrates (unsurprisingly) that such illiberal attitudes were to be found in the Metropolitan officers of the day.

There is a slightly suspect conclusion drawn regarding certain racial characteristics (as demonstrated in the sexually 'abandoned' dancers) – the sensuality of the dancing is posited as an indicator of racial background. It's important not to be politically correct in taking the film to task for this; after all, Oscar Hammerstein and Jerome Kern utilised similar unmistakable music-related signs for the mixed-race character Julie (passing as white) in the then-challenging musical *Show Boat*. Once again, it would be facile to lament such dated notions; at least important issues were being tackled in a largely responsible fashion in a piece of popular entertainment.

In *Sapphire*, the attitude to miscegenation (the latter term, of course, is itself contentious in the twenty-first century) is based around this hidden series of racial indicators (the dead woman's liberal attitude towards sexuality is something that has been kept secret from her unworldly white innamorato) and the revelation of the killer devolves on an attempt to protect someone close to Sapphire from her 'contaminating' influence. If this plot development seems crass today, it nevertheless retains a vestige of moral force in an era of non-white so-called 'honour' killings, with the murder of young women utilised as a way of extirpating unacceptable behaviour. Such murders devolve principally on one offence in that most incendiary of arenas: the sexual impulse.

The later racially-aggravated Brixton riots in 1981 subsequently resulted in a radical rethinking of police tactics, and the film (for all its naivety) could be subtly seen to reject the simple notion that a more liberal approach to racial issues is a panacea. Here, as in the case of the Brixton riots, a solution which addressed only white racism while ignoring certain aspects of behaviour within the black community is facile. *Sapphire* posits the notion that there are rarely straightforward solutions to complex issues. Not everything, in other words (and in a double sense), can be seen in simple black-and-white terms. Labour administrations are traditionally regarded as being more attentive to problems relating to racial tension, but Relph and Dearden suggest that whatever party is in power (Conservative, Labour or Liberal), those obliged to dispense immediate solutions are the foot soldiers serving at the sharp end: the police. And the fact that this film demonstrates the inadequacy of such a response ensures that (for all its dated qualities), it remains very much a demonstration of *plus ça change*.

Homosexuality as a plot element in films is now relatively mainstream. *Victim* (1961), also from the Dearden/Relph team, presents something of a conundrum for modern audiences in its treatment of a theme which is now quotidian but which was considered shocking at the time of the film's original release. The eponymous 'victim' (or one of them) in this blackmail drama is a young gay man who has been arrested for stealing money that belonged to his employers. He commits suicide in his cell, and the real reason for this death (which was readable to alert viewers of the day and is crystal clear to more knowing audiences today) is his desperate desire to conceal the secret of his sexuality. Among the young man's sexual partners was a married barrister, Melville Farr, with the most propitious of prospects. The character is played by Dirk Bogarde (some distance from his juvenile delinquents of earlier years – a decade or so previously he might have been astute casting for the young suicide victim). Farr is a QC whose prospects for the Bench are very good indeed. Inevitably, Farr is himself blackmailed for his liaison and is painfully confronted with a slew of courses of action: he can pay off the blackmailer (which would involve breaking the law, an action which would entail a variety of consequences for him), contact and reveal all to the police (thus maintaining his own integrity while throwing away his reputation and career in a society still hidebound by convention) or he can attempt to discover the identity of the blackmailer himself and perhaps turn the tables by blackmailing his tormentor. This last course of action, of course, will make Farr a criminal himself, but would inevitably have suggested to audiences the course of action inevitably followed by the proactive hero of many crime films.

The writers Janet Green and John McCormack, in creating this then-challenging scenario, utilised existing generic conventions of the day, but nevertheless succeeded in throwing up several queasy moral choices for the conflicted central character (such as the fact that had a barrister with a gay past not become the target of the blackmail ring, his progress to the Bench would have resulted in him becoming an integral part of a legal system which was antipathetic to him – and against which he had offended).

Inevitably, as in so many movies of the day confronting 'problem' issues such as homosexuality, the dialogue spoken by the characters is frequently tendentious, rehearsing the much-exercised arguments of the day, in the case of *Victim* either for or against the Wolfenden Report which brought about a liberalisation of British society's treatment of homosexuality. However, the arguments (while sometimes quaint-seeming today) still have a degree of moral force and might be even more à propos in twenty-first-century America, where the rights painfully won by gay men and women are under threat from a resurgent Republican Party. The dramatic situations created in the film to encapsulate these arguments have an incisive dramatic force, such as the scene in which the barrister is forced by his dismayed wife (played by Sylvia Sims) to talk about his feelings for the boy who committed suicide ('I wanted him!') and admit his sexual attraction; similarly, a scene in which a star of the theatre played by Dennis Price (another actor, like Bogarde, who would have been well aware of the hidden sexual world the film describes) is allowed to defend his transgressive way of life and his reluctant decision to pay off blackmailers.

Where the film is most successful is in suggesting that moral decisions taken lower down the social scale from the professional classes are more problematic; while the money to pay off blackmailers may be less readily available, there is the same possibility of the destruction of lives. As in the production team's earlier problem picture *Sapphire*, the narrative occasionally slips into the realms of the well-intentioned didactic (and the blackmailers themselves are under-characterised), but, nevertheless, there is certainly a brave (for the time) identification of unbending religiosity and repressed sexuality as the elements inspiring the actions of the unsympathetic characters in the film. Finally, the approach of Dearden, Green and McCormack in *Victim* is largely speaking unsensational – what *was* sensational was the seismic effect that the film had in adjusting public perceptions of homosexuality.

Attitudes towards sexuality by the police in the crime films made in the UK were – after a period of censor-enforced innocence (as in the American model) – finally allowed to reflect the real world, both in terms of demonstrating society's liberality and illiberality. While a picture of police rectitude (as encapsulated in John Ford's unchallenging British-made *Gideon's Day* (1958), based on John Creasy's novels) was consigned to the dustbin of history, there were still old-fashioned views to be found in the coppers played by the avuncular Jack Warner, as (for instance) an ageing policeman in Val Guest's assured *Jigsaw* in 1962, in which the actor who had earlier played the homily-dispensing bobby on the beat PC George Dixon in *The Blue Lamp* now, older and stouter, made frequent despairing pronouncements on the (as he saw it) downward trajectory of society – an ironic viewpoint, given the more radical developments that would be shaking society's entrenched attitudes in just three or four years' time. The difference now, of course, was the fact that the film-makers did not necessarily share the retrograde (or, to put it more generously, traditional) views of its dyspeptic protagonist. And by the time of the nigh-psychotic policeman played by an intense Sean Connery in Sidney Lumet's *The Offence* (1972), a much colder eye was being cast on the force and the sometimes disturbed individuals within it. Once again, sexual disapproval by the police protagonist was a theme, but this time, the central character's disapproval is of an unacceptable predatory behaviour, rather than simple sexual licence, as was the case with Warner's old-fashioned copper. Connery (firmly consolidating his acting credentials) is DS Johnson, who, despite his commanding appearance and tough-as-nails persona, is a man who has seen far too much of the less admirable side of human nature and is beginning to pay a damaging psychological price. His unreconstructed attitude towards those who he perceives as paedophiles reflects the view maintained in British prisons, where 'nonces' are regarded as utterly beneath contempt and representatives of a moral vacuum for their despicable crimes. In the prisoners' view (as reflected in DS Johnson), there are less contemptible crimes. But if the attitude of the criminals themselves in prison (frequently reflected in films which treated the subject) was a fairly specious stratification of crime, allowing prisoners some feeling of moral superiority over the *really* depraved, the reality for Johnson is somewhat different, although his contempt for the suspected pederast played (in repellent fashion) by the excellent Ian Bannen is more to do with Johnson's own self-loathing than an exteriorisation of other elements hidden within his personality. When the Bannen character – clearly possessed of his own measure of self-loathing – forces the damaged policeman who is his opponent into an act of extreme violence, the moral mire into which Lumet's film moves allows for no easy answers.

The film, like the John Hopkins play on which it was based (Hopkins also wrote the screenplay), enjoyed a certain degree of controversy – enhanced by the fact that Lumet underlined the ideological debate of the narrative, demonstrating the American director's command of the English idiom, and offered proof (if proof were needed) that there was far more to Connery as an actor than insouciantly conveying the urbane sophistication of James Bond.

Though relatively little-seen today, *Yield to the Night* (1956) created a considerable stir in its day, both for its controversial subject matter and its establishment of one of this country's most underrated actresses as something more than a pouting sexpot with an unlikely embonpoint. As an eloquent anti-hanging diatribe, J. Lee Thompson's film was something of a British riposte to Robert Wise's trenchant American film *I Want to Live!* (which performed precisely the same trick for the under-regarded actress Susan Hayward, giving her a certain dramatic credibility). Wise's film, however, was written, acted and directed in a more forceful and adrenaline-generating fashion, with the nervous jazz score by Johnny Mandel accentuating this edginess; *Yield to the Night* was an altogether more low-key affair, though hardly lacking forcefulness.

The British film appeared during a period when the abolition of the death penalty was a hotly contested issue in the UK, with a great deal of argument (on either side) for and against abolition. The inspiration for the film was the case of the last woman to be hanged in Britain, Ruth Ellis, although Thompson's film fictionalised these events (unlike the later Mike Newell film *Dance with a Stranger* (1985), which upped the ante in terms of the potentially destructive effects of sexual passion while retaining some of the names of the real-life protagonists involved).

At the time of *Yield to the Night*, the filmmakers were quick to point out that they were not following a particular agenda and were not specifically advocating the abolition of the death penalty, but such is the power of the film's final scenes that these remarks might be retrospectively seen as disingenuous. In fact, by the time the film was showing in cinemas (1956), hanging had been abolished as a punishment for capital crimes. Looking at J. Lee Thompson's film in the twenty-first century, when the late actress Diana Dors had long been accepted as a character actor of distinction, it is easy to forget that this process was to some degree dependent on a marked change in the star's appearance. Dors' days as Britain's answer to Marilyn Monroe were over, and a marked increase in weight opened up a secondary career for her with distinctive cameos in such films as Jerzy Skolimowski's *Deep End* (1970) (to some degree parodying her earlier sexpot image). At the time of *Yield to the Night*, however, efforts were made to play down the cleavage-accentuating Hollywood glamour so associated with the actress's appearance, and the most familiar stills from the film to be seen today show her with her hair swept back in prison gabardine, looking nothing like the bottle-blonde parody of voluptuousness that was the hallmark of most of her career.

Of course, making a film about a controversial young woman whose notoriety depended as much on her openly-expressed sexuality as anything else (audiences were well aware that the film's 'Mary Hilton' was clearly based on the real Ruth Ellis) parlayed certain elements from Diana Dors' own life, where the least consequential of her sexual peccadilloes was the subject of much media attention. In the early part of the film, before disaster befalls her character, Dors is able to utilise the erotic elements of her standard persona, but in a more subtle, nuanced way than she was invited to do in other films. The efficient J. Lee Thompson (who ended his career with unambitious exploitation movies considerably less accomplished than this work from his heyday) astutely commented on the sexual hypocrisy of the day, in which a woman's sexuality could be minutely examined as long as the requisite moral disapproval was built into the examination. Thompson and his actress are also not afraid to present Mary as a complex character, particularly after her killing of her faithless lover – there are no easy attempts to gain sympathy for her and she does not demonstrate remorse for the murder she has committed. What's more, Mary remains as fixated upon the man who treated her so badly (and who paid such a heavy price for so doing) that the grim final execution scenes (reminiscent of similar sequences in *I Want to Live!*) produced a complex response in the audience – although, needless to say, a revulsion at Mary's fate is the overriding consideration.

Yield to the Night was an undoubted career-high for its director, who had worked on such films as *The Weak and the Wicked*, *Woman in a Dressing Gown* and even the censor-baiting *The Yellow Balloon*, which was one of the first recipients of the British Board of Film Censors' 'X' certificate. Later big-budget movies such as *The Guns of Navarone* finessed Thompson's director's bank balance, but his reputation was assured with this strong mid-period film.

In 1985, the director Mike Newell tackled the same subject in *Dance with a Stranger*, this time with the much-acclaimed (and highly versatile) actress Miranda Richardson now allowed to play an undisguised Ruth Ellis. Richardson had no preconceived perceptions to change in the minds of cinema audiences, having long demonstrated that she was an actress ready to tackle a variety of provocative and even unsympathetic parts. Ruth Ellis in *Dance with a Stranger* is allowed to be a more self-loathing character than the Mary Hilton of the earlier film, and a more liberal age permitted a franker treatment of the story's sexual elements. As Ellis becomes erotically obsessed with the alcoholic David Blakely (played as attractive but oversmooth by Rupert Everett), she virtually ensures that everything that is important in her life will evaporate, damaging her relationship with her son and creating despair in the other man with whom she has a relationship, Desmond Cussen (played in desolate fashion by the excellent Ian Holm). When she has virtually cast off everything of importance in her life, there are two final nihilistic acts she is able to perform: the destruction of her worthless lover and, accordingly,

herself. Ellis (as played by Richardson) is allowed a notably dyspeptic view of the male sex (we hear about an abusive earlier marriage)
and to some degree – as in several films with feminist subjects made
by male filmmakers – the view of male sexuality could not be more
caustically expressed in an all-women separatist commune of the
1970s (it is notable that even Ellis' generally sympathetic neglected
lover Cussen is shown to be misogynist in his views by the end of
the film). But if *Dance with a Stranger* conforms to certain accepted
feminist viewpoints in its overwhelmingly negative view of the
male sex, it can hardly be said to ennoble its female characters.
What's more, Newell was to lose any feminist friends he might have
acquired via his film's outlook with his next project, *The Good Father*
(1986), which appeared to argue for the under-threat paternal rights
of fathers, generally regarded as a target for feminist ire. Much of that
ire was directed at Newell for his apparent espousal of such views in
the film. *Dance with a Stranger*, however, retains its power and authority to this day, not least for Miranda Richardson's uncomfortable and
painfully truthful performance.

12
Corporate Crime: Curtains for the Maverick

The recurrent themes of free agent individuals against institutions have inevitably been attractive to the makers of crime films, given the ready-made dramatic (and violent) possibilities of such conflicts. Another, similar, theme involves the new corporate crime, reluctantly tolerating – then eliminating – those who threaten the status quo (and profits). Variations on this theme have served as metaphors for a larger conflict between bloody-minded, solitary protagonists and establishment interests. The complex reaction (attraction/disapproval) inspired in audiences regarding these anti-heroes is instructive, particularly when the filmmakers have refused to make moral judgements, disingenuously or otherwise, on such figures.

The game of cards with which *The Criminal* (1960, a prime example of the theme) begins acts as an index of the skilfulness (and thoughtfulness) with which various hands are played throughout the course of the film, with an indication given (even in this opening sequence) that the stakes involved are of the highest order. The revelation that follows is that the game of cards is taking place in a prison. With this sequence, director Joseph Losey vouchsafes a key element of the film's strategy, in which the viewer is presented with a microcosm: of society, its attitudes and its strategies for coexistence. And the prison Losey utilises for this notion is both apposite and satisfyingly worked-through. As is so often the case in the many excellent films he made during his years as one of Britain's most capable (and in-demand) tough-guy actors, Stanley Baker suggests both the flawed qualities and the strengths of his character Johnny Banyon (the eponymous 'criminal'). Unlike many of the erratic figures around

him, he is largely in control of his behaviour and pursues his aims
with a single-mindedness that grants them a kind of tarnished grace –
until, of course, the inevitable fall and destruction. The bad end
to which criminals habitually come in both British and American
movies is inevitably made to seem like a corollary of the organic
functioning of society in which the corrupt and maladjusted are
expunged, but Losey is far too sophisticated a filmmaker for such
banal equations and manages to render 'society' – as presented in
such unsympathetic figures as the martinet prison officer played by
Patrick Magee – as compromised and as constricted as the criminals
in their charge. But the levels of society in the film are presented
with an equally cold eye, notably the prison governor, depicted as a
liberal capable of acknowledging (and respecting) the stoicism and
intelligence of Banyon.

Inevitably, of course, when Banyon returns to the outside world,
the condition of his life is barely ameliorated. He is shown to be
the victim of a continuing confinement, with even the availability
of sex, as proffered by his lover (played by Margit Saad), hardly a
source of liberation. In relentless pursuit of the money that he has
been cheated out of, Banyon's fate is as clearly marked out as one
of Shakespeare's tragic anti-heroes, with the final ignoble image of
his death a reminder that society's prison without bars remains as
impregnable as the government institution we are shown at the
beginning of the film. If the vision of the various strata of British life
offered in *The Criminal* is a dyspeptic one, it is no less rigorous for
that. Losey's own personal circumstances as an involuntary ex-pat
(combined with his intractable, combative personality) meant that
he was not in the business of offering any kind of ameliorative solution to the problems of surviving in the modern world. Yet, despite
this, the final effect of his best films is not, in fact, negative; the positive, energetic qualities of his doomed heroes (however misdirected)
still offers a sense of the unquenchableness of the life force – even if
that life force is (nine times out of ten) doomed to be extinguished
by a society that will not tolerate the destabilising influences those
heroes represent.

Joseph Losey had already demonstrated his skills in the crime
film genre (in such movies as *The Prowler*, which was efficiently
dispatched in only 17 days). Obliged to tackle the very different
studio system in the UK when his persona non grata status in

Hollywood as a blacklistee obliged him to work in this country, the director quickly familiarised himself with a very different new regime, and the combination of this readiness to change with a bloody-minded tenaciousness when it came to getting his own way meant that he was soon able to turn out a great deal of exemplary work in the crime genre in the UK. To some degree, he remained constrained by the subjects he was obliged to take on (it was only by the late 1960s and his creative association with the playwright Harold Pinter that he was able to choose the screenplays that spoke most personally to him). But he was still able to impose (to some extent) his own caustic personality and worldview on what might initially have been perceived as merely generic subjects and material.

To a certain degree, compromise became a default element in Losey's career (and this was a director not temperamentally disposed to any easy notions of compromise) and his British crime films rarely appeared in the form that he wished them to. For *The Criminal*, he found that he was unable to film certain important sequences as there simply wasn't the time available. One of these sequences involved Jill Bennett's character and was designed to illuminate her drug addiction; the fact that Bennett's character makes such a considerable mark in only a handful of scenes is a testament to the director and the striking abilities of the late actress. Above all, Losey was aware that he was, to some degree, a director for hire, and quickly accommodated himself to the notion that if he were to create something personal in his work, it would be in the interstices of the material he had been hired to bring to the screen.

As an American outsider, Losey felt that he was eminently qualified to comment on the absurdities (and nuances) of the British class system. Despite the notably sceptical eye he cast upon such things, he noted that Britons of every class had colluded in creating a smoothly functioning mechanism in the class structure, an efficiently functioning social system. And although his perceptions regarding such matters informed all his British work, his most direct commentary on this particular phenomenon was not to achieve its fullest fruition until the time of such films as *The Servant* (scripted by Harold Pinter from Robin Maugham's novel). Nevertheless, his early fascination with the subject found expression even in his

British crime films (along with the many other aperçus that Losey offered on the curiosities and vicissitudes of British life). Of the earlier films made in the UK, he was wont to regard *The Criminal* as the piece of work which had come closest to his original vision; he was less pleased with *The Sleeping Tiger* (1954), featuring a curious ménage involving psychiatrist Alexander Knox, his disaffected wife Alexis Smith and a disturbed young man (a miscast Dirk Bogarde), regarding the film as something of a thing of shreds and patches; certainly, the heated sexual frisson clearly designed to power the narrative was notably absent. The extremely creative working relationship with Bogarde was not to follow for several years, after the actor had made strenuous efforts to shake off his matinee idol persona.

There are those who consider that the first serious British gangster movie (pitting individual against organisation) is Mike Hodges' *Get Carter*. The cinema re-release in the twenty-first century of *Brighton Rock* (Roy Boulting, 1947), the original gritty adaptation of Graham Greene's lacerating crime novel, is a salutary reminder that the Boulting Brothers had been there before. The film stars Richard Attenborough in a role that is light years away from his current image as a cosy British 'luvvie' figure: he is utterly mesmerising as the psychotic Pinkie Brown, a small-time hoodlum running a protection racket at a Brighton racecourse. Following the murder of a visiting journalist, Pinkie becomes involved with Rose (Carol Marsh), a café waitress and potentially dangerous witness. Despite his aversion to sex (a product, perhaps, of his own pitiless version of Roman Catholic belief), Pinkie marries her to guarantee her silence, but a Damoclean sword hangs over him and his own precipitate actions loosens it, bringing about his own destruction. Also starring Hermione Baddeley as Ida (relentlessly on the tail of her youthful nemesis) and a menacing William Hartnell (the first Dr Who), the film was adapted for the screen by Greene himself – who famously changed his own ending after some pressure. It remains mesmerising viewing, not least for Attenborough's chilling turn as the psychotic Pinkie. The famous censorship cuts of the day (notably Pinkie's razor wielding) contributed to the film's notoriety – and celebrity.

Rowan Joffe's 2010 remake was a very different kettle of fish, and the director was repeatedly obliged to remark upon the fact that it was not a remake of the Boulting Brothers film but a new version of Graham Greene's novel. To a large degree, this was a truthful observation, but one egregious miscalculation gave the lie to the notion and proved that the earlier film version was very much in the filmmaker's mind when filming in the twenty-first century. Ironically, both versions were criticised for downplaying the Catholic elements of Greene's novel, but in neither case did this criticism have any real validity. There had, in fact, been some pre-censorship in this regard before the filming of the first version, which was reluctantly undertaken, as it was felt that Catholics would be offended by the film's association of the creed with a murderous psychopath at the centre of the narrative, but the queasy conflict of moral values actually remained intact in the Boulting Brothers version and the newer Joffe film. Crucially, both films retained (in different forms) the author/convert's curious espousal of Catholic values which appear to run counter to the proselytising aspects of the religion. There could rarely be said to be a positive presentation of Catholicism in either film (an echo of the author's original bleak conception, in fact); Pinkie in the new version is clearly the remnant of an abused childhood and has been imbued by his cradle Catholicism with a fatalistic vision of hell (the rewards of heaven have no place in his Manichean worldview: Rose is 'good', he is 'bad') – and, more precisely than Attenborough, Sam Reilly, the Pinkie of the new version, present the character's belief in a truly cold-eyed and negative fashion. Similarly, no special case is made for Catholicism in the character of the waitress Rose who falls under the youthful thug's spell: Carol Marsh, adequate in the first film at conveying the naivety and unworldliness of the character, presents no positive aspects that belief has brought her, while Andrea Riseborough in the Joffe film (in an assumption of the role which is far better written and played) presents the vulnerable waitress as something of a lamb to the slaughter, with a simple-minded unthought-through acceptance of the tenets of her faith. Certainly, both films maintain the notion that it is hard to believe that reading a Graham Greene novel (or, for that matter, watching a film adaptation of the same) ever converted anyone to Catholicism. The incendiary issue for the more rigorous adherent of the faith is, of course, sex, and the latter film is able to treat Pinkie's stunted sexuality in a more frank fashion – his clumsy, maladroit forcing of his hand between Rose's thighs on the couple's wedding night is emblematic of both his crude approach to sex and his perception of the expectations his new wife will have (it's a realistic touch that we see a post-coital Rose unfazed by this approach – her perception of sex, courtesy of the couple's shared religious beliefs, accords with that of her insensitive husband).

Perhaps the signal achievement of Joffe's film is the fact that it managed to establish its own identity under the massive shadow of its predecessor; before the film was made, the director and his associates were aware of the response accorded to Gus Van Sant's shot-for-shot colour remake of Hitchcock's *Psycho*, which was generally regarded as pointless. Similarly, it was asked, why remake *Brighton Rock*? Initially, a viewing of the film suggests that Sam Reilly possesses not an iota of the basilisk intensity of Attenborough's original assumption of the role of Pinkie, but Reilly's more lower-case incarnation pays dividends and makes his destruction the more telling; Pinkie is always destined for a grim end, with his combination of hubris and innocence (the latter not a million miles away from that of Rose). And in an echo of the extreme razor-wielding violence of the original film (which so upset the censors), a new and far more gruesome death is devised for the young killer; in a struggle with a another gangster, a vial of acid that Pinkie is struggling to use is crushed above his own face, reducing it to raw meat – he staggers to the edge of a cliff and ends up a broken and bloody object on the shales below.

There are many significant changes effected for the relationships between the various characters in the novel (avenging angel Ida, for instance, is now the owner of a café that employs Rose – and, ironically, the always-reliable Helen Mirren is able to make considerably less impression in this role than Hermione Baddeley in the far more conventionally written original film); having the setting updated to 1964 (allowing for Mods-versus-Rockers riots to cover one of the more violent murders) is largely felicitous, and Rowan Joffe has a particularly strong sense of Brighton itself, even though (unlike the earlier film) much of it is not filmed on location in the town, as Eastbourne down the coast, which is far less developed, retains more of the character that Greene's original setting possessed.

With the noir-ish violence cranked up to appropriate levels for modern sensibilities (though knives largely replace the famous razors), Joffe makes the most of the other elements (such as some dramatic cinematography showing the sea as a dark and threatening presence) to grant the narrative and almost elemental quality, while the various integuments of life in 1960s Brighton (clothes and other fashions, modes of speech, etc.) are handled in an intelligent fashion that does intelligent service to the demands of the narrative rather than drawing attention to itself in pointlessly pictorial fashion.

Returning to Rowan Joffe's claim that his *Brighton Rock* was not a remake of the Boulting Brothers version but a new take on the novel, the least successful moment in the modern film is in fact a re-creation of a compromise arrived at in the earlier movie. As Rose is listening to the recording reluctantly made for her in a pierside booth by Pinkie, she is spared from hearing the outpouring of bile and dislike from her lover by the simple expedient of the needle sticking in the groove as Pinkie utters the words 'I love you' (and before he makes clear his true feelings of hatred). In both films, the horror of what Rose is to hear when she takes a record home is (unlike Greene's novel) spared the character for the sake of what appears to be a sentimental ending – doubly ironic, given that both Attenborough and Reilly strongly convey the character's pathological inability to love. This compromise is further compounded in the new version by a shot of a crucifix (a shot that appears to be divested of irony) and a burst of choral music on the soundtrack – a rare miscalculation in the latter regard, given that the scoring by Martin Phipps of Joffe's film is truly unorthodox, with everything from ominous Bernard Herrmann style brass chords to nervous jazz scoring combined to considerable effect. What Joffe's largely commendable effort lacks, though, is the sheer visceral intensity of the earlier version, and it seems likely that the judgement of history on both films will not shake the primacy of the earlier film's hold on the public imagination.

The maverick is very often a criminal – or an ex-criminal. Looking at *Hell Drivers* (1957) today is a reminder that the House Un-American Activities Committee did British cinema a favour by consigning left-leaning directors such as Joseph Losey to professional exile in the UK in the 1950s. Another casualty of the communist witch-hunt was Cy Endfield, who similarly produced excellent work when exiled to the UK – as with *Hell Drivers*, one of the most incisive Brit Crime movies ever made – Endfield's lean, taut movie about corruption among truck drivers, as aficionados will know, is clearly indebted to Henri-Georges Clouzot's *The Wages of Fear*, with its truck-drivers-in-peril scenario (here matched to criminality and cruelty), but so what? Endfield (whose symbiotic professional relationship with blue-collar actor Stanley Baker was to result in the memorable *Zulu*) rings the changes very satisfyingly – and there's the matchless cast (one that would not have been affordable a decade or so later): Baker as the ex-con protagonist, Patrick McGoohan as a sadistic, cigarette-chewing heavy, a pre-007 Sean Connery, Peggy Cummins, Sidney James, Herbert Lom *et al...*

While the in-your-face ethos of *Hell Drivers* may present most of its characters in bright primary colours, there is no gainsaying its ambition (or, for that matter, its achievement), not least the palm-sweating action sequences with recklessly speeding lorries. One expects the central character – the quiet ex-con struggling to keep his head down – to be fashioned with Stanley Baker's characteristic assurance, but there are also several sharply delineated subsidiary characters, such as the sensitive, pious Italian lorry driver played by Herbert Lom (like fellow character actor Warren Mitchell, Lom was able to provide whatever ethnicity was required by any project he was hired for, a skill that assured him of a long and varied acting career). To some degree, Lom is the kind of 'sacrificial lamb' character to be found in so many James Bond films, whose function, essentially, is to die and provide a visceral impetus for the hero (here, Baker's truck driver) in the latter's final inevitable confrontation with the heavies. Interestingly, in an era when religion was rarely questioned, Endfield treats the Roman Catholic Lom character's belief (as evinced by the shrine he prays to) as a naive response to the hard realities of the world he lives in – a response, moreover, which doesn't save his life.

John Lemont's *The Shakedown* (which the director made from a screenplay he had written with Leigh Vance in 1959) is a fairly inert attempt to wring some provocative notions from a familiar scenario, with a piquant leavening of exploitation elements: a con released from prison attempting to reclaim the prostitution racket he once ran from a slimy successor. Terence Morgan (as the ill-fated maverick up against a more unpleasant opponent) delivers a fairly standard performance, but this is one of those British 'B' movies whose interesting backup cast just about makes up for its maladroit execution and now seems far more cherishable than in its heyday: a nicely underplayed performance by Donald Pleasence as a down-on-his luck photographer set up by Morgan in a studio as part of a blackmail scheme (in a piece of egregious plotting, the character simply vanishes from the film), Hammer Films stalwart Hazel Court undoes her blouse to provide discreetly glacial sexuality and Harry H. Corbett chews the scenery as Morgan's ruthless usurper. Like many films of the period (such as Michael Powell's *Peeping Tom*), *The Shakedown* samples the world of sleazy erotica and fairly decorous late-1950s nude pin-ups (there is nudity here, which is unusual for the era, but it is minimal). *Inter alia*, the film freights in some interesting comments about polite society's complaisance with the less salubrious elements that offered once-a-week entertainment (with catchpenny moralising overlay) in the Sunday papers (clearly pushing the envelope with its mentions of prostitution, but still crushingly twee in the 'model school' that is the cover for the blackmail racket). The characterless Soho depicted here is less persuasively sleazy than in the same team's superior *Piccadilly Third Stop*.

One measure of assessing the national character is, of course, to present it in contrast to other nationalities, so that perceived strengths (or, equally, weaknesses) might be set in relief. Alvin Rakoff's tale of criminal mavericks, *On Friday at Eleven* (1961), was an international co-production utilising both British and German money, and employed a multinational cast that guaranteed sales within the host countries of the actors involved (a characteristic almost par for the course in later in Italo-German productions). By the 1970s, such productions were routinely dismissed as characterless, badly post-synched 'Europuddings' in which the various national traits of the protagonists cancelled each other out in favour of a bland American ethos. But Rakoff's film precedes and trumps such uninspiring efforts, and manages to juggle its variety of elements with a certain degree of sophistication. Representing Britain is the capable character actor (and sometime juvenile lead) Ian Bannen, who is more than able to hold his own against such international heavyweights as Rod Steiger (from the USA),

Germany's Peter Van Eyck and (as the French contingent) Jean Servais. The sexual element is provided by Nadja Tiller. The multinational criminal group putting together an ambitious heist is encouraged by Rakoff to demonstrate certain national characteristics, although not (generally speaking) in any crass fashion (needless to say, all the protagonists are obliged to share at least one common supranational characteristic: ruthlessness and amorality). It's instructive that the Brit in this particular mix (Bannen) is actually a Scot, and this canny piece of casting may be said to anticipate the choice of Sean Connery as Ian Fleming's super-efficient secret agent; while American audiences may not have known that Connery was a Scot, they could at least sense that he had none of the effete quality that in the early 1960s was still perceived as a peculiarly English characteristic. The fact that James Bond is currently played by an Englishman, Daniel Craig, demonstrates that international audiences have acquired a touch more sophistication in this area.

In *On Friday at Eleven*, the Brit/Scot doesn't make it to the end of the film, and with international audiences this might have been perceived as a logical dramatic imperative – after all, it is the resourceful American (whatever his faults) who was customarily considered most likely to survive. Viewed today, in the light of the problems that have followed European integration and the loosening up of international borders, it might be said that *On Friday at Eleven*'s central metaphor – international cooperation will always be a fraught enterprise – was prophetic. Certainly, in Britain, political parties such as the United Kingdom Independence Party (not to mention certain strands of the Conservative Party) might prefer to read the film's message in this fashion.

Mavericks can be disillusioned ex-establishment types. While Cliff Owen's lean and economical 1962 film *A Prize of Arms* is essentially a well-turned heist movie, it is also (*inter alia*) a multi-layered picture of the workings of the British army on all its levels – a picture, moreover, which takes into account hectoring, bull-necked sergeant majors, sardonic squaddies, chinless wonder officers and all the multifarious petty tyrannies of the service. But it is a vision which is not unaffectionate and which celebrates the fact that for all the customary breakdowns of communication and obfuscatory lines of command, things in the army (eventually) get done. (This subtly worked pro-establishment line is all the more surprising given the presence of a young Nicolas Roeg among the writers – his own subsequent career would hardly suggest a vestige of respect for such a monolithic organisation.) In some ways, Owen's film reflects certain strands of Basil Dearden and Bryan Forbes' *The League of Gentlemen,* with its central notion of an embittered officer who feels the army is not providing sufficient recompense for the years he has given (although Stanley Baker's tight-lipped leader of the ex-army squad has, in fact, been dishonourably discharged for black market activity; the once-honest Jack Hawkins, at least, had more reason to feel resentment at his consigning to the scrapheap). In fact, it is the presence of Stanley Baker which locates the film precisely in a more working-class ethos, a fact further emphasised by the presence of an actor from the (then) next generation, Liverpool-born Tom Bell, who carried many of the same working-class associations as the ever-reliable Baker (the presence of Helmut Schmid as the third member of the trio attempting an audacious payroll heist is somewhat confusing, given his pronounced German accent, though the latter is built cleverly into the plot; for suspense purposes, it is important that Schmid is obliged to conceal his accent to fool the British soldiers he is deceiving). *A Prize of Arms,* as a film, has its foot on the pedal from virtually the first sequence, and Owen's capable cutting for tension and suspense keeps things moving *accelerando.* The corollary of this kinetic quality, though, is that the characters have little chance to develop beyond what we can be conveyed by their actions as they attempt to fool an entire army base with a series of complex double bluffs. But Baker, as ever, is able to delineate the resentment and sense of quiet desperation of his character with just a few terse sentences delivered on the hoof.

What is perhaps most interesting about this film is not its ambiguous attitude towards the army milieu within which it is set, but the almost geometrical precision of the plotting. The scenario here affords a particular, unfolding pleasure as the viewer realises that seemingly meaningless actions performed by the protagonists early in the film have a logic that will only become clear as the narrative unfolds, and elements of the planning of the robbery (involving flame-throwers, stretchers, sabotaged fire alarms and even mysterious tracks deliberately made in grass by a car) fall into place.

Inevitably, any criticism of the military regime in *A Prize of Arms* has to be seen in context. The individual effort and organisation demonstrated by the robbers has an inevitable conclusion – a conclusion that is not the result of (for instance) the carefully signalled short fuse of the Tom Bell character, but of the ineluctable, sometimes chaotic yet (as Owens seems to suggest) inevitably effective army machine. Needless to say, the precision with which the robbers execute the robbery – not to mention their improvisatory skills when things go wrong – bespeaks their military training.

Far less celebrated films than the adaptations of Graham Greene's *Brighton Rock* regularly depicted criminal loners who become *de trop* for their corporate bosses. Michael Dryhurst's *The Hard Way* (1979), originally made for TV, was a choice example. This modestly budgeted pared-to-the-bone piece utilises its neo-noir elements as cannily as it does its bleak Irish setting. Patrick McGoohan and Lee Van Cleef underplay with considerable skill their underworld figures, making the elliptical dialogue telling. Interestingly, 'The Troubles' are not a key element here – this is a film about individual responsibility.

Given that it is one of the most stripped-down, nihilistic crime dramas ever filmed (the executive producer is John Boorman) and that it stars a particularly charismatic and challenging actor (McGoohan), it's something of a surprise that *The Hard Way* functions only fitfully. But there is a John Buchan-like vision of dangerous landscape and moments of bleak effectiveness, not least concerning the edgy interaction between two hard-bitten hitmen, the laconic Irishman Conner (McGoohan) and his American contact McNeal (played by ageing genre stalwart Lee Van Cleef). The interaction between McGoohan and his estranged wife (played by the Irish novelist Edna O'Brien) is non-existent; they have one wordless, cold scene together as he packs her off to safety when she is in the line of fire, and it's hard not to discern McGoohan's well-known Catholic aversion to any kind of emotional or sexual involvement with women in his work (a stance rigorously maintained in his two cult TV series *Danger Man* and *The Prisoner*). But this hole at the centre of the narrative (admittedly justified by the withholding Conner's solitary personality) is further emphasised by the ill-judged direct-to-camera monologues O'Brien is obliged to deliver about her absent spouse – underlined by the fact that O'Brien is a better novelist than an actress. Nevertheless, Dryhurst's paring down of narrative, dialogue and performance to a bare minimum pays dividends and the film has a cold, affectless sheen which commands attention.

The mavericks, however, were shortly to be transmogrified into more efficiently functioning entities (at least on a small scale – and until internecine disagreements sowed havoc) in a new London-set wave of British films, with criminal protagonists born within the sound of Bow bells.

13
Mockney Menace: The New Wave

For any student of popular culture, it is instructive to notice how quickly a trend can pass, or at least descend into the realms of exhaustion and self-parody. Of course, such a progression is often mirrored by the fall from grace of key progenitors of such trends – and nothing illustrates this sobering thesis more lucidly than the example of the British director Guy Ritchie and the movement he was instrumental in launching: the streetwise, comedically-inclined hyper-violent London gangster movie of the late 1990s, invariably featuring either wisecracking Cockney wide-boys out of their depth or massively cruel, stone-faced psychopathic killers (often in the same films, the former relentlessly pursued by the latter). It's a film trend which is still producing a variety of examples today, but the kind of acclaim and audience enthusiasm which accompanied the early work in the field now largely seems a distant memory.

Such films are routinely described as 'Mockney gangster' fare, vainly struggling for a kind of street-smart authenticity and a desperate, hopeful alignment with the real gangsters who are sometimes called upon to appear in such films, struggling to act; critical response has been particularly vituperative, given the middle-class, well-educated credentials of the filmmakers aspiring to present themselves as East End hard men (the syndrome is not confined to the film world and directors such as Guy Ritchie; the highly acclaimed violinist Nigel Kennedy similarly adopted street slang and glottal stops to distance himself from his middle-class origins and finesse an image of a man of the streets). As with Guy Ritchie, the comfortable lifestyle of both men accruing from their considerable commercial success has made this 'working-class hero' status suspect for many commentators, as it was for the lower middle-class John Lennon in an earlier era. Needless to say, the kind of films that Ritchie and his colleagues and imitators created did not come into the world fully formed without the influence of such pithy earlier work as John Mackenzie's *The Long Good Friday*, but there is no denying the sheer energy and exuberance of the new approach forged by Ritchie and co. – and one film in particular as the standard-bearer for this new movement, a film once enthusiastically acclaimed but now acrimoniously blamed for a host of increasingly desperate and shopworn imitators. That film was *Lock, Stock and Two Smoking Barrels* and, apart from striking a resonant note with audiences in its day, it launched a variety of careers, many of which are still going strong today. The director himself, after seriously losing his way (not least for vanity projects with his then wife, the rock star and sometime actress Madonna, who lived in some splendour with Ritchie in this country), has recently discovered a way of re-connecting solidly with audiences in a controversial but generally well-received rebooting of the Sherlock Holmes franchise.

It is not difficult to see why Guy Ritchie's exuberant film made such an impact in 1998, with its stylish, mannered cinematography, ingeniously constructed (and often very funny) screenplay and notably canny casting, mixing hungry young actors (Jason Flemyng, Dexter Fletcher and Jason Statham, whose broken-nosed Cockney persona was to be parleyed into a highly successful series of thick-ear thrillers) with experienced pros and a sprinkling of real-life masters of the art of menace. The narrative devolves on a motley group of likely lads from the East End who unwisely put their money in a crooked high-stakes card game. Needless to say, they lose disastrously, and the attempts to recoup their losses put the young chancers in the most extreme danger from a variety of different criminals. While this plot device gives the narrative its energy, other pleasures are afforded by the presentation of the different strata of criminal life in modern London, with the various illegal pursuits (drugs, of course, money-laundering and, inevitably, guns offering a microcosm of both this violent subculture and – without any over-emphasis – a picture of the wheeling and dealing in the wider business world in London, which by extension sails similarly close to the wind). And while the consequences of the criminal activity here are frequently shown to be violent in the extreme (though usually in a blackly comic fashion), the sardonic humour that Ritchie (who also wrote the screenplay) trades in is never far away, with the protagonists (including a car dealer, a chef and two dealers in stolen goods) mostly on the receiving end of the accumulated menace that is the lingua franca of this world.

In the first *Godfather* film, Francis Ford Coppola used a certain legerdemain in the presentation of the murderous Don Corleone (as played by Marlon Brando); in order not to alienate the audience, we were only ever allowed to see the old man being avuncular and statesmanlike – the bloody violence with which he maintained his empire was executed by others, and audiences were even manipulated into feeling sympathy for the old monster after an assassination attempt. Similarly, Ritchie, like so many young directors (including his American contemporary Quentin Tarantino), is nothing if not cine-literate and pulls off a similar trick with the wide-boy heroes of his film. We are encouraged to sympathise with their desire to pay off their enormous debt without the alienation of seeing them actually practise violence themselves; they are, as Ritchie presents them, likeable semi-criminals.

Ritchie made no secret of the fact that he was a drinking companion of various individuals on the wrong side of the law (quite the reverse – we were made well aware of these associations) and it was perhaps easy to understand the attraction of those who led this glamorous but violent life outside the law – more edgy and real, perhaps, than (say) obtaining finance for and putting together a film. Reaction to this relatively sympathetic treatment of criminals was fairly swift in coming, as soon as Ritchie – after the great success of this film – became something of a celebrity himself (a process further finessed by his marriage to Madonna). In the final analysis, of course, what really counts is what is on the screen, and in this first film there is no gainsaying the assurance with which Ritchie juggles the various elements in his seductive package. He is particularly good at directing his cast of youthful actors (all male – the only woman to be seen in the film is not given any lines, but achieves a degree of respect by her casual way with violence). And accompanying the witty and kinetically delivered screenplay is a cleverly chosen soundtrack of various rock and pop hits that enhance the mood the director is striving for as well as reflecting the musical tastes of the central characters.

However, what is perhaps most impressive about the film is its level of ambition in coordinating the various narrative strands while negotiating the abrupt changes of tone. The influence of such film-makers as Tarantino is instantly apparent (not least in the shocking violence unleashed at regular intervals, but also in the surrealistic humour with which the entire film is shot through). As the hapless poker player Eddie, Nick Moran delivers just the right note of insouciant Cockney charm, while the three friends who bankrolled him are equally adroit. One piece of stunt casting in the film doesn't come off: the rock star Sting, playing Eddie's father (who owns a pub). Eddie may be sacrificed if the friends are not able to come up with the money; various limbs and appendages will be lopped off by the associates of the fearsome Hatchet Harry (P.H. Moriarty). The ex-footballer Vinnie Jones forged an entirely new career himself here, channelling the violence he was known for as a player into the shotgun-toting debt collector dispensing mayhem throughout the film (a nice touch is this brutal enforcer's touching concern for his son, who accompanies him on the violent errands and is clearly destined for the same career as his father).

The sheer number of characters introduced in *Lock, Stock and Two Smoking Barrels* has a tendency to obfuscate the narrative, but this hardly matters given the panache with which it is dispensed. It may well be a fair criticism to say that the film represents a triumph of style over content, but a healthy measure of social commentary is freighted into the ruthless picture of an acquisitive, money-led modern Britain (the director's ex-wife famously presented the persona of a material girl, but the protagonists of Ritchie's most famous film are unquestionably material boys and are allowed to undergo what is, in the end, only a glancing punishment). The success of the film, however, was a double-edged sword. It was the progenitor of an increasingly dispiriting series of successors, vainly attempting to recapture the elements that made the first film such an audience-pleaser. And among those caught up in this increasingly vain endeavour was, in fact, director Guy Ritchie himself, who would struggle to re-create the career success that this debut film bought in before achieving it again with *Sherlock Holmes*.

To some degree, it was almost inevitable that Ritchie's follow-up film to *Lock, Stock and Two Smoking Barrels* would be more controversially received. In both the literary and film worlds, the second piece of work after a stunning initial success always seems to conform to something as unbending as the laws of physics: the work itself will be met with less enthusiasm than its predecessor and it will not be as impressive an achievement, with (customarily) a sense that time is being marked before the third effort, which will hopefully confirm the promise of the debut piece.

That second film for Ritchie was *Snatch* (2000), in which crooked boxing promoters, threatening bookies, scowling gangsters and maladroit cheeky cock-er-nee thieves are on the trail of a stolen object; the Maguffin here is a stolen diamond worth millions. The film once again sports a strongly cast and varied *dramatis personae* with (for the second time) Jason Statham and several heavy-hitting imported names, including Dennis Farina, Benicio Del Toro and (most controversially) Brad Pitt as an Irish gypsy bare-knuckle boxer, here attempting a crusty accent that audiences on both sides of the Atlantic found largely incomprehensible. Once again, the universe we are shown is that of organised (and barely organised) crime, and the complex and confusing narrative also stirs into the brew a bounty hunter and an arms dealer with a past in the KGB.

The original response to *Snatch* was one more of mystification than disappointment, particularly as it showcased one of Brad Pitt's periodic attempts to distance himself from the pretty boy stardom that he had come to find such an anathema – hence his brutal character's nigh-impenetrable Oirish accent. However, subsequent viewings of the film have somewhat modified those initial responses and it has now acquired something of a cult status. Certainly, Ritchie's kinetic directing style was fully in evidence again, as was the Tarantino-style *pot pourri* approach to the film's music. If the wittily written screenplay by Ritchie (recycling familiar elements) and labyrinthine narrative did not match the sheer exuberance of his debut film – and both the eccentric names for the characters (e.g. 'Brick Top') and lazy mythologising of the salt-of-the-earth Cockney ethos already looked shopworn – time is proving kinder to it than subsequent work by Ritchie or those he inspired.

Among the filmmakers who Guy Ritchie may be said to have inspired is in fact an ex-partner, the *Lock, Stock and Two Smoking Barrels* producer Matthew Vaughn, who directed his own striking and individual crime film in 2004. As well as being a considerable piece of work in its own right (and one of the better British crime movies appearing when the great majority of such work was already proving dispiriting and underachieving), *Layer Cake* also showcases a career-making performance by an ice-cool Daniel Craig, whose assumption of the role of James Bond was two years in the future. Craig plays a moderately successful London cocaine dealer (the film grants him no name and makes no moral judgement on his dubious choice of career) and the narrative describes the protagonist's dizzying journey from small-time dealer to top-of-the-tree success, even as he aids the search for a young woman, the daughter of a colleague of his boss. His other agenda while undertaking this task is to shift a large amount of the stolen drug ecstasy. The author of the original novel, J.J. Connolly, had been conscious that much fiction portrayed London criminals as none-too-bright thugs, and had personal experience of men involved in criminality who were far from stupid – and to whom violence was very much a last resort. Their reasons for being in the crime business did not involve enhancing any macho reputation but were directly – and simply – pecuniary. The illegality of drugs paved the way for such enterprise. The notion that crime was being written about by observers who were naive about professional criminals inspired Connolly to insert a new level of verisimilitude into his writing. And as the narrator of *Layer Cake* suggests, 'everyone likes to walk through a door marked private'. This is, in effect, the key to the whole book (and the subsequent film). We are shown that the reality of selling drugs is that it is a brutal, difficult and unglamorous way to make money, even if you don't get caught by the police. As Connolly demonstrates in no uncertain terms in *Layer Cake*, you have more to fear from other criminals than you do from the police. The novel is a criminal procedural rather than a police procedural, written from the criminal's point of view.

Regarding the film, the novelist was realistic in his responses:

As soon as you sell your property to film producers [he said to me] it's *their* property, and no longer yours. My experience was a good one. I was curious as to how they would adapt it – and I was pleased that they asked me to write the screenplay. It's one of the few films that did do justice to the novel but it's a totally different entity. Coming from a culture that suggests that nothing is 'as good as the book' you've got your work cut out. Matthew Vaughn, the producer and director, knew that if you try to diligently replicate the novel you're on a loser. You have to create a whole, new, autonomous piece of work – one that lasts an hour and 40 minutes. The book opens up a deeper, more concentrated world. With *Layer Cake*, the whole novel would be about 30 hours of screen time, so as a writer, you can't afford to be too precious. Scenes you love simply have to go.

Matthew Vaughn's career was to take unexpected turns in the future (with such crowd-pleasing pieces as the over-the-top and parodic superhero fantasy *Kick-Ass*), but at this point in his career, he was content to deliver a piece that is much more linear and integrated than the work of his ex-colleague Guy Ritchie. *Layer Cake* boasts the strikingly authoritative Daniel Craig performance mentioned above (which trades in understatement, one of the actor's strongest suits), but it also delivers the goods when high-voltage action sequences are required. Interestingly, despite the film's attempts to retain a cool distance from its protagonist, it was clear from early showings that audience involvement was considerable, something of a testament to both Craig's performance and Vaughn's direction, along with the readiness of viewers to maintain a certain moral equivocation, whatever their view of drug dealers.

By the time he made *Sexy Beast* (2000), the east London actor Ray Winstone had become something of a British national treasure. Making his mark as a younger man in such pieces as the caustic borstal-set *Scum* (Alan Clarke, 1979), Winstone's career as a hard man was largely mapped out for him, and his bruised, abrasive Cockney charm has been to some degree his stock in trade since his youthful days. However, by the time of *Sexy Beast*, an interesting transmogrification has occurred. Winstone's performance as top safe-cracker Gal Dove functions on several levels: its own straightforward naturalistic level, as a parody of itself and also as a wry and knowing commentary on what audiences had come to expect from such characters. Dove, after a successful London criminal career, has decided to retire and has moved with his wife to an exquisite villa in Spain. Needless to say, this idyllic hiatus is to be short-lived when another criminal appears to throw his life into disarray. This criminal is a psychopath, the monstrous, diminutive Don Logan, a violent criminal who is unable to complete a sentence without the most colourful of epithets. His job is to persuade the retired Dove to take part in a bank robbery back in London and he is utterly determined not to take no for an answer. There is absolutely nothing that the reluctant Dove can do to dissuade his snarling criminal colleague from trying to persuade him. If Winstone's casting as the suntan-oiled and slightly laid-back Dove plays on audience expectations of earlier performances, a similar piece of doublethink is evident in the casting of the psychopathic Logan, played by the modestly-proportioned (but here terrifying) Ben Kingsley. To have the actor who is most famous for playing Gandhi as a psychotic criminal was not quite as audacious a piece of casting as it might once have seemed, as Kingsley had latterly made something of a speciality of such characters. But the film's real achievement is to make explicit the dynamic that audiences will read into the off-screen lives of the two characters: the fact that the Royal Shakespeare Company stalwart Kingsley could offer such a threat to the genuine East End hard man Winstone demonstrates just how impressive both men's performances are, which is not to underestimate the direction by Jonathan Glazer. The screenplay by Louis Mellis and David Scinto effortlessly sounds all the right notes, although it should be pointed out that the tone of the film shifts alarmingly at times, a factor not always negotiated smoothly by its director. Glazer was a debut director who was perhaps to some degree in awe of his two heavyweight stars, but, unlike so many filmmakers who made a mark in advertising (including, in Glazer's case, alcohol commercials), he shows a grasp of storytelling that matches his edgy stylishness in terms of the film's vision. Particularly well found are the excellent Spanish settings, which counterpoint the audience's knowledge that London is where these two sparring partners really belong. The film is further finessed by excellent supporting performances from such reliable players as Ian McShane, Amanda Redman and James Fox.

Director Paul McGuigan's entry in the burgeoning London gangster genre was markedly different from many of those films beginning to appear, most notably in its commendable (and refreshing) lack of 'Mockney' humour. This was truly a scarifying piece of work, building its razor-sharp narrative around the picture of a British criminal of almost preternatural force, only ever identified in the film as 'gangster'. Audaciously, *Gangster No. 1* begins with the violent protagonist, played by Malcolm McDowell (an actor with a resonance of menace stretching back to Stanley Kubrick's *A Clockwork Orange*), who is shown to be luxuriating in the position he has so brutally achieved. But the great majority of the film treats (in flashback) the gangster's younger days, when in 1968 he is played by the smooth-faced Paul Bettany (although the voiceover for the character is still handled by McDowell). Bettany's character is the protégé of a criminal known as the 'Butcher of Mayfair', Freddie Mays (chillingly played by David Thewlis), who is a more smooth piece of work than his violent pupil. The bloody, all-stops-out story is told in a completely uncompromising fashion, with some striking pieces of technique (such as the image on the screen shattering then coming together again). The story of a mobster's rise to power through a series of murderous acts is of course desperately overfamiliar, but McGuigan manages to give everything a dark and unfeeling sheen, relying on some particularly striking performances (notably from Bettany, knowingly ushering in a stellar career). There is, of course, the inevitable conflict between the self-made killer and the man who was his patron (Mays has been languishing in prison, put there by his protégé), and this confrontation is handled in as eye-opening a fashion as anything else in the film. The visceral violence in the film is utterly unsparing and makes *Gangster No. 1* a poor choice for squeamish audiences. We are shown that unbending force of personality is required to achieve success in this pitiless world, and once again a metaphor for success in the unshown non-criminal world is stressed.

14
The Age of Acquisition:
New Crime

The notion of instant gratification/acquisition as a motivation for crime (as opposed to careful, methodical planning) is hardly a new one, and while modern instances of the phenomenon (both in the cinema and the society which it reflects) are generally ascribed to the Thatcher era and its celebration of entitlement values throughout the country, it is also a theme in several recent British crime films. It is ever more apropos, particularly after the looting and burning of shops in the riots of 2011 that spread through the country. Needless to say, of course, there are lengthy and detailed examples of the syndrome to be found within much of Western society and the literature which is held up as a mirror. Flaubert's Madame Bovary, for instance, is shown by her creator to be a woman at the service of her instincts for acquisition. Leaving aside her desire for both romantic love and physical gratification (the latter being a suitable catalyst for self-destruction in an era when the Church's attitude to female sexuality was hardly enlightened), her desire to indulge her love of such expensive items as furniture and clothes are similarly shown to be pursued with a relentless disregard for the consequences – it is the latter (rather than an indulgence in the erotic) which might be seen to be the author's identification of Emma Bovary's fatal flaw.

Similarly, filmmakers utilising the crime film form are usually well aware of the baubles, the seductive accoutrements with which criminals surround themselves. Our moral opprobrium is dissolved in a vicarious enjoyment of these various objects of desire – both animate and inanimate. What the more intelligent filmmakers interpolate into such scenarios is the sense of *mauvais foi* practised (consciously or otherwise) by the lawbreaking protagonists. They may not know (or care) about the consequences in human misery suffered by others directly because of their actions, but we, the viewers, are not allowed the luxury of such indulgence – for these crime films, the discussion of the price to be paid is the contract agreed (more or less willingly) between filmmaker and audience.

Certain writers and filmmakers have attempted to destabilise this equation; the late American writer Donald Westlake, for instance, in his series written under the pseudonym of Richard Stark and featuring the ruthless hitman Parker, occasionally invited the reader to examine the bloody consequences of his charismatic but appalling hero's actions on innocent bystanders – Westlake/Stark knew that his readers (and the viewers of the several films made of his books) would be happy to see mayhem unleashed on brutal criminals who were even worse than the compunction-free Parker, but tried to instil feelings of guilt in his audience for their participation. There is, we were being reminded, a price to be paid for spending guiltily pleasurable time in such violent company. However, this was clearly a case of a creative artist wanting to have his cake and eat it. And there are inevitably many crime films which play the same game – interestingly, most of them are to be found on the other side of the Atlantic. British crime films tend to express less equivocation in their attitude towards the protagonists than their American counterparts. In the UK, the moral battle lines are drawn and we are well aware that death and destruction is the price on the ticket for the amoral protagonists we are identifying with.

Paul Anderson's full-throttle crime film *Shopping* (1994) did not find an audience in its day, but nevertheless made an ambitious attempt to identify a strand of crime which had not previously been treated in the cinema: the consumerist, small-scale criminals for whom expensive trainers and digital electronic equipment were the principal objects of aspiration. Attempting to balance a disdain for its lawbreaking protagonists with a certain grudging admiration, Anderson never quite decides what his final attitude towards his characters is (though inclining to the latter), but incidentally creates an impressively uninspiring London setting for his film, with some well-chosen Isle of Dogs locales along with other grim and blighted urban landscapes. In some ways, the treatment of these settings (reminiscent of the 1987 film *Empire State*) is Anderson's most cogent achievement, with the director finding a bleak and haunting poetry in the dispiriting capital we are shown, perhaps not a million miles away from the vision presented by the most celebrated chronicler of London subcultures, writer Iain Sinclair, in such books as *Lights Out for the Territory*.

During the London riots of August 2011, disenfranchised youths (and some who were not disenfranchised) used the catalyst of a police operation in which a young black man with a gun was fatally shot to lay waste to large areas of the capital and loot sports goods and electronics stores. Paul Anderson's film may be said to be prescient in showing young people utterly outside any kind of parental influence (after the riots, the media cry regarding the looting youths was 'Where are the parents?', a cry that is comprehensively answered by Anderson's film: the influence and control of parents is completely eroded and invisible). The protagonist Billy (played by Jude Law) has just been released from jail at the beginning of the film and is caustic about the rehabilitation effect that prison has had upon him. Upon meeting a young Irish woman, Jo (played by Sadie Frost), Billy begins a descent into consumerist criminality in which such items as a BMW are shown as grist to the mill for the young couple's acquisitiveness. But Billy has reckoned without another, slightly older, criminal, Tommy (played by Sean Pertwee), who has consolidated his pole position in Billy's absence and regards Billy as a divisive, irrational force – in short, bad for business. Although the film ends in the kind of violent confrontation that has always been a crime film lingua franca, Anderson's real concerns lie in rendering an image of modern youth crime with total amorality as the order of the day (Billy is never presented in any heroic fashion and exploits his underlings with as much ruthlessness as do those higher up the social scale that he so despises). To his credit, Anderson has no easy answers to dispense after presenting us with this downbeat scenario. Certainly, there is no idealising of the working-class characters (portrayed, to a man and a woman, in deeply unsympathetic fashion), and the authorities (as encapsulated in the beginning of the film by Jonathan Pryce's well-meaning but ineffectual prison governor) offer no further facile solutions. However, where Anderson perhaps comes unstuck is in what may be read as his grudging admiration for the youthful, nihilistic energy of his protagonists who are at least presented as possessors of impressive force in contrast to the inertia around them, and the attractiveness of his players contains echoes of the director Arthur Penn's casting of the photogenic Warren Beatty and Faye Dunaway in two similarly blithely acquisitive characters in *Bonnie and Clyde*, where physical attractiveness guarantees audience sympathy despite the actions of the protagonists. It is also significant that Anderson appears to admire his anti-heroes' forensic knowledge of the objects of desire that power their actions. And it is perhaps this engaging of the director's sympathy that keeps *Shopping* from attaining a balance and cool-headedness that would allow the viewer more leeway in seeing the different facets of the characters.

Shallow Grave (1994) demonstrated a certain ambitiousness (along with a readiness to challenge viewer expectations), and if the film's achievements are decidedly mixed, director Danny Boyle deserves credit for his imagination and inventiveness (even if there are several shades hovering behind the film's inspiration: the Coen Brothers and Quentin Tarantino in particular). At the centre of the film (and in the memory of those who have seen it) is one abiding – and unsettling – image: the naked corpse of the actor Keith Allen. There is a certain iconic resonance in the use of the actor here – until middle age brought about a marked change in lifestyle, Allen was best known for his hellraising and rebellious ways, perhaps overshadowing a memorable career playing a series of villains and criminals. The fact that Allen ends up dead and unclothed in this film – and is looked at in that way by the protagonists (and the audience) for some considerable time – is perhaps a comment by Boyle (along with writer John Hodges), but perhaps *Shallow Grave* was designed to represent a moratorium on other British crime films of recent vintage. In fact, if that were the intention, it is not achieved, although there are fresh things here; for instance, foregrounding a female character as a major element in the plot rather than as a piece of window-dressing (and who is refreshingly shown to be as crassly venal as the male characters). The writer-director team (along with producer Andrew Macdonald) would subsequently go on to make the highly successful *Trainspotting*, which genuinely offered an alternative to standard, by-the-numbers crime narratives – and that leap into the unknown is given a preliminary exploration here. With a healthy dose of a sardonic black wit that was to distinguish much of the director's later work, the central premise here is the dangerous effect of money (stolen, of course) and the deleterious effect it has on the lives of all the protagonists, who basically fall into the criminal world by their discovery of stolen loot in the possession of the Allen character. The three principal characters are from a middle-class background – three self-assured professional types living together and seeking a flatmate in Edinburgh. One is a journalist (played by Ewan McGregor), the second is an accountant (Christopher Eccleston) and the female member of the group is a doctor (Juliet Fox); the three are living comfortably in their impressive flat and are auditioning a possible fourth rent-sharer. One applicant, the louche Hugo (Allen), tells them he is a novelist, and after his death from a drug overdose, they discover that his suitcase is crammed with a great deal of money. After some discussion, they decide to keep it – being clearly non-film-literate and unaware of the inevitably disastrous consequences of such actions in films. The implacable villains on the trail of the money are more than ready to torture and maim to recover the money, but (as Boyle and his writer suggest) the worm in the bud is already eating away at the souls of the outwardly law-abiding protagonists, and violent deaths and betrayal are to take their toll – and not just at the hands of the pursuing criminals.

If a salutary point is being made about the corrupting power of money (and corruptibility of those putatively on the right side of the law), it is sharply undercut by the film's grim but ambiguous ending, with one character nailed to the floor by a knife, but grimly aware that the bloodstained money will be theirs – if, that is, there is not a shallow grave beckoning. The truly dyspeptic vision on offer here clearly equates the amorality of professional criminals with the serviceable moral standards of the yuppie protagonists, and the absence of the police as any mediating factor in the bloodshed here moves the film into a very parlous moral territory; whether or not the critique of the central characters' values represents a lazy shorthand on the part of the filmmakers (before the low esteem in which bankers are now held after the world recession, yuppies had been high in the list of unpopular groups – ironically, even by those who might have been said to belong to this despised cadre), so broader points about moral equivocation are dampened down by the easy targeting here.

Crime cinema has long been reactive rather than proactive, but many of the most ambitious directors have traditionally utilised the form to make prescient points about society – a welcome syndrome which is particularly pronounced in the early years of the twenty-first century.

An intriguing phenomenon of the new era is the fashion in which the genre has reflected a certain nihilistic affectless attitude on the part of its protagonists (whether criminal or otherwise), and it might be said that these new anti-heroes suggest nothing so much as the refusal to prioritise physical objects over personal relationships (as espoused by such French existentialist writers as Sartre and Camus in the 1940s and 1950s). There is the same studied refusal to be owned by objects coupled with an antithetical acquisitiveness – but the new objects of desire are regarded in a utilitarian fashion rather than being fetishised (as, say, jewels might be in a crime film of an earlier era). The unconscious emphasis on the development of personality (or, conversely, the deflection from any natural organic growth of the same) is a recurrent theme of modern crime films. And as in the 1950s, the notion of an alienated, disenfranchised youth is often central to these new films.

The films of black director/actor Noel Clarke incorporate these notions. The unfortunately-titled *Kidulthood* in 2005 suggested a visceral power and vision which had already been formulated, if not fully thought through. This efficient British film, written by Clarke, possesses a genuinely fresh, contemporary vision in its picture of young people drifting in and out of crime on the streets of west London. Several 15-year-old schoolchildren are given a day off when a suicide has a destabilising effect on their school. The viewer is then presented with a vivid, sometimes overwrought picture of the fashion in which the group spends the next day: bitter/affectionate squabbling – verbal arguments of (what might seem to the outside observer) terrible ferocity are the *sine qua non* for these youngsters, having grubby sex, drinking in Olympian quantities and (when these stimulants proves insufficient) fighting, thieving and attempting to develop 'respect'-engendering expertise in the use of knives and guns.

Clarke wisely avoids a tongue-clucking moral disapproval of his underage reprobates, and foregrounds energy and crude wit as driving forces for his protagonists. An earlier film, *Bullet Boy* (2004, directed by Saul Dibb), covers much of the same territory with its cast augmented by rappers who knew the world of drugs and guns personally, but the movie lacked Clarke's clearly authenticated film sense, and it was perhaps inevitable that *Kidulthood* would be compared to Fernando Meirelles' sprawling *City of God* (2002) in its unvarnished panoply of young lives being squandered in pointless criminality and excess. Clarke has nothing like the visionary qualities of Meirelles, but the British director's refusal to condemn or condone demonstrated a refreshing willingness to allow audiences to make up their own minds. Coaxing natural performances from his well-chosen group of young actors, Clarke allows (perhaps encourages) the viewer to share their enthusiasms, whether fumbling sexual activity or sticking two fingers up to authority. And he is happy to include many of the issues that keenly affect teenage lives today with (thankfully) an attitude that suggests inclusivity rather than throwing in a barrage of elements for easy effect. While adults are largely conspicuous by their absence, this does not suggest a lionising of the teenagers in the film, who are presented with cool objectivity. Certainly, younger audiences responded to the film with great enthusiasm, feeling that they were not being talked down to or moralised to. As an actor himself, Clarke showed a strong response to dialogue, and the ludicrously over-the-top abuse and sexual imagery of the wordplay here has an almost Joycean exuberance (if that's not too grandiose an analogy). But as well as the erotic activity shown in the film, Clarke demonstrates how sexual imagery infuses most of the caustic verbal exchanges between these young people. However, though it might be noted that the attitude is (in its way) as anti-sex as might be heard from any pulpit, the difference here is that these individuals treat sex in unblushing, full-on fashion; contempt for people not in the immediate circle is not based on sexual transgression, but on the bitterness of betrayal – and the film is full of that, with the protagonists constantly behaving towards each other in the most callously faithless of fashions. It's here perhaps that Clarke allows himself a straightforward value judgement. He is also clearly deeply unhappy with bullying, and there is an intensely unpleasant scene here showing bullying between girls – and it is shown to be just as cruel and pitiless as that practised by boys on their peers.

The energy of the film is matched by a carefully chosen soundtrack (mostly of music not calculated to appeal to a demographic beyond that of young protagonists) and the director also presents an unglamorous image of London that is not seen too often. It might be argued that Clarke's refusal to editorialise suggested either a strong-mindedness on his part or a laziness in terms of formulating any overarching directorial vision. Similarly, his clear awareness that adult viewers will mostly look on the activities of the film with a fascinated horror is not perhaps a sufficiently objective stance.

Such misgivings about Clarke's rigour as a director were confirmed by the film's successor, *Adulthood* (2008), in which the innovative elements shown earlier have now experienced a hardening of the arteries, with the narrative progressing along much more well-worn lines than the earlier film. Clarke himself plays Sam, returning home after a prison sentence for murder and discovering that new young criminals have taken over the block, and it is only a matter of time before a knife is driven into his heart or stomach. In the course of the day, Sam comes to realise that there are three things he must tackle: his enemies, those who he had victimised and his own attitude to his behaviour and his society. The picture of London society presented here is even bleaker than in the earlier film, with gun and knife crime now accepted as an essential part of life for these young people, but much of the film feels warmed over with elements adapted from such models as *Trainspotting* (1996, Danny Boyle's film of Irvine Welsh's novel, which showed a similarly unvarnished picture of young British adults, cast adrift and at the mercy of violent criminals and drug dealers). For all its incidental virtues, the misfiring *Adulthood* took some of the gloss from Clarke's reputation – which he will hopefully reclaim.

The 2011 riots (which began in London and then quickly spread throughout Britain) occasioned a great deal of soul-searching and hand-wringing throughout the country, particularly regarding the role of the police, who (it was initially felt) had adopted an ill-advised 'softly softly' approach when the violence began and had not intervened in the early stages of rioting and looting. Whatever the rights and wrongs of this particular aspect of a troubled period, there was one significant development. While the right-wing press inevitably called for the draconian treatment of the rioters (who were described by some politicians as members of a feral underclass, but who had among their numbers teachers and other professionals), the expected liberal critique of such calls to action from more left-of-centre members of society was not as forthcoming as might be expected. Was this because Britons of most classes had been able to see the smoke of burning stores (either on TV or from their own windows) and had experienced a revision of the customary attempts to understand the causes of such behaviour? Daniel Barber's film *Harry Brown* (2009) pre-dated the looting of electronics and clothes stores, but featured in prescient fashion one much-discussed aspect of the riots: the dangers of ordinary people attempting to intervene when violence erupts.

The film begins with a group of teenagers smashing the windows of a car and knocking the owner to the ground when he attempts to stop them. Pedestrian tunnels are sources of danger, as young men loiter at the entrances ready to assault anyone who dares to traverse this risky territory. While the film in fact presents the vision of Britain fondly held by readers of such right-wing newspapers as the *Daily Mail* (in which out-of-control youth gangs rule the streets and ordinary citizens are cannon fodder for this new breed of urban monster), it initially appears to present a more nuanced view of society. But does it? Barber's film was received with some dismay by liberal-leaning critics on its release in 2009; it's intriguing to speculate what the critical response would have been had the film been released after the riots. The audience surrogate here is a mature ex-marine played by Michael Caine (now a British elder statesman of film), who is standing in for all respectable, older inner-city inhabitants, but deals with the thuggish murder of a friend by arming himself and setting out to summarily eliminate the thugs à la Charles Bronson in Michael Winner's *Death Wish*. But even in the light of the less indulgent stance towards the causes of teenage violence in 2011, Barber's film can hardly be said to offer a realistic solution to the problems it addresses: while it may afford the viewer (by proxy) a cathartic resolution for the ordinary citizen via violent action (the Michael Douglas film *Falling Down* had offered similar vicarious pleasures), the acquisition of heavy artillery by the elderly is hardly a realistic solution to such problems. Gary Young's screenplay sets down its basic thesis in relatively straightforward terms and eschews any evidence of psychological effects on the ageing protagonist, despite initially establishing him as a lonely man whose life appears to have ground to a halt and whose service to his country was ill rewarded (another parallel here might be Clint Eastwood's film *Gran Torino*, which offers a more complex and intelligent resolution to similar issues). The police in *Harry Brown* (as ever in such scenarios) afford no help. There is some strongly-etched detail in the scarifying vision of inner-city Britain portrayed here, and there is no reason why a filmmaker should furnish any kind of easy amelioration. The problem with Barber's film, however, is that there is little evidence that such debate ever took place between writer and director, either before or during filming.

Ill Manors (2012), written and directed by rapper Ben Drew (aka Plan B), was a striking, if muddled, vision of a broken Britain, scored with a relentless hip-hop soundtrack; moral redemption is at a premium in this bleak urban setting.

Nirpal Bhogal's *Sket* (2011) was hardly more illuminating, offering an unvarnished picture of life among British girl gangs (in which rape by members of the male gangs that also prowl the blighted estates was endemic). Bhogal's film offers the possibility of retaliation for the brutalised young women (whose lives of drug dealing and violence are lived to the soundtrack of high-decibel 'girl grime' music), but at a cost to the vulnerable tyro members, who are forced to be as tough as the rest of the group to survive. In a piece by Megan Walsh related to the film (*The Times*, 22 October 2011), it was noted that 'females accounted for 22% of all proven offences in 2009/10' and that 'violent attacks are the most common first-time crime for girls under 17', which begs the following question: are films such as *Sket* salutary in their readiness to address such issues or do they add to the self-mythologising of the gang members in the fashion of 'gangsta rap', which is similarly accused of celebrating a violent creed?

15
Twenty-First-Century Hybrids

It is interesting to speculate on the future of the crime film. Like all durable genres in the cinema, the crime movie is cyclical, with familiar tropes making periodic reappearances (after a suitable interval) for new audiences who – in many cases – will be unfamiliar with the material or its presentation. If a cursory examination of the crime field suggests that it is now tougher and colder than it has ever been, with a rock-hard carapace that allows no gentler moments, this is to some extent an illusion. The earliest crime films (particularly those of American vintage, such as Howard Hawks' *Scarface*) are quite as unforgiving and bleak as anything being made in the early twenty-first century. But there are innovations appearing, and some of these are symptomatic of a phenomenon flourishing in other fields of the arts: the hybrid or 'mash-up', fusing two disparate genres. In an era in which the Britart *enfants terribles* Jake and Dinos Chapman add smiley faces to Goya's *Disasters of War* and Jane Austen's genteel, crinolined characters encounter bone-crunching representatives of the living dead in literary mash-ups, it is hardly surprising that the cinema is attempting similar syntheses of disparate elements, shoehorning them together with grotesque results. In some cases, such experiments are a concomitant of creative exhaustion – desperate attempts to cast around for something new to reinvigorate a shopworn format. But some directors have, in fact, forged something rich and strange, in which the seemingly incompatible elements coagulate to create something quite new. And given that (in the first ten years of the new century) the horror genre was enjoying something of a new lease of life (or death), it was perhaps inevitable that ambitious directors might see a way of combining the Gothic with the equally durable crime fiction format. The fact that this unholy but stimulating marriage has already produced at least one remarkable film (to be discussed later) bodes well for the future.

Christopher Smith's lively (and ensanguinated) *Severance* attempted the crime/horror melding in 2006 (it was, of course, by no means a new syndrome – Michael Powell had tried it with career-stalling results in *Peeping Tom* in 1960). The Smith film incorporated some wry and telling points about modern team-building exercises and slippery business ethics, as a sales group from an international arms-dealing firm are bloodily slaughtered during a group exercise designed to inspire sales acumen, but even though the lopping off of limbs and slicing off brainpans seemed to engage Smith somewhat more than the character-based aperçus to be found in the piece, he deserved credit for trying something different.

To some degree, Sean Hogan's *The Devil's Business* (2011) was something of a canny multiple synthesis: the tough crime drama married to the Pinteresque character study/chamber piece, with dialogue of studiedly naturalistic character (imprecision, pauses and so forth), plus a striking dose of pitch-black sardonic humour amid the verbal menace. Of course, the traffic concerning the English playwright Harold Pinter's influence is unquestionably two-way. While the impact of his writing (via Samuel Beckett) is clearly evident in such films as Roman Polanski's *Cul-de-Sac* (notably the bitter sparring between the two ineffectual gangsters), Pinter himself explored this very territory in such plays as *The Dumb Waiter*, which combined a *Waiting for Godot*-style inertia with a narrative concerning two hitmen waiting to perform a killing; the kind of narrative, in fact, which has done much service in straightforward crime films. And perhaps the most influential of Pinter's plays (in this area) is *The Birthday Party*, with its two terrifying criminals (one Jewish and one Irish) producing an astonishing stream of witty and brutal verbal invective that most crime screenwriters are clearly in awe of. Given that one of Britain's leading playwrights was so adept at minatory wordplay (with an ever-present threat of violence – in actuality rarely delivered), it was hardly surprising that younger filmmakers with an ear for dialogue (which, fortunately, seems to be a great many of the new breed) would customise the Pinter template to their own ends.

The most impressive use of this model (utilised within the context of a crime/horror hybrid) is Ben Wheatley's *Kill List* (2011), but before looking at that, it is worth considering a couple of other films. Hogan's *The Devil's Business* commendably avoids surgical shots for much of its length in order to generate tension through dialogue and character interaction rather than under-motivated mayhem (the besetting sin of many journeymen filmmakers in both the crime and horror fields). To say that the budget of *The Devil's Business* was restricted might be said to be litotes (in fact, the producer, Jennifer Handorf, utilised the house of her in-laws for the film's settings), but the film is a sterling example of how inventiveness can triumph over the most limited of resources. The central charters are two hitmen, Cully (played by Jack Gordon) and the more savvy Pinner (Billy Clarke), and Hogan begins his film with the duo assigned to their next target, sent there by sinister mobster Bruno (Harry Miller). What follows is the kind of colloquy between the team that theatre-literate audiences might expect, in which the two men begin to swap stories – and Pinner delivers a pithily written monologue about their boss' slightly demented sexual fixation on a dancer (the story has a grim and violent finale). But as the two men wander about the house of their victim, they discover bizarre evidence of some kind of unholy ritual. Ultimately, of course, they encounter the man they have been sent to kill, the civilised, opera-loving Kist (memorably played by Jonathan Hansler), and the steady pace increases towards a dramatically handled (if not entirely convincing) resolution. The device – virtually patented by Pinter – of the more experienced interlocutor (in this case the seen-it-all Pinner – note the name) detailing the lie of the land for his tyro assistant offers no radical contrast to earlier usages, but the arrival of their 'mark' – a character quite unlike that we have been led to expect – allows the director to pull off something of a *coup de théatre*, genuinely surprising the viewer. But Hogan's real achievement lies in the intelligent melding of the crime fiction and macabre elements. However, it is another director, Ben Wheatley, with a very similar scenario, who was subsequently to take this experiment several stages further.

In 2009, Wheatley, bristling with ambition, delivered a calling card movie with *Down Terrace*, a claustrophobic study (set largely in a cluttered house in Brighton) of twisted human behaviour that fused the mechanics of the crime thriller with quirky character

observation à la Mike Leigh. While the result here is sometimes tor-
pedoed by the inexperience of the non-professional actors involved
(the cast includes Julia Deakin, Kerry Peacock and Robert Hill), there
is undoubtedly evidence here of a truly original (if unpolished) cinematic sensibility – one that was destined to do idiomatic work in the
future (as proved to be the case with the director's next film, which
was undoubtedly his breakthrough work). *Down Terrace* investigates
the eccentricities and betrayals within a bizarre family unit, pepper-
ing its unconventional narrative with the incendiary behaviour of
its volatile characters and (at intervals) some particularly savage and
gruesome killings – it is a crime movie, after all. The father and son in
the family which Wheatley presents to us are bottom-feeding, minor-
league drug dealers who have managed to escape jail after a court
hearing goes (surprisingly) in their favour. What follows is the pursuit of the person who sold them down the river, but these two are
not smoothly functioning crime machines. The father has shreds of
leftover attitudes from his counterculture days and he is saddled with
a son who can barely hold together a succession of incandescent
rages. As the cryptic and banal banter between the two (principally
concerning substance abuse) is ratcheted ever higher, the audience
appears to be presented with a dark social comedy, but memories of
Mike Leigh and co. are summarily obliterated as the corpses begin to
bloodily pile up. But if Wheatley's concatenation of different genres
here is only a qualified success, his subsequent film was to prove a
much more considerable achievement.

That film was the remarkable and edgy *Kill List* (2011), which
began to glean critical praise fairly early via that most reliable of tried-
and-tested methods: word of mouth. The extra authority and command of the film medium that Ben Wheatley had gained since the
hit-or-miss *Down Terrace* was immediately apparent here, although
initially the spliced-together elements appear to consist once again of
Pinteresque comedy of menace and the over-familiar machinations
of two hitmen (yes, again) attempting to carry out a murder in the
face of a series of disasters. More than in his previous film, Wheatley
establishes a verisimilitude in his detailed portrayal of a very contemporary Britain, with an Afghanistan war veteran, Jay (mordantly
played by Neil Maskell), living an unsatisfying life in an unprepos-
sessing house with his wife and son. Jay is in desperate need of a
lifeline (his debts are prodigious) and after a deeply uncomfortable

dinner party (redolent once again, in its embarrassment, of the serio-comic British director Mike Leigh, as was Wheatley's earlier film), he decides to get the money he needs by taking on some contract kill-ings with Gal (Michael Stanley) for a sinister figure played by Struan Rodger. Once again, we have the odd couple relationship between two hitmen, although this is a much more sophisticated treatment of the theme than in previous films dealing with similar ideas (the social realist director Ken Loach also appears to be an influence in the unsentimental treatment of the characters, and the non-linear editing creates a subtly destabilising effect). But then Wheatley takes the viewer by the throat and the film begins a slow and terrifying journey into a true heart of darkness, starting with a confrontation with a group of Christians in a restaurant which brilliantly balances very dark humour with a truly unsettling atmosphere. And as the two hapless protagonists come face-to-face with the horror that is at the end of their assignment (some distance from the opening scenario – we are now firmly in another genre), the shifting of gears between crime and horror is handled adroitly. What's more, this audacious mixture of themes does not (as was often the case in the past) bring about a cancelling out of the most potent parts of both elements. And if this skilfulness were not enough, Wheatley manages to incorporate several trenchant points about modern society and its serviceable attitude towards morality.

The notion of the crime/other genre mash-up produced much interesting work in the first decade (and beyond) of the twenty-first century, not least (for instance) Joe Cornish's lively and intelligent (if ideologically confusing) *Attack the Block* (2011), which pitched the menacing young black hoodies of a drug-ridden council estate against marauding, monstrous aliens. Managing to incorporate sociopoliti-cal commentary alongside pulse-racing excitement, the film's basic premise (the invasion of a deprived south London housing estate) shows the influence of several films with similar themes, notably John Carpenter's *Assault on Precinct 13* (the siege in a rundown area) and Walter Hill's *The Warriors* (teenaged gangs as beleaguered heroes). But Cornish (whose background was in TV comedy) makes some relatively audacious decisions when it comes to the characteri-sation of his teenage protagonists. Within the context of a fictional tower block, the Wyndham Tower estate, he incorporates a certain level of critical commentary on his low-achieving, youthful black protagonists (there is even a reference to the better career prospects of the female relatives of these young men). And to some degree, these women (rather as in the Westerns of the director John Ford) represent a civilising influence – it is for them that the young males are obliged to come up with alibis for their behaviour. Cornish is even able to incorporate the different levels of 'street cred' within the various strata of the gangs: the teenage members are viewed askance by the older professional 'gangstas', but are themselves admirable role models for the pre-teen aspirant children whose bleak futures the viewer is clearly able to discern from their misplaced admiration. There is even a more affluent young white man, a 'wannabe black' who attempts street jargon and patois to ingratiate himself with the gang (to some degree, Cornish allows him to stand in for the many white aficionados of 'gangsta rap', who similarly attempt an unconvincing version of rap argot). But perhaps the director's most challenging tactic lies in the first encounter, where the white trainee nurse Sam (played by Jodie Whitaker) is the victim of a very threatening mugging by the group before the invading aliens force everyone onto the same side. It's a moot point as to whether Cornish is (after this indelible scene) able to allow us to feel sympathy for the default heroes, even though the presentation of the aliens as something utterly 'other' points to such a strategy, and he permits us to see the vulnerability behind some of the threatening exteriors. Nevertheless, the picture of low-level street crime presented by *Attack the Block* has a pungent verisimilitude.

Other films of this period to mix genres included *The Cottage* (2008, written and directed by Paul Andrew Williams), which attempted a crime/horror comedy mélange, beginning as a kidnapping drama and modulating into full-blown horror for the film's final reel. Williams chooses an andante tempo for the early part of the film (a risky move, given audience expectations with this kind of narrative) and the humour lacks the edge of similar material by Simon Pegg and director Edgar Wright, but the eccentric playing of Andy Serkis as one of the criminals ensures that audience interest is maintained. However, by far the best modern utilising of the kidnapping theme was in director J. Blakeson's highly successful *The Disappearance of Alice Creed* (2009), a film made on the most restricted of budgets but which nevertheless demonstrated a constant command of film language. Two crooks snatch a wealthy young woman, Alice (Gemma Arterton), from her moneyed father. Apart from the remarkable, exposed performance by Arterton as the kidnap victim, the director is able to find a variety of new wrinkles in the kidnap scenario, as well as delivering a rich panoply of jawdropping narrative twists.

So is a marriage of horror and crime the wave of the future? Many felt that the writer Thomas Harris, when conflating the two genres in such books as *Red Dragon* and *The Silence of the Lambs,* had effectively put paid to both as discrete entities. The risky offspring of this marriage has been ruling crime fiction on the printed page since Harris comprehensively galvanised the genre, and the auguries are that cinema will continue to nourish its own visceral version of this hybridisation process. But the crime genre is infinitely malleable and the possibilities for future commingling of elements are infinite. One thing is certain: the crime film (and, in particular, the British variety) is in the rudest health.

Appendix 1: The Directors: Makers of Key Crime Films

Anthony Asquith (1902–1968)

The patrician Anthony Asquith's reputation as a director (once unassailable, subsequently in flux) is enjoying something of a new dawn, with his handful of entries in the crime genre worthy of reassessment. In recent years the adjective 'worthy' has told against Asquith (who was the son of the Liberal prime minister of the early twentieth century) as anti-establishment and subversive values began to gain ascendancy in modern critical circles – though a close view of the director's films suggests a more complex picture than this reductive assessment allows. Asquith followed many of his public school-educated colleagues into the film industry of the early 1920s, initially working on documentaries and films with natural history subjects. After the usual process of working his way up through the ranks, he made well-crafted films in a variety of genres, but only when he became a secure member of the Gainsborough Pictures personnel in 1932 did he begin to find his *métier* in (among other things) sophisticated comedies. By the 1930s, he had shown a taste for the intelligent theatrical adaptation (notably Shaw's *Pygmalion*, one of several theatrical classics that he was to direct) and his famous association with the playwright Terence Rattigan (the latter now enjoying a revival of interest after years of neglect) was one of the most significant achievements of his career. Some of his best work was to be found in the less high-profile crime-related projects such as *The Woman in Question* (1950) and the understated and effective *Orders to Kill* (1958). His film of Francis Clifford's atmospheric novel *Act of Mercy* (filmed as *Guns of Darkness* in 1962) was generally seen as evidence of the director's decline, but has its modest virtues. Looked at retrospectively, it is clear that Asquith allowed elements of individuality into his less prestigious projects (such as his crime films).

Robert S. Baker (1916–2009) and Monty Berman (1912–2006)

In their day, this hardworking director/producer duo were generally regarded as catchpenny (though highly successful) exploitation merchants, and there is no doubt that they always kept an eye on the main chance when it came to the box office; they were, for instance, one of the most ambitious imitators of the Hammer Films style when that studio began to enjoy immense popularity with crowd-pleasing (if unrespectable) product. The Baker/Berman company, Tempean Films, which began to produce low-budget supporting films from the 1940s onwards, showed a predilection for crime subjects (filmed in 'stronger', more explicit versions with the sex and violence quotient increased for the more tolerant continental market) and enjoyed steady success while finessing the careers of such directors as the prolific John Gilling (a director with whom the duo liked to work and who helmed several of their films). The Baker/Berman film of *Jack the Ripper* in 1958 was one of the most bleakly vigorous emulators of the Hammer style, and even in the truncated version in which it is largely known remains an intelligent if unsubtle piece of work. One of the duo's most intriguing films is *The Siege of Sidney Street* (1960), a sober treatment of the gun battle between the police and anarchists in early twentieth-century London – a film that demonstrated a certain intelligent political and historical engagement. The crime genre was to be the calling card for the team when they moved to television, with such solid series as *Gideon's Way* in 1965, the long-running if superficial *The Saint* (1962–1969) and other less esteemed but popular series.

Roy Ward Baker (1916–2010)

Like Hitchcock (with whom he worked), Roy Ward Baker learned much of his craft at Islington's Gainsborough Pictures, initially, like the then-youthful master, taking whatever jobs he could find but gradually assimilating the nuts and bolts of the business with work on such films as *The Lady Vanishes* (1938). A memorable encounter with the crime genre took place when the respected left-wing novelist Eric Ambler requested that Baker handle his production of *The October Man* in 1947, one of the first films to demonstrate the underrated

John Mills' remarkable skills. The film inaugurated a fruitful professional collaboration between actor and director, and marked Baker
out as a director to watch, albeit a journeyman filmmaker rather than
an auteur. Leaving aside such camp extravaganzas as the homoerotic
The Singer Not the Song (1961), with one of Mills' least impressive
performances, Baker began to demonstrate his utilitarian versatility
in a variety of genres (notably horror), but kept his hand in with the
crime field by directing for television efficient if by-the-numbers episodes of such shows as *The Saint* and *The Avengers*. Other impressive
crime films on a crowded CV included the American *Don't Bother to
Knock* (1952) and the tense and colourful *Inferno* (1953).

Antonia Bird (1959–)

Antonia Bird began her professional life working in the theatre
(notably at London's Royal Court) but also directed for television
a variety of ambitious dramas and better-than-average soap operas.
She showed a firm and continuing commitment to social issues with
the pertinent drama *Safe* (1993), dealing with homelessness. Moving
into the crime genre, she made the kinetic *Mad Love* (1995) about a
young couple running from the law, but enjoyed favourable reviews
for the dark-hued *Priest* (1994), a typically scabrous Jimmy McGovern
screenplay about a gay Catholic priest. Her most significant contribution to the crime genre was the edgy and uncompromising *Face*
(1997), dealing with a robbery (and written by Ronan Bennett),
with the intense Robert Carlyle as a young man who switches from
what he sees as useless agitprop to criminal activity. The movie
ambitiously tried to do several disparate things (apart from its crime
genre underpinnings) and perhaps misfired on a variety of levels,
but nevertheless showed the kind of astringent intelligence that has
always been the hallmark of Bird's work. A later film, *The Hamburg
Cell* (2004, also written by the talented Ronan Bennett), dealt with
the events leading up to 9/11.

John Boulting (1913–1985) and Roy Boulting (1913–2001)

One of the most significant family partnerships in the history of
British cinema, the Boulting Brothers were a double-threat director/

producer duo who created striking and individual work in a variety of genres. Their film *Thunder Rock* (1942), with its anti-isolationist stance, was tendentious but impressive, and the duo's first impressive work in the crime genre was their adaptation of Graham Greene's *Brighton Rock* (1947), which conjured up its seedy, violent seaside world with great skill. The Boultings enjoyed considerable critical acclaim for the ticking-clock narrative of *Seven Days to Noon* (1950), which dealt with the desperate search for a bomber with confused motives. The film itself has worn well and now contains pre-echoes of the threat from bombs planted by religious fundamentalists in the twenty-first century. A workaday remake of *The Most Dangerous Game* as *Run for the Sun* (1956) was one of their less impressive efforts, and their series of sardonic and cutting social satires (of which the best was probably *I'm All Right Jack* (1959)) may be the duo's most lasting legacy, although certain, broader aspects have (perhaps inevitably) not worn well. Other impressive entries in the crime genre included *Suspect* (1960), and their last outing in the field was the controversial and misfiring *Twisted Nerve* (1968), which drew much criticism for its linking of certain forms of mental illness with psychopathic behaviour. While crime films may have been only one part of a varied joint CV, the Boulting Brothers demonstrated that, had they ploughed only this particular furrow, they would be remembered for their achievements in that field alone.

Alberto Cavalcanti (1897–1982)

In a lengthy filmmaking career, the quixotically talented Alberto Cavalcanti (who was born in Brazil) became one of the most significant talents in British cinema, his exotic name a metaphor for his introduction of a striking poetic strain which raised his films (however generic) above most other commercial product of the time. Working on impressive early documentaries with Humphrey Jennings, it was only a matter of time before Cavalcanti began to establish himself as a nonpareil director of tense crime or thriller-based subjects, such as his trenchant film of Graham Greene's *Went the Day Well?* (1942), in which a subdued English village proves itself capable of massive violence against intruders. The high point of his career (many would consider) was the chilling ventriloquist's dummy episode in Ealing's single horror film, *Dead of Night* (1945), which is one of the great psychological studies in the genre. In 1947, he made what may be his most significant contribution to the crime genre with the celebrated *They Made Me a Fugitive*, an uncompromising crime scenario in which an RAF officer (played by Trevor Howard) makes a disastrous foray into the world of criminality. For many critics, this bleak film is the single most significant example of British Noir, and the very fact that it was so excoriated on its first release has given it a kind of retroactive glamour. Such is the achievement of the film that it is to be regretted that Cavalcanti made so few forays into the crime field.

Don Chaffey (1917–1990)

In the early days of Don Chaffey's lengthy film career, he consistently showed invention and inspiration when directing a wide range of subjects (including one of the most memorable of the colourful fantasy films featuring Ray Harryhausen's stop-motion animation, *Jason and the Argonauts* (1963)), but perhaps his most long-lasting contribution was to home-grown crime cinema. Chaffey, who was born in Hastings, learned his craft toiling at the Lime Grove Studios art department and initially appeared to be set for a career in production design, working with such directors as Lewis Gilbert. An early example of his skill with popular genres was the economical *The Man Upstairs* (1958), with Richard Attenborough giving a memorable (if actorly) performance as a man at the end of his tether. A variety of comedies followed (such as 1960's underwhelming *Dentist in the Chair*) and Chaffey demonstrated a surefooted approach to the fantasy genre, with, for example, the Ray Harryhausen film mentioned earlier and another venture with the animator, *One Million Years B.C.* (1966). But Chaffey had worked in the crime genre on a variety of television series, such as *The Four Just Men* (1959–1960) and *The Avengers* (1968–1969), and perhaps his most memorable work was in this field, including (for the cinema) *The Flesh is Weak* (1957) and *The Crooked Road* (1965).

Basil Dearden (1911–1971)

To say that the reputation of the director Basil Dearden has been in flux is not, perhaps, accurate; for some years he has been regarded as a journeyman filmmaker with impressive ambition who occasionally rose to some memorable levels of inspiration but generally demonstrated a quotidian approach to his subjects. This lacklustre judgement is not quite fair, as Dearden's level of achievement over a lengthy career included several high spots and the commitment to his various subjects was never in doubt. Born in Essex, he spent several stultifying years in insurance before work in the amateur theatre led him to more congenial work at Associated Talking Pictures. A long-lasting partnership with the producer Michael Relph (who was also a collaborator on the screenplays the men filmed) led to such films as the haunting *The Halfway House* (1944), one of Ealing's rare forays into the supernatural (although lacking the distinction of the studio's most impressive work in this field, *Dead of Night* (1945)). Relph and Dearden quickly acquired a reputation for professionalism and speed, qualities that were very highly valued in the high-pressure British film industry of the day. What really distinguished their work, however, was their readiness to engage with difficult social issues, even though detractors claim that these issues were rarely integrated into the fabric of the plot but were utilised in a slightly exploitative fashion (the American filmmaker Stanley Kramer was to suffer from the same accusations). The exploitative tag would not, perhaps, have been levelled at the duo had their films not appeared to aspire towards a seriousness of purpose that it was felt they were not able to achieve.

Their first film in the 'social issues' genre, *Frieda* (1947), was a post-war examination of prejudice, but *The Blue Lamp* (1950) inaugurated their commitment to the crime genre, although the crime trappings were often incidental to the central 'engaged' subject of the screenplays. *Violent Playground* (1958), like *The Blue Lamp*, also dealt with juvenile delinquency, in a more bitter and confrontational fashion than its cosier predecessor, but 1959's *Sapphire* set a then-daring examination of attitudes towards race within the context of a relatively conventional police procedural. Similarly, the groundbreaking *Victim* (1961) utilised the same format, with homosexuality as its plot engine (again, the controversial theme was wrapped in one of the standard mechanisms of the crime film, in this case blackmail). Later work by Dearden and Relph such as *Life for Ruth* (1962) still utilised the 'issue' concept (in this film, religious fundamentalism putting the life of a young girl at risk), but eschewed any 'crime' motifs. The duo's careers were studded with intriguing crime melodramas such as the astringent *Pool of London* (1950) and the later *The League of Gentlemen* (1960). Succeeding films were very much a mixed bunch as the search for new issues demonstrated signs of fatigue, but if the social problem films have dated, there are many commendable and challenging elements in them that still work for a modern audience.

Cy Endfield (1914–1995)

Born in Scranton, Pennsylvania, Cy (sometimes 'C. Raker') Endfield showed promise shortly after leaving Yale University, but in a field other than that of his ultimate *métier*, the cinema: he was a tyro magician. A significant (and fateful) association began in his younger days when he joined the Young Communist League, a decision that was to both change the course of his life and (indirectly) grant British cinema one of its most interesting expatriate talents when he was obliged to work in the UK after he became unemployable in red-baiting Hollywood. But before this, a series of low-budget films in America such as *The Sound of Fury* (1950) had marked Endfield out as a trenchant and economical talent, rather in the vein of another much-acclaimed director who also dealt in unrespectable genre subjects, Don Siegel. But in 1951, when the House Un-American Activities Committee identified Endfield as a communist, he was obliged to either name fellow travellers or be blacklisted. Like many of his contemporaries, including Joseph Losey, he abandoned Hollywood to work in Britain on television series such as *Colonel March of Scotland Yard* (1956–1957), in which the eponymous police-man was played by Boris Karloff. Endfield's first really distinctive film in Britain (and the sign that he was able to customise indigenous subject to his particular satisfaction) was the energetic *Hell Drivers* (1957; his credit reads C. Raker Endfield), with Stanley Baker as an ex-con finding himself inadvertently engaged in criminality again and up against a rogue's gallery of tough lorry drivers, notably a psychopathic Patrick McGoohan. The film had a markedly American feel despite its British cast and also inaugurated a lengthy associa-tion with the actor Stanley Baker, with whom Endfield made the less interesting *Sea Fury* (1958). The greatest success for the actor/writer duo was, of course, the intelligent epic *Zulu* (1964), detailing the Battle of Rorke's Drift, but the team returned to characteristically tense thriller material with the fitfully successful *Sands of the Kalahari* (1965), their last film together. Time has been kind to Endfield's reputation and his body of work looks ever-more impressive with the passing years.

Bryan Forbes (1926–)

Bryan Forbes is one of the reliable, multi-talented professionals of British film; never displaying the brio (as actor, writer or director) of more coruscating talents, but nearly always producing solid, accomplished work in whatever field he is essaying, be it acting, directing or writing (the last of these three may be his most pertinent legacy for the cinema; the acting was quickly sidelined when his behind-the-camera skills proved more impressive). Born in Stratford, his original ambitions lay in the acting realm and he underwent training at RADA, but left before the completion of his final term. Initially making his mark as an actor in films (including in Michael Powell's *The Small Back Room* in 1949), he then began to exercise his nascent skills as a writer and director. His first significant success was the witty and artfully constructed screenplay for *The League of Gentlemen* (1960, directed by Basil Dearden), with its ingenious heist committed by a group of alienated ex-servicemen led by Jack Hawkins. Success in other fields followed (such as the gentle, wistful drama *Whistle Down the Wind* (1961) and the quintessential kitchen-sink film *The L-Shaped Room* (1962), with Leslie Caron glumly considering abortion). Other films in the crime genre were to follow, such as the deeply flawed but interesting *Deadfall* (1968) with its vaguely *Du Rififi Chez les Hommes* style robbery. The versatile Forbes' secret (apart from his considerable screenwriting skills) was his fellow-feeling sympathy for actors, and all of his films feature some exemplary work from the group he always continued to regard himself as part of – the thespian community. The most frequently used member of that community (who features in many of his films) was his wife, the actress Nanette Newman.

David Greene (1921–2003)

After David Greene left the merchant navy in 1941, his studies at RADA were followed by a brief film acting career, but he finally settled on directing with the much-acclaimed *The Shuttered Room* (1967), a memorably unsettling adaptation of the writings of H.P. Lovecraft and August Derleth, heavily filtered through the film's curious attempt to pass off Britain as America (the film's principal actors were American, but smaller parts were played by British players such as Oliver Reed, who is menacing as ever). This film established Greene's highly individual way with landscape and setting (a skill that was to distinguish his work throughout his career), along with a particularly dexterous approach to cutting and editing. *The Strange Affair* (1968) incorporated an ambiguous view of both the burgeoning hippie culture and an unsparing examination of police corruption, but other crime/thriller subjects (such as the modish *Sebastian* (1968) and *I Start Counting* (1969)) were less well received. The director's middle-aged vision of swinging London in *The Strange Affair* was as jaundiced as that of the English director John Schlesinger's phantasmagoric America in the latter's adaption of James Leo Herlihy's *Midnight Cowboy*, and the extreme violence of Greene's film made an impression (and may have rendered this, his most striking work, unseeable in subsequent years). The occasional interesting film followed (along with a steady if quotidian employment directing for television), but Greene's career faltered – a source of regret given the considerable skills he had demonstrated in his early films.

Val Guest (1911–2006)

The much-employed and urbane Val Guest may be regarded as one of the most versatile journeyman directors to have worked steadily in the British film industry – or (less charitably) as a jack of all trades who delivered professional work without often being really engaged with his subject. The former, however, is probably the more accurate assessment. Like many directors, Guest began his career as an actor and even had a period in journalism (an experience that was to stand him in good stead for the pungent, persuasive realisation of the journalistic world in such films as *The Day the Earth Caught Fire* (1961)). Born in Maida Vale, Guest was brought up in India before coming to London. His first films involved venerable music hall comedians of the day such as Will Hay, but as a director with an early grasp of commercial imperatives, he began to make his mark with such studios as Hammer, for whom he created the trendsetting (and still impressive) *The Quatermass Xperiment* (1955), the film which inaugurated the studio's long and profitable association with the fantasy/horror field, even before it reinvigorated the Dracula and Frankenstein myths. Perhaps drawing on the long journalistic fascination with crime that clearly engaged his own interest, Guest demonstrated a marked sympathy with and enthusiasm for the crime genre, although his best work in the 1960s may be found in *The Day the Earth Caught Fire*, which is one of the great British dooms-day movies. However, the ambitious *Hell is a City* (1960) and *Jigsaw* (1962) showed his considerable expertise with crime-related subjects (as did, to a lesser extent, *80,000 Suspects* (1963)). Later films such as *The Diamond Mercenaries* (1976) showed a notable falling-off of his economical and highly professional filmmaking skills, but his career in the cinema was a long and distinguished one.

Robert Hamer (1911–1963)

Born in Kidderminster, Robert Hamer made his mark in the edit-ing studios of Gaumont British in the early 1930s and worked with such directors as Alfred Hitchcock (on the latter's *Jamaica Inn* (1939)). Joining the GPO Film Unit, he worked with the equally talented Alberto Cavalcanti and with such broad comedians as George Formby. Like Cavalcanti, some of Hamer's most memorable work is to be found in the Ealing supernatural anthology *Dead of Night* (1945), but his personality (difficult, quixotic and immensely creative) began to demonstrate its first flowering in such films as the multi-faceted *Pink String and Sealing Wax* (1946), which dealt in expressive fashion with the subjects of murder and suicide. His considerable achievement in this film was topped by *It Always Rains on Sunday* (1947), adapted from the novel by Arthur La Bern, which created a remarkably detailed picture of the East End Bethnal Green community (Googie Withers lives a life of quiet desperation until her worthless criminal lover turns up on the run to destabilise her quotidian existence). Bristling with wonderful character finessing (such as the Jewish community in Bethnal Green, which is shown without sentimental gloss), the film was exquisitely photographed by Douglas Slocombe. Not for the first (or last) time in the direc-tor's career, his work bore the influence of art films from abroad. His great black comedy of murder, *Kind Hearts and Coronets* (1949), looks as glitteringly ruthless in the twenty-first century as when it was made, and (along with Alexander Mackendrick's *The Ladykillers*) is perhaps the most uncompromising film made under the Ealing banner, eschewing the studio's bourgeois (if comforting) cosiness. *The Spider and the Fly* (1949) began to show evidence of his decline (his personal problems had begun to interfere with his work) but was still an intriguing melodrama in which a policeman (played by the saturnine Eric Portman) tracks down an ingenious criminal (Guy Rolfe). *The Long Memory* (1952) is also highly regarded, with John Mills giving one of a series of memorable performances as a convict released from jail after serving time for a murder he did not commit and pursuing those responsible. It is a trenchant film, with the director's bleak vision fully in evidence. Hamer's film adaptation of G.K. Chesterton's detective stories in *Father Brown* (1954) produced a gentle comedy with an unassuming performance by Alec Guinness, but hardly showed the director at full throttle, and his alcoholism began to affect the success of his projects. Later comedies such as the slight but winning *School for Scoundrels* (1960) showed that his skills had not deserted him, but this film was to represent his last work in the cinema.

Sidney Hayers (1921–2000)

For many years, the reputation of the talented Sidney Hayers as one of the most highly regarded auteurs to work in the British film industry was unassailable, even though he had begun to make a living in television with some relatively undistinguished work. Hayers was born in Edinburgh and worked as an editor in the early part of his career (on such films as Jack Lee's *A Town Like Alice* (1956)). Working with J. Lee Thompson on *Tiger Bay* (1959), his association with genre films was marked out (his delirious 1960 horror opus *Circus of Horrors* is now considered one of the most outrageous and strikingly Sadean films made in the UK, in the same year as Michael Powell's *Peeping Tom*). Perhaps his finest hour was the chilling *Night of the Eagle* (1962), but *Payroll* (1961) was one of the most commandingly made heist movies in British cinema, filmed largely on location in Newcastle (a city that was to provide an equally vivid locale for the later *Get Carter* (1971)). Later films in the crime genre by the director did not build to any degree on this success, and *Revenge* and *All*

Coppers Are... (both 1971) were far less successful and were workaday in their casual and unthinking use of exploitation techniques. Later films such as *Deadly Strangers* (1976) demonstrated a less sure grasp of the vocabulary of crime film vocabulary even as the director upped the ante in terms of violent incident. By now, Hayers was taking on bread-and-butter work such as second-unit direction for Richard Attenborough on *A Bridge Too Far* (1977) and his long, profitable but unexciting career in television began. His earlier work, however, remains immensely impressive and his name retains its cachet.

Alfred Hitchcock (1899–1980)

The inclusion of Leytonstone-born Alfred Hitchcock in any study of the history of film is a given, so towering is his achievement in both his British and American films. While there are those who have made a case for more mainstream directors who tackle more respectable genres (such as David Lean), many would argue that Hitchcock is the most influential creator the British cinema has ever produced in any genre. And looking at his British films (before his move to the USA and the creation of such complex masterpieces as *Vertigo* and *Psycho*) remains a salutary experience. Early admirers (who were not prepared to accept the director's own slightly disingenuous assessment of his talents as simply the 'Master of Suspense' – notably French critics writing for *Cahiers du Cinéma*) prioritised the director's exuberant British films over his later American work, but that assessment has now been radically re-evaluated. Nevertheless, the British films remain an astonishing body of work, brimming with a young man's fizzing intoxication with both his own talent and the medium he loved, from the early silent classics such as *The Lodger* in 1926 (with its precocious visual flourishes) through the first British sound film, the innovative *Blackmail*, three years later and up to the sublimely eccentric British version of *The Man Who Knew Too Much* (1934). Hitchcock's willingness to combine a playful attitude to the crime/thriller genre with a commitment to colourfully-drawn character and setting (freighting in a richness not hitherto to be found in the field) remains as winning today as when the films were first made. Of course, these films (and such vintage crowd-pleasers as *The 39 Steps* (1935) and *The Lady Vanishes* (1938)) also began to explore the more complex and intriguing themes first identified by his more informed followers, notably the famous 'transference of guilt' theme and an examination of the limits of heroism as adumbrated in his studies of ordinary men caught up in dangerous circumstances beyond their control. But even if Hitchcock had not been tempted overseas – and had never made his remarkable American films – his legacy of work in the UK would be considerable – not least for its influence, which continues to this day, both in the UK and throughout the world.

Mike Hodges (1932–)

To say that the film *Get Carter* (1971) has been something of an albatross round the neck of the director Mike Hodges is only partially true. Certainly, the filmmaker, who was born in Bristol, has never matched the cult success of this film, but he has nevertheless created a corpus of films that are full of accomplishment and imagination (a certain cult reputation has grown up around such work as the dark science fiction thriller *The Terminal Man*). What is more, several of these films are in the crime genre, although each is invariably compared (usually, it has to be said, unfavourably) with the director's magnum opus. Working in television, Hodges was a cine-literate director well aware of the developments of other countries, and with his first feature, *Get Carter*, created perhaps the most seminal of British gangster films. Its successor, the comedic *Pulp* (1972), which was based on a story written by the director himself, once again featured Michael Caine, but the comedy-thriller format found far less favour with audiences, and even though the film has its supporters, it remains something of a slight *jeu d'esprit* when considered in the context of the director's career. Big commissions were to follow, such as the outrageously camp *Flash Gordon* (1980), in which – despite the money thrown at it by producer Dino de Laurentiis – the director showed little sympathy for the subject material, and the unspeakable *Morons from Outer Space* (1985) was a career low. But Hodges' Indian summer was in the wings. *A Prayer for the Dying* (1987) was a pungent thriller with Mickey Rourke as an IRA hitman trying to leave his career of bloodshed behind him.

More recently, the veteran director regained some of the inventiveness and inspiration that distinguished his best work, notably *Croupier* (1998) with Clive Owen as the morally compromised title character. Hodges aficionados, while acknowledging that later films such as *Croupier* and *I'll Sleep When I'm Dead* (2003) do not match the achievement of his signature film, nevertheless argue that he still has much to offer the cinema. In the early twenty-first century, the director began to write quirky crime fiction, but it is to be hoped that he can find the financing to continue adding to a very respectful filmography.

Seth Holt (1924–1971)

The history of the cinema (both in the UK and the USA) is littered with talents that flickered and were extinguished all too soon before promising careers could achieve their fullest expression. While this notion is undoubtedly true of such filmmakers as Michael Reeves (who died young after completing only one totally successful film), it only peripherally applies to the equally talented Seth Holt, who left behind a slim but highly accomplished body of work. Of the films that he did manage to complete, the evidence is clear that had Holt's personal problems not intervened, a career of considerable distinction would have been his legacy.

Holt was born in Palestine but received his education at Blackheath School in London. His early work as an editor in 1942 for a documentary company led to more ambitious film work (perhaps a certain nepotism played a part – Holt's brother-in-law was the much-acclaimed director Robert Hamer; both men were to share a career-crippling love of the bottle). Working for Ealing, Holt polished his skills as an editor working with such directors as Alberto Cavalcanti and Charles Frend, and his first experience with the crime genre (albeit comic crime) was working as an editor on Charles Crichton's *The Lavender Hill Mob* in 1951 and working as associate producer on Alexander Mackendrick's *The Ladykillers* four years later. While enjoying this work, Holt nurtured one burning desire: to direct. Regrettably, however, the once-great Ealing Studios was becoming moribund, but before Michael Balcon finally closed the doors, Holt was able to direct his highly accomplished (if flawed) debut movie *Nowhere to Go* in 1958 (discussed earlier). Working with Mackendrick inspired Holt in making a film which – even more than *The Ladykillers* – seemed to represent the antithesis of everything that the Ealing Studios represented, not least via the bleak vision enshrined in this economical crime drama. The film was cut by the distributor MGM, but the director's obvious talent shone through even in this compromised version. However, it was to be three years before Holt made what is generally regarded as his masterpiece, this time for Hammer Film studios. *Taste of Fear* (1961; *Scream of Fear* in the USA) is a stunningly atmospheric, beautifully shot example of malign misdirection, one of the many riffs on the genre of psychological thriller popularised by the French crime writers Pierre Boileau and Thomas Narcejac (notably Clouzot's *Les Diaboliques*, with which this film shares a constantly-popping-up waterlogged corpse), but so total was Holt's command of his material (notably in the chiaroscuro finesse of the monochrome visuals) that the elaborate criminal machinations in *Taste of Fear* (via the unlikely twists of Jimmy Sangster's derivative screenplay) are immensely satisfying. Tension was more fitfully present in *Station Six-Sahara* a year later, with a sweatily seductive Carroll Baker inspiring lust in all the even more perspiring males around her. The most famous image from the film – Baker provocatively sunbathing in black bra with both straps falling down – suggests the simmering sexuality which was inevitably played up in the film's posters, but the opening scenes of *Station Six-Sahara* (prior to Baker's sudden appearance via an unlikely car crash) actually have more of the authority of Holt's other work, with a remote oil station in the Sahara peopled by a variety of variously uptight or volatile characters, all representing particular characteristics of their various nationalities (Germans, Scots, Englishmen and Spaniards) with the sharply-drawn hostility between the members of the group finely tuned by the director. After the destabilising Baker's appearance, the tensions take a very specific direction and the film traverses a more familiar road and (to some degree) dissipates the effectiveness the opening scenes.

The Nanny in 1965 was a considerable return to form, with more elaborate criminal obfuscation keeping the audience guessing (and Holt even manages to achieve some splendid underplaying from Bette Davis in the title role – not an easy task). After that, the director's career began something of a decline, with the listless *Danger Route* in 1967 a fag-end entry in the Bond imitation stakes. Holt had plans to direct *if...* (a project that he worked on), but was obliged to relinquish it to Lindsay Anderson, as his reliance on alcohol now began to seriously sabotage his projects. For Hammer, Holt began to direct a horror film in 1971 based on Bram Stoker, but died before the end of shooting. His is a brief, splendid vibrant career, possibly more about failure than success, but he remains one of the most intriguing talents in British cinema.

Neil Jordan (1950–)

Neil Jordan's varied and protean careers have all produced some cherishable work, but his renaissance talent was perhaps too butterfly-like in his approach to various media (had he only remained a novelist, he would be regarded as one of the most promising writers of his generation). Born in County Sligo in Ireland, Jordan made his mark as a novelist, before beginning work in the film industry with John Boorman on the latter's Arthurian epic *Excalibur* in 1981. The first film Jordan himself directed was the highly individual *Angel* (1982), in which a young musician is present at the murder of his manager and a woman friend – a crime he takes it upon himself to revenge. The film was the beginning of a long professional relationship with the talented actor Stephen Rea, who became something of an alter ego for the director. Jordan's first sizeable success was with *The Company of Wolves*, a 1984 fantasy inspired by the writings of Angela Carter, but it was with his subsequent film, *Mona Lisa* (1986), that he made his most singular contribution to the crime fiction genre. With Bob Hoskins as a sympathetic gangster becoming involved with a luckless prostitute played by Cathy Tyson, Jordan was able to conjure a dark and minatory world of pimps and criminals set within a sophisticated evocation of a Britain in which corruption is endemic. Influence of Italian neorealism could also be detected in this incisive and highly effective drama. The director's Irishness found expression in several films, notably *The Crying Game* and *Michael Collins*, his study of the Irish revolutionary, although he resisted special pleading for his nation and the demonisation of British characters to be found in the work of such filmmakers as Mel Gibson.

A fallow stretch beckoned for Jordan. Many felt that the director's talent had utterly deserted him with such woeful, heavy-handed comedies as *High Spirits* and *We're No Angels*, the box-office failure of both being matched by the critical opprobrium heaped upon them. But more good work lay in the future for the director, such as an arresting adaptation of Patrick McCabe's *The Butcher Boy* in

1997, a film boasting some deft insights into the influence of the media. And another ambitious crime film was Jordan's version of Jean-Pierre Melville's *Bob le Flambeur* (as *The Good Thief*) in 2002, which demonstrated (if nothing else) the director's chutzpah in taking on Melville in this territory and showcased a magnetic turn from Nick Nolte as the drug-addicted gambler protagonist. While never neglecting his Celtic origins, Jordan has repeatedly shown his willingness to work on a large canvas and tackle subjects far removed from the Dublin of his college years.

Quentin Lawrence (1920–1979)

The name of Quentin Lawrence is primarily known (if at all) to those with a knowledge of the more obscure byways of British cinema, and his reputation can hardly be said to match that of more stellar names in the genre. But in a relatively small body of work, Lawrence was able to produce films of a certain individuality and even panache, while always working within the constraints (budgetary and otherwise) of commercial cinema. After some experience in films in the late 1940s, Lawrence (who was born in Gravesend, Kent) began to make a mark in television, with two challenging (if crudely made) science fiction serials to his credit, *The Strange World of Planet X* in 1956 and *The Trollenberg Terror* in the same year (he was later to helm the cinema version of the latter for Baker & Berman films, retaining much of the original's eccentric quality despite the restrictions of low-budget special effects). The first film on which he was able to display his conscientiously acquired filmmaking credentials was the taut *Cash on Demand* in 1961, a highly effective adaptation of a television play by Jacques Gillies in which Lawrence's economical direction is immeasurably aided by the nonpareil acting of Peter Cushing and André Morell.

Lawrence's next assignment promised much, not least for its boasting of a truly impressive cast which (in retrospect) might have appeared absolutely sure-fire in producing a memorable crime drama. But despite several highly commendable elements, *The Man Who Finally Died* (1962) remains a thing of shreds and patches, intermittently successful and owing more to its copper-bottomed cast (Stanley Baker, Peter Cushing, Mai Zetterling, Eric Portman and Nigel Green) than to Lawrence's efficient (if relatively uninspired) contribution. The film's lack of success forced Lawrence to say yes to some low-prestige work in the poorly regarded and long-running Edgar Wallace crime 'B' features, although both *Playback* (1962) and *We Shall See* (1964) have fleeting – very fleeting – moments reminiscent of his best work. Back in his alma mater of television, Lawrence's association with crime continued with the routine adventure series *The Baron* in 1966, with a great deal of work in TV soap operas to round off his career.

Alexander Mackendrick (1912–1993)

It has become something of a cliché to describe the late Alexander Mackendrick as one of the great glories of the British cinema, a director whose talent stretched from glorious Ealing comedies such as *The Ladykillers* (1955) to one of the most brittle and malevolent American films ever made about the media, *Sweet Smell of Success* (1957). Regrettably, however, it is also true to say that despite the acclaim the wry Mackendrick enjoyed in his later years, mostly spent teaching film (and it is refreshing that he lived long enough to see this level of celebrity), this truly major talent was notably under-employed after his heyday. Mackendrick was, in fact, born in Boston, Massachusetts, but moved to Glasgow in 1919. He worked on propaganda films in the Second World War before establishing himself at Ealing Studios (working as a production designer on Basil Dearden's *Saraband for Dead Lovers* in 1948). The films he directed for the studio are now recognised as among some of the most mordant and unsentimental work in the British cinema of the era, notably *The Ladykillers*, the celebrated comedy of robbery and multiple murder mentioned earlier, along with less caustic (but memorable) fare such as *The Man in the White Suit* in 1951. His last films (made in a variety of countries) included such highly interesting work as his adaptation of Richard Hughes' *A High Wind in Jamaica* in 1965, but it is something of a tragedy that so many years after his last films of the 1960s that Mackendrick was not having money thrown at him (as would have happened in an ideal world) to film his unfulfilled projects.

Cliff Owen (1919–1993)

Born in London, the highly professional Cliff Owen inaugurated his career in the cinema in 1937, ultimately working as assistant director on such films as John Boulting's Friese-Greene biopic *The Magic Box* in 1951. He continued to hone his craft in television, working on a series of prestigious drama adaptations (including plays by Terence Rattigan and Arthur Miller) while burnishing his crime credentials on such series as *The Third Man* in 1959. His initial forays as director in the cinema were both in the crime genre: *Offbeat* (1960), in which a maverick policeman played by William Sylvester takes on some ruthless criminals, and the highly impressive *A Prize of Arms* a year later (discussed earlier) in which the default tough man of British cinema Stanley Baker masterminds the robbery of a payroll office in an army camp. Both films showed a director full of fresh ideas and fully prepared to stretch the parameters of the genre to create work that had something unusual and unconventional to say (such as the grudging respect shown by the undercover man for the criminals he is investigating in *Offbeat*). The mildly diverting comic crime film *The Wrong Arm of the Law* followed in 1962 and suggested that comedy might be another *métier* for this talented director, a notion swiftly disproved by such maladroit and unfunny comedies as *That Riviera Touch* in 1966 and the dismal *Ooh... You Are Awful* in 1972. Later work as second unit director on a variety of big-budget productions paid the bills, but Owen was not given the opportunity again to display the talent so confidently exercised in his early work.

Chris Petit (1949–)

For readers of a certain generation, the name Chris Petit evokes particularly percipient film criticism in the pages of the influential London magazine *Time Out*, but the ambitious Petit persuaded the German director Wim Wenders to facilitate his debut film *Radio On* in 1979. This was a truly unusual and ambitious piece of work presenting an almost Antonioni-like vision of an urban Britain as bleakly existential (and uningratiating) as the British cinema had seen. An intelligent adaptation of the crime writer P.D. James' novel *An Unsuitable Job for a Woman* in 1981 (a version that much bemused the novel's author) was followed by two cryptic but mesmeric films, *Flight to Berlin* in 1983 and the challenging *Chinese Boxes* a year later. Sharing a fascination with the Soho subculture of seedy bookshops and louche living with the novelist Iain Sinclair (whose concept of psychogeography was massively influential on many other writers), the two collaborated on a trilogy of films for television which profitably ignored established rules of narrative structure. The most controversial of these was *The Falconer* in 1997, which studiously avoided linearity in pursuit of a textured hyperreality (Sinclair has ironically remarked on the tendency of Petit's films – notably *Radio On* – to play to empty cinemas of all but the most committed viewers). A connection with the crime genre continued for Petit with an unlikely version of an Agatha Christie story (an author who was hardly a natural fit for the strictly uncosy Petit), but the majority of his work remains markedly unclassifiable, albeit curiously British, even though (as Sinclair said of him) Petit's London was overlaid with a European cinema sensibility. In the manner of such British filmmakers as Nicolas Roeg and Donald Cammell, Petit is one of the most uncompromising artists to have worked in UK cinema.

Michael Powell (1905–1990)

It's relatively easy to celebrate Michael Powell's exuberant talent (and his position as one of Britain's most visionary filmmakers, which is now assured), but few have managed to convey the peculiarly English genius of the man in prose that matches his poetic vision.

Powell's earliest films were firmly in genre territory, notably the lively *The Spy in Black* in 1939, in which he began his long and fruitful association with the writer Emeric Pressburger. The credit 'Written produced and directed by the Archers' (the name that the duo chose for their association) became a long-standing guarantee of quality (and often delirious visual flourishes) in British cinemas over many years. When Powell directed *The Spy In Black*, he was yet to establish his particular style, one that combined a fey mysticism with an intense evocation of the English landscape (the latter was perhaps to be his most lasting legacy for future filmmakers), but already demonstrated a gift for utilising genre elements when necessary. Interestingly, such remarkable later films as *A Canterbury Tale* with its element of Chaucerian narrative and understated magical realism nevertheless utilised the familiar crime scenario of the tracking down of a sinister figure – in this case a mysterious man who pours glue into women's hair, though the 'whodunit' elements are peripheral; the identity of the (possibly) sexually deviant culprit isn't a mystery for too long.

Apart from later masterpieces such as *The Red Shoes* and one of the definitive opera films in Powell's version of Offenbach's *The Tales of Hoffmann*, a watershed in the director's life was approaching – a then-shocking film that would come to be regarded as one of his supreme masterpieces and would also virtually bring his career to a close until he was able (after a fashion) to revivify it. The *Peeping Tom* debacle is discussed separately, but other films which touched on the crime/thriller genre included *The Small Back Room* in 1949 (after Nigel Balchin) and even the early *The Rasp* in 1932, which featured Philip MacDonald's sleuth Anthony Gethryn (better known for the later *The List of Adrian Messenger*).

Carol Reed (1906–1976)

An interest in the performing arts was perhaps hereditary for Sir Carol Reed. Born in Putney, London, Reed was the son of the celebrated actor Sir Herbert Beerbohm Tree. After a conventional public-school upbringing, he tried his hand at an abortive career in the army. However, the then-massively popular crime writer Edgar Wallace had created a theatrical company to present stage versions of his work, and thus began Reed's association with the theatre – and the crime genre. For Wallace, he undertook double duty as both actor and stage manager. A film career was inevitable, which began for Reed by directing several quotidian but efficiently handled apprentice efforts. Early success came with an adaptation of A.J. Cronin's novel *The Stars Look Down* in 1939, but Reed's enjoyably Hitchcockian *Night Train to Munich* in 1940 showed a particular flair for the crime/thriller genre, aided by the fact that it was written by the witty screenwriters Frank Launder and Sydney Gilliat, who had delivered the triumph of Hitchcock's *The Lady Vanishes*. More upmarket fare followed with a series of literary adaptations, but Reed's reacquaintance with the thriller was memorably established in 1947 with the masterful *Odd Man Out* (from a novel by F.L. Green), which successfully synthesised the requisite delivery of tension with some nuances of characterisation. Subsequently, the director's adaptation of Graham Greene's *The Fallen Idol* in 1948 once again utilised a scenario predicated on violent death as a catalyst for the action, but a year later, Reed moved from the sewers of Vienna to the top of the Prater Wheel to create his most celebrated film, *The Third Man* (once again an adaptation of Graham Greene and once again built around themes of betrayal and responsibility). The film forged a template for the modern multi-textured espionage/crime thriller and was a massive hit. Later Reed films such as *The Man Between* (1953) failed to rekindle the spark of these earlier classics, but another Greene adaptation, *Our Man in Havana* in 1959, showed something of a return to form. Reed's hard-earned skills seemed to desert him in the workaday *The Running Man* in 1963 (a handsome-looking but vacuous piece) and his last sizeable hit was a large-scale adaptation of the Lionel Bart Dickens musical *Oliver!* in 1968.

Guy Ritchie (1968–)

Early success, stasis and disappointment, followed by finding the lost chord a second time. It's a familiar progression with which the director Guy Ritchie is fully acquainted. Born in Hatfield, Ritchie began his film career in what was once the centre of the British film industry, London's Wardour Street, with a succession of undemanding jobs (including directing commercials). Attention was paid to his short film *The Hard Case* in 1995 and enabled him to put together the requisite financial and other elements to direct his first feature film, *Lock, Stock and Two Smoking Barrels* in 1998. Utilising familiar elements of the gangster genre, he was neverthe-less able to create something fresh, kinetic and unusual – not least by inaugurating a major new trend: the hardboiled East End gang-ster film (with the added ingredients of sardonic dialogue and a large cast of violently squabbling criminals). After the success of the first film, money was thrown at its successor, *Snatch*, in 2000, but this time Ritchie was able to draw upon the services of such major stars as Brad Pitt and Benicio Del Toro (although he encouraged both actors to disguise both their physical appearance and their accents). The film had a mixed reception, and a tabloid-pleasing marriage to the pop star Madonna led to the erotic desert island film *Swept Away* in 2002 which unleashed a torrent of dismissive critical reviews. Ritchie was able to re-charm his admirers to some degree with the complex gangster movie *Revolver* in 2005 (which some saw as a partial return to form), but it was the director's auda-cious, if controversial, reinvention of Sherlock Holmes as an action hero with the American actor Robert Downey Jr. that re-established him as a force to be reckoned with in the British cinema. The fact that Ritchie's first Sherlock Holmes film made over $200 million in the USA and £25 million in the UK (with a worldwide tally of $524 million) ensured that the filmmakers' (and actors') desire for a sequel would inevitably be realised, and a variety of new elements could now be brought into the fray to counterpoint the eccentric byplay between Robert Downey Jr.'s Holmes and Jude Law's Watson, notably Stephen Fry as the detective's equally brilliant brother, the heavyweight Mycroft, the sultry Noomi Rapace as the gypsy Sim and, crucially, Jared Harris as Holmes' nemesis Moriarty. Casting here was, of course, crucial, with such remarkable actors as George Zucco, Lionel Atwill and Eric Porter having etched such chilling portrayals of the master criminal in the past. Harris was an apposite choice – little-known, but having created memorable performances in otherwise unsuccessful films such as *Lost in Space*. The son of the actor Richard Harris (but not inheriting his father's good looks), Harris *fils* had made a mark in such films as Todd Solondz's *Happiness* and is able to combine a dark charisma with the appearance of an intimidating intelligence – perfect casting, in fact, for a twenty-first-century Moriarty. With the success of these films and the television franchise, it was clear that Conan Doyle's creation was a figure for the ages.

Don Sharp (1922–2011)

Cinéastes who are admirers of commercial British cinema show a keen appreciation of Don Sharp, who again and again triumphed over intractable subjects (not to mention equally intractable actors and producers) to produce work of imagination and nimble technique. A 'cult' director who has earned the sobriquet over and over again, Sharp is widely regarded as one of the minor unsung glories of British commercial cinema; a director who could take conventional genre cinema and wring something individual and iconoclastic from it, while still delivering the imperatives for those who were paying his wages. The crime drama *A Taste of Excitement* (1970) is perhaps his most neglected and little-known film, but is further proof that he could take shopworn material and give it a bracing makeover.

Born in Hobart, Tasmania, Sharp came to the UK in the late 1940s and began to learn his craft in a series of modestly budgeted films.

His adroitness in the horror genre was demonstrated for Hammer with films such as *The Kiss of the Vampire* in 1963 and the sombre *Witchcraft* a year later. These films made it clear that Sharp was a director ready to shake up the familiar troops of genre filmmaking, creating something innovative and energetic. His version of Sax Rohmer's Oriental master criminal in *The Face of Fu Manchu* reinvigorated (while embracing) some tired stereotypes and delivered a colourful and splendidly staged piece (with Christopher Lee's master criminal more than matched by the splendid Nigel Green as his implacable opponent). Sharp continued to produce highly professional work. By the 1970s, expectations for adaptations of the thriller writer Alistair MacLean (who had begun to write by-the-numbers novels that read like treatment for the inevitable screen adaptation) were low in terms of everything except box-office success, but Sharp's pared-to-the-bone version of *Puppet on a Chain* in 1970 was generally considered a triumph of style over content, a shot of adrenaline applied to moribund material. The IRA thriller *Hennessy* (with an unusually understated Rod Steiger as an Irishman drawn back into the killing cycle) showed a level of political sophistication rarely found in such fare, and his remake of John Buchan's *The Thirty-Nine Steps* boasted a period charm without ever really rivalling Alfred Hitchcock's matchless version. Another Alistair MacLean adaptation, *Bear Island* in 1979, showed unmistakable signs of faltering inspiration, but by now the director's admirers could at least savour the memory of many superior films he had made over the years.

Peter Yates (1929–)

Born into an army family in Aldershot, Hampshire, Peter Yates sampled a variety of careers, but it was his time in the theatre that led to his decision to attempt films, and he began work as an editor before assuming assistant director duties with such filmmakers as J. Lee Thompson and Mark Robson. Yates' predilection for the crime/thriller field was demonstrated in some sharp and economical episodes of the Patrick McGoohan television series *Danger Man*, but then came his first major break. There are those who say they can discern elements of Yates' already considerable skills in the anodyne Cliff Richard musical *Summer Holiday*, which was his debut film feature in 1963, and the director's admirers may find themselves inclined to watch it again for a re-evaluation. But it was with the taut *Robbery* in 1967, a sober black-and-white fictionalised version of the Great Train Robbery, that Yates was really able to demonstrate his credentials. The film (with its economical characterisation of the large cadre of thieves) is best remembered for its career-defining (and tyre-burning) car chase, the most exhilarating (and exhilaratingly edited) the cinema had – up to that point – witnessed. In fact, the film – and that sequence – led directly to Yates' hiring by Hollywood for the Steve McQueen thriller *Bullitt*, which even managed to top the car chase of the earlier British film. Other thrillers in the USA followed, such as *The Hot Rock* (known in the UK as *How to Steal a Diamond in Four Uneasy Lessons*), but critical opinion was beginning to harden against the director, as it was felt that such unambitious thrillers as *Mother, Jugs and Speed* (1976), constructed largely as a showcase for Raquel Welch's pneumatic superstructure, were demonstrating that his promise was now in evidence less frequently. But that assessment is to reckon without the splendid *The Friends of Eddie Coyle* (1973), a beautifully understated version of the classic George V. Higgins novel, with a perfectly judged, world-weary performance by Robert Mitchum as an ageing gunrunner. Other estimable films would follow, such as the charming *Breaking Away* in 1979, but later work by the director was more hit-or-miss, with only the Irish-set *The Run of the Country* in 1995 showing continuing evidence of the director's considerable skills.

Appendix 2: TV Crime

Arthur Conan Doyle's Sherlock Holmes and Colin Dexter's Inspector Morse were played by actors who nailed the characters' traits as defined by their creators (multiple incarnations in the case of the Great Detective); other great detectives have been only fitfully successful in their screen versions. In the cinema, Agatha Christie's Miss Marple was played several times by Margaret Rutherford – and though Rutherford was one of the greatest comic performers this country has ever produced, the generously proportioned, larger-than-life actress was hardly Christie's wiry, quietly observant spinster. What was worse, Christie's plots were largely played for laughs – a tendency that has insinuated itself into several otherwise admirable TV versions of the character. The quirky Geraldine McEwan – another national treasure – always managed to suggest that she didn't really take the character seriously when playing Marple, and while the latest version of St Mary Mead's amateur sleuth, Julia McKenzie, plays the character straight, most of those around her are encouraged to give massively broad, primary-colour performances. For most Christie aficionados, the great Joan Hickson remains the definitive screen Marple – played without parody, but with a gentle and self-deprecating humour in adaptations that did full justice to the Queen of Crime's skilfully wrought mysteries.

It seems that the appetite of audiences for Agatha Christie on TV is undiminished and each generation feels obliged to take its shot at the iconic characters. But new adaptations shouldn't erase the achievements of earlier efforts, and the ten episodes of *The Agatha Christie Hour* from the 1980s are (when viewed in the twenty-first century) a particularly piquant excavation from the past, as this largely ignored series eschews the customary Marple/Poirot/Tommy and Tuppence tales in favour of some of the British Queen of Crime's lesser-known protagonists. These include the unflappable Parker Pyne (eccentrically played here by the great Maurice Denham), whose investigations all have a romantic element: the elderly statistician sorts out the problems of warring couples and other lovelorn characters. More a dated curio than any kind of filmic achievement,

the novelty value of the series in nevertheless worthy of some attention and it is packed with sterling British character actors who more
than make up for the extremely modest production values and the
occasional over-pitched performance (such things did not, unfor-
tunately, begin with Julia McKenzie's Marple series).

As for Sherlock Holmes on television, the most notable aspect of
these adaptations has been their consistently high quality. Over the
years, considerable justice has been done to nearly all the immortal
sleuths of crime fiction. Take the cocaine-dependent resident of
221b Baker Street. Conan Doyle's masterly creation – virtually the
blueprint for every super-intelligent investigator who followed him
(Agatha Christie's Hercule Poirot, for instance, is one of the detective's illegitimate offspring) – would still be one of the world's best-
known fictional characters if he had never left the page, but a small
army of accomplished actors have reproduced the hawkish profile,
clipped consonants and patrician disdain. For many of us, Jeremy
Brett's fascinatingly mannered, nervy performance is definitive –
at least until the actor's personal problems and ballooning weight
rendered the performances too idiosyncratic for comfort.

Adapted from Doyle's original stories and novels, *Sherlock Holmes,
The Adventures* and *The Return* featured Brett's charismatic turn as the
erudite sleuth and the under-regarded David Burke as Dr Watson in
such nonpareil adaptations as *Speckled Band, The Solitary Cyclist, Sign
of Four* and *The Hound of the Baskervilles*, while *Sherlock Holmes: The
Case-Book* and *The Memoirs* incorporated the long-serving Edward
Hardwicke (excellent in the role, but rather unfairly erasing memo-
ries of his predecessor David Burke) in such adaptations as *The Golden
Pince-Nez, The Boscombe Valley Mystery, The Master Blackmailer* and
The Red Circle.

This immensely popular series ran from 1984 to 1994 and is widely
considered to be the most faithful representation of Conan Doyle's
stories to date – and its success in both the UK and the USA cemented
221b Baker Street as one of London's most famous addresses. Even
the sad decline of the series in its last few episodes (not entirely the
result of its central performer's health problems, though they were
clearly a factor) has not dimmed its lustre.

The Great Detective's first name was all that was used in 2011/2012
for perhaps the most radical reimagining of Conan Doyle's master
ratiocinator in the BBC TV series *Sherlock*.

It was a high-risk strategy, updating Sherlock Holmes to the twenty-first century. The two principal objections? Firstly, that a fog-bound nineteenth-century London is crucial to the Holmes ethos; and, secondly, the fact that another new Holmes film franchise (with Robert Downey Jr.) was a palpable hit. However, the BBC series proved mega-successful in terms of critical acclaim and audience enthusiasm. In Season 2, we were presented with a brilliant rejigging of two of Holmes' key nemeses: Irene Adler is now a dominatrix who nonplusses Holmes by greeting him naked and there is a glee-fully lunatic Moriarty who comes across as an intellectual version of Batman's enemy, the Joker. Much of the praise that has been show-ered upon this modern Holmesian rethink is, of course, due to the unorthodox casting of Benedict Cumberbatch and Martin Freeman as Holmes and Watson. Cumberbatch's very modern, neurasthenic portrayal of Holmes as a sociopath to rival (in his own way) Lisbeth Salander is fascinating, but Freeman's underplayed support should not be underestimated. And there's the wonderfully inventive writ-ing by Steven Moffat and Mark Gatiss, full of affection for (and infin-itesimal knowledge of) the source material but perfectly prepared to spin elaborate modern filigrees on the familiar tropes. (In his parallel career as an actor, Gatiss also added to a distinguished gallery as the detective's equally neurotic brother, creating a memorable Mycroft.)

For Holmes aficionados, the fondly remembered detective drama *The Rivals of Sherlock Holmes* sported many cherishable elements. Adapted from Hugh Carleton Greene's much-acclaimed anthology of Victorian and Edwardian detective fiction, the series presented adroitly acted renditions of the Great Detective's sleuthing rivals in London, each tackling baffling mysteries. The series (which won a BAFTA) was able to persuade a nonpareil cadre of actors to come aboard (to play such stalwarts of the field as Dr Thorndyke and Carnacki), including John Neville, Robert Stephens, Peter Vaughan, Roy Dotrice, Donald Pleasence, Ronald Hines, Peter Barkworth and Donald Sinden. The by-rote shooting on video rather than film makes for problematic viewing in the twenty-first century. The sec-ond series is as fascinating as the first; no pale pastiches on offer here, but inspired efforts, paying homage to the Great Detective, adding fresh spins and unusual notions.

Accruing solid viewing figures on its first showing in 1992, the intriguing Victorian murder mystery series *The Blackheath Poisonings* was based on the celebrated novel by Julian Symons and was put together by producer Kenny McBain (who also had under his belt the TV adaptations of Inspector Morse). The tone of this atmospheric period drama is nicely judged by director Stuart Orme: there's a subtly sardonic air, but no parody – and there are lashings of nicely calculated suspense. It is essentially a family drama: the Collards and the Vandervents are the two distinguished families in the moneyed, comfortable setting of Albert Villa, near the London suburb of Blackheath. But the bourgeois respectability conceals a disturbing turbulence beneath the surface, with internecine squabbles over control of the family toy business. A Machiavellian stranger arrives and Albert Villa is thrown into barely disguised chaos, with – inevitably – murder on the menu. The production looks splendid, but the top-notch cast is the thing here: Zoe Wanamaker, Judy Parfitt and (most divertingly) the saturnine Patrick Malahide using all their considerable skills to stir the ingredients of a heady brew.

Many 'classic' British crime and thriller series were formulaic and uninspired: viewed today, such crime shows as *The Saint* and *The Persuaders!* have little to offer beyond foggy memories. But there is an exception to this rule: Patrick McGoohan's economically filmed series *Danger Man*, which enjoyed a healthy run as both half-hour and hour shows before metamorphosing into the cult series *The Prisoner*. The inaugural 30-minute shows have many virtues and identify the transnational aspirations of British television of the day – while no one could claim that these earlier episodes (in which McGoohan was forced to sport a mid-Atlantic accent for American sales, which was subsequently dropped) have the richness and sophistication of the subsequent hour-long shows, these are all highly accomplished, fast-moving mini-dramas, with a wealth of British acting and directing talent making an early mark (Bond director John Glen, for instance, demonstrates his editing skills before his groundbreaking 007 stint). Patrick McGoohan is always impressive: stern, sexually attractive to women, but always maintaining a monk-like celibacy. A maverick talent and a prickly man who never quite achieved the Hollywood stardom that appeared to be his due (possibly because of his unbending moral code – the very code that made him turn down the libertine role of 007) still appears, with distinction, in such films as *A Time to Kill* and *Braveheart*. And while the enigmatic *The Prisoner* remains his magnum opus (as co-creator and actor), *Danger Man* is a brisk and effective series that wears very well. The first half-hour episode of Series 1 was broadcast in the UK on 11 September 1960. Each episode began with Special Agent John Drake walking from a Washington Federal Building (although the series was nearly always filmed in Britain), lighting a cigarette and then ducking across the streets to his white sports car. The viewer is then presented with economically written, sophisticated, pared-to-the-bone espionage dramas, often written by series creator Ralph Smart.

But it is the subsequent hour-long episodes on which the show's reputation rests. These are much more rewarding, with none of the rushed feeling which inevitably resulted from such brief timeslots. Now the team (utilising many of the same personnel and directors, with such luminaries as Don Chaffey providing some of the best shows) had a chance to layer in an extra dimension of characterisation and plotting, with McGoohan now able to exercise his acting chops. The new dimension of tackling complex moral issues, which was frequently and profitably explored, resulted from Drake's disgust with some of the dirty jobs he was obliged to undertake – the expedient betrayal of old friends by Drake was a recurrent theme, always explored in a non-clichéd fashion, and McGoohan and his writers generally gave extended opportunities to some of the finest British acting talent available at the time – there are some first-rate performances threaded throughout the series. While McGoohan/ Drake's avoidance of guns looks positively suicidal at times, the bouts of action are kinetically handled, with the engendering of suspense always a priority. Drake's sexual abstinence, while more realistic (in an espionage context) than Bond's libidinousness, sometimes seems cruel when he leads on lonely or damaged women with the promise of a relationship with this attractive man, only for him to priggishly stop short at the bedroom door. As the series progressed, hints of the paranoia and surrealism of the subsequent *The Prisoner* – which McGoohan pitched to Lew Grade as a successor to *Danger Man* – make fascinating appearances (as in the episode 'The Ubiquitous Mr Lovegrove'), but leaving that aside, *Danger Man* remains quite simply the most sophisticated and intelligent adventure series ever made for television.

Like the more celebrated *Danger Man* (with which it shares the adroit British composer Edwin Astley), *The Baron* (various directors,

1965/1966) was a Monty Berman-produced series which utilised a cadre of British acting luminaries and conjured up its ersatz foreign settings with as much ingenuity as producer Ralph Smart had demonstrated on the similarly studio-bound *Danger Man*. Foreign forestry was usually conveyed with a few serviceable fronds, while reliable British all-purpose character actors such as Warren Mitchell supplied a variety of strongly characterised foreigners. *Danger Man's* transatlantic sales were finessed (in the first half-hour-long series) by having Patrick McGoohan adopt a mid-Atlantic accent; no such problems here, as Monty Berman hired the American Steve Forrest to incarnate John Creasey's protagonist and ensure US TV audiences.

Anglia's celebrated adaptations of P.D. James' crime novels (as *The Adam Dalgliesh Chronicles*) do considerable justice to the originals, and the virtues of this series speak for themselves. In a more civilised TV age, Anglia was able to adapt the James novels at a more generous length than would be afforded to a crime series these days, so many of the subtleties of the original books survived intact in the leisurely adaptations. And speaking of subtleties, Roy Marsden's performance as the doughty Commander Adam Dalgliesh is full of them, perhaps as the result of his attempts to enliven the task of playing the same character over such a long period.

For decades, P.D. James has been the virtually unchallenged queen of British crime writing. The secret of her supremacy in the genre is perhaps due to a synthesis of various elements: stylish writing, a gift for multi-faceted characterisation (not just of her of her long-serving copper Commander Adam Dalgliesh but also of his striking rendered fellow detectives). But James is also celebrated for her reluctance to repeat herself – as so many of her rivals do – even though certain notions are prone (rather pleasingly) to re-surface. There is little room for debate that James (despite rival claims from Ruth Rendell and such modern-day successors as Minette Walters and Frances Fyfield) is the heir apparent to the female titans of British crime writing, Agatha Christie and Dorothy L. Sayers.

Television interest in the Dalgliesh novels was, of course, inevitable – and the fact that P.D. James herself was so pleased with the results must have been a relief to her nervous producers.

All of the signature crime fiction expertise that makes James' writing so individual (even when utilising classic themes and techniques) were sympathetically transmuted into televisual terms in the long-running Anglia series, such as the author's much-favoured use of an isolated setting (a homage to her writing forebears who enjoyed this challenge), and there is no denying that James is unbeatable in the area of malign deeds in a secluded setting. Such notions lend themselves seamlessly to filmic adaptation (e.g. the baroque Thameside publishing house that is the setting of the murders in *Original Sin*, here located in Wapping). For the strip-mining of psychological insight and plotting of consummate skill, her books set any potential adapter major problems in doing justice to these elements. That the lavishly mounted series, with Roy Marsden as an impeccably cast Dalgliesh supplying everything any P.D. James aficionado could wish for, is a reminder that British fictional detectives have (largely speaking) been fortunate in their translation to the television format – think of Colin Dexter's Inspector Morse, for instance – but few have been afforded such deluxe treatment as James' copper, incarnated in a tightly written, strikingly filmed series with the excellent Marsden as the author's poetry-writing policeman.

Utilising the apparatus of the 'Golden Age' crime novel, James imbued it with far greater psychological acuity than her celebrated predecessors (although Dorothy L. Sayers had examined the psychology of her protagonist with intelligence) and forged a detective figure who was a much more realistic figure than Christie's Poirot, who was largely a synthesis of eccentricities modelled after the template of Conan Doyle's Holmes. James' first really impressive novel was 1971's *Shroud for a Nightingale*, where the timbre of her writing echoed that of many a more overtly serious 'literary' novel. But it is for her lengthy sequence of books featuring her highly civilised detective that she is most celebrated. Dalgliesh uses his busy professional life to cover the missing elements in his private life (he is left emotionally scarred by the death of his wife in childbirth) and is essentially a lonely man – elements incorporated fully (but with refreshing subtlety) into the TV series. In later books, the detective acquired two assistants, Sergeants Piers Tarrant and Kate Miskin, both of whom James has satisfyingly developed through subsequent novels – and who are used creatively in the TV adaptations (Kate, in particular, is a richly drawn character and is in some ways a more intriguing female protagonist than James' earlier private investigator, Cordelia Gray). The responsibility of getting all this right in the television adaptations was a heavy one, but the legion of admirers of James' novels were firmly in the mind of the producers as much as a new TV audience who had yet to make the acquaintance of the characters, and in every aspect (from the casting of Dalgliesh and his associates to the impressive roster of guest actors who appeared in different episodes to murder or be murdered) the filmmakers demonstrated a shrewd grasp of all the key elements. The distinctive results established a new benchmark for television adaptations of crime fiction. James herself noted that Anglia Television had been the first broadcasting company to dramatise the Adam Dalgliesh novels, and in Roy Marsden (she felt) provided the first and most memorable Dalgliesh. The novels were shown in more episodes than is possible today, to the great advantage of the stories, and the acting, direction and camera work were of cinema-level quality.

Marsden remarked that one of the most rewarding things about the series – and one that gave it a real distinction at the time – was the fact that Adam Dalgliesh wasn't simply a TV copper for whom adventures had to be concocted each week; the production company were filming individual P.D. James books and each one was a separate entity. Playing a relatively reined-in character like Dalgliesh represented a considerable challenge for the actor, as Marsden was not able to allow the detective to openly display his emotions (British reserve is something that both James and her adapters clearly admired, allowing comments on certain aspects of the English character to filter into the books and, subsequently, the TV series). Other actors (in fact, the cream of the British acting profession who were employed in the series) often had showier parts. Marsden made a virtue of necessity by making the most of Dalgliesh's peculiar insularity. The audience is always studying the detective's reaction to the things that people are saying to him – it was important for Marsden to convey things in the non-verbal way, through emotions or thought processes that the audience could read in his eyes.

Marsden also tackles the more unlikely facets of the detective's character: the fact that a well-read, literary man like Dalgliesh – a man who writes poetry, in fact – could be a real London copper. This is something of an uphill struggle, in light of the fact that most of the real-life senior policemen seen on television hardly suggest they might have an acquaintance with the work of William Blake or Coleridge.

The TV adaptations were very faithful, but there were changes relating to the structure of the books when they were adapted to another medium. A crime is committed, and it is often halfway through the book before Dalgliesh appears in order to solve the crime. This is, of course, perfectly acceptable in literary terms, Marsden noted, but works less well in a visual medium where it was necessary to introduce the character to the audience at an earlier stage – and this had to be done in such a way as to do no damage to the original structure of the novel.

But it's not just vintage sleuths who have had TV versions that strayed quite a distance from their literary origins. Ian Rankin's Rebus is one of the great modern detectives, pounding the mean streets of Edinburgh. Inspector Jack Rebus, heavily built, short-fused, struggling with alcoholism and problems with authority, was always a natural for TV adaptation. But when Rankin admirers heard that the first TV Rebus was to be the actor John Hannah, eyebrows were raised. Hannah was a fine actor, yes, but one who always looked slight and boyish – hardly Rankin's dangerous, burly, middle-aged copper. Rankin took the storm of criticism on the chin, perhaps biding his time, until the recasting of the paunchier, more lived-in persona of the actor Ken Stott finally caught the image most of us had of the bolshie Rebus. Ian Rankin (born in 1960) is the UK's bestselling male crime writer. At one point, his sales accounted for 10 per cent of all UK crime fiction, and his protagonist Rebus has been allowed to age in real time; as the character was born in 1947, his creator has now allowed him to retire. Rankin noted that *Exit Music* (2007) would be the valedictory Rebus novel, but the character's status as an iconic copper is assured.

Rebus is confrontational, struggles with the bottle, ignores the rules and, in thematic terms, carries echoes of two of the author's key influences, Robert Louis Stevenson's *The Strange Case of Dr Jekyll and Mr Hyde* and James Hogg's *The Private Memoirs and Confessions of a Justified Sinner*, notably in terms of the duality of Rebus and even of his stamping ground of the city of Edinburgh, which bifurcates into the modern New Town and the history-heavy, atmospheric Old Town (with its repressive Calvinist history). All of these elements were to surface in the TV adaptations.

The fondly remembered Callan had an interesting genesis. James Mitchell, aka James Munro (1926–2002), was a versatile and professional writer, successfully forging three distinctive and individual fictional franchises: the book and television espionage series *Callan*; a drama concerning a Northern shipyard trade unionist, *When the Boat Comes In*; and (as James Munro) penning one of the most inventive riffs on the James Bond books with his series featuring tough secret agent John Craig.

Mitchell, who was born in Tyneside, sampled a wide variety of career options (including the civil service and the teaching profession), but during most of these non-vocational choices, he was always an assiduous writer of fiction, and his first professional work was as a playwright, with a play performed in a modest drama group in his native South Shields. Mitchell's real *métier*, however, was the novel, and after a short struggle to be published, he wrote many, both under his own name and under the pseudonym James Munro. His low-key, unglamorous secret agent Callan first appeared in a one-off TV drama (for ITV's *Armchair Theatre*) in 1967 entitled *A Magnum for Schneider*. This immediately established the rebellious anti-establishment protagonist (not a million miles away from Len Deighton's unnamed operative in *The Ipcress File*), and so striking was the character that it was hardly a surprise that a series followed, which ran from 1967 to 1972. Edward Woodward perfectly incarnated Mitchell's surly antihero, and while the series was occasionally dismissed as Deighton/le Carré-lite, it was immensely popular – and, regarded dispassionately in the twenty-first century, still wears well. Such novels as *A Magnum for Schneider* (1969) – the Callan TV premier – *Russian Roulette* (1973) and *Death and Bright Water* (1974) were books written with an unassuming craftsmanship and skill, creating a queasy moral universe in which Mitchell's undercover hero is frequently obliged to choose between pragmatism and altruism; the resolutions were usually bleak. Writing as James Munro, Mitchell delivered surprisingly adept results in what was clearly a commercial enterprise: feeding the public's insatiable appetite in the 1960s for Fleming-style sybaritic espionage adventure. John Craig, the best of the would-be Bonds, was a tenacious and rootless British agent reporting to Department K in British Intelligence. Carefully synthesising the elements that Fleming had burnished to perfection, Mitchell upped the ante in terms of violent action and soon located his protagonist in a more realistic world than other, similar entries in the ersatz-Bond field. Such books as *The Man Who Sold Death* (1964) incorporated jaw-droppingly outrageous plotting into an eminently readable narrative, guaranteeing a succession of sequels.

The original pilot 'Regan' in 1974 marked the genesis of the gritty cop show *The Sweeney*, which appeared a year later. Originally transmitted as part of the then-highly successful *Armchair Theatre*, Regan was the brainchild of Ian Kennedy Martin (who had created *Z-Cars*) and acquainted audiences with a pre-Morse John Thaw and Dennis Waterman. It was shot on location in and around central London. In the gritty inaugural show, a cop is murdered by a gang of thugs, with Regan and Carter assigned to nail the killers, encountering non-cooperation from other members of the Flying Squad. The succeeding series, *The Sweeney*, was influential on many British television police series that followed with its unvarnished picture of British coppers lower down the social scale than the traditionally upper middle-class officers previously seen in the cinema.

Even grittier was *Sharman*. This series (which came a cropper in the hysteria following the Dunblane killings) features a charismatic, pre-Hollywood Clive Owen as the eponymous detective created by the crime writer Mark Timlin. The series, originally aired in 1996, was criticised for its violence – resolutely mainstream by today's standards. The pilot episode, transmitted in 1995, was *The Turnaround*, which has a striking and nuanced performance by Bill Patterson in an ambiguous role. The series showcased screenplay storylines from, among others, Tony Hoare of *The Sweeney* and the now-famous Paul Abbott. And with such actors as Ray Winstone and Keith Allen among the casts, one can forgive the few blemishes (some uncertain pacing, and nondescript music and title sequence – the show called out for a striking and kinetic credit sequence to match Mark Timlin's edgy character). And questions were asked at the time: why weren't more of Mark Timlin's original novels used as source material?

1999's *The Vice* was a series of caustic crime dramas now remembered for a pre-*Rebus* Ken Stott as an uncompromising copper DI Chappel. All the usual ingredients make an appearance: prostitution, pornography and murder are all part of the daily workload for the cynical vice team as they investigate the capital's grimmer secrets and encounter a veritable Metropolitan Sodom and Gomorrah. *The Vice* customarily portrayed London as a city of striking social contrasts, moving swiftly from the backstreets of King's Cross to the bars of Park Lane hotels. Ken Stott burnished his pre-*Rebus* credentials and Anna Chancellor shored up the authoritative acting.

Inspector Morse – in his television incarnation – is an institution. Sullen and difficult he may be, given to browbeating his subordinates and demonstrating his knowledge of the arts (notably poetry and opera) in a somewhat self-aggrandising fashion. But Colin Dexter's Oxford copper is one of the defining figures in British detective fiction – a multi-faceted, fascinating protagonist who readers have followed avidly through a series of sharply turned and ingenious novels. In a line of descent that extends back to Arthur Conan Doyle's Sherlock Holmes (notably via the laser-sharp intellect), Morse is a character who can stand shoulder to shoulder with the very best in the genre. Interestingly, his creator, Colin Dexter, shares several characteristics and traits with his hero: he is erudite (with a particular love of the countryside-set poetry of A.E. Housman – Dexter quotes the latter's *A Shropshire Lad* at the drop of a hat) and shrewdly analytical in terms of the varied personalities he encounters. But Dexter himself is the polar opposite of Morse in terms of his character: extremely affable, immensely charming and humorous – and (most of all) sensitive to the feelings of those around him: an anti-Morse, in fact.

Of course, the popularity of the character is not entirely due to the exemplary novels which gave birth to him – the long-running TV series featuring (over the years) a series of cannily underplayed performances by the late John Thaw as the eponymous Morse cemented the popularity of Dexter's policeman, moving the sales of the books into ever-more stratospheric reaches and establishing a Morse fanbase throughout the world, notably in the USA. Most significantly, however, the TV series even had an influence on the books, actually bringing about changes in the characters – not a unique syndrome, but perhaps the most often remarked-on case of this (not least by Dexter himself, who was happy to acknowledge these changes – something that many writers might have been reluctant to do, even in the face of the evidence).

Over a series of ever-more impressive novels, Dexter cannily developed his complex and combative central character, revealing deeper aspects of his rebarbative copper. Simultaneously, Dexter conjured a panoramic vision of the city of Oxford in all its aspects (from council estates to the leafy groves of academe) that has few equals in literary backdrops for series characters (not even Ian Rankin's vividly evoked Edinburgh for DI Rebus matches Dexter's richly drawn settings). For both of these achievements – not to mention plotting of immense ingenuity and symmetry – the Morse legacy will live as long as the crime genre itself.

Regarding the actor John Thaw's lengthy stint as Inspector Morse, the detective's creator smiled benignly on the productions (even after filmmakers ran out of Dexter novels to adapt) for their achingly romantic vision of the dreaming spires of Oxford and Thaw's wonderfully tetchy, parsimonious version of Morse (though Dexter often wryly remarked on the staggering body count that both the Morse books and the TV series were racking up in the historical streets and academic quadrangles of the city).

Detective Inspector Tom Thorne's accession to the airwaves in a strongly cast television series was a fait accompli before it became a fait accompli – the only question was how well (or cack-handedly) it would be done when the inevitable transfer to another medium happened. Thorne's 'onlie begetter', the writer Mark Billingham, had made a considerable impression with both *Sleepyhead* (2001) and *Scaredy Cat* (2002), two tough and heavily atmospheric novels that instantly marked him out him as one of the most visceral (and trenchant) writers on the overcrowded British crime scene. Subsequently, *Lazybones* showed the author's continuing willingness to tackle uncomfortable themes, dealing as it did with convicted rapists being savagely killed after their release from prison. Billingham's astringent protagonist, copper Tom Thorne, is always ready to plumb the darker reaches of the human psyche – as is his creator. And it has to be said that Billingham's novels take no prisoners in terms of scarifying violence – he will never be a favourite read among those who want polite mayhem amidst the tea-cosies.

Lifeless was a novel that added more lustre to Billingham's achievement, not least for the element of social critique folded into it. A strong central character, strong writing, strong social critique – who would be the first to be smart enough pick this package up for TV?

It was Sky TV (in 2009) that took up the option on the Billingham Thorne novels, and a considerable amount of money was spent on the first three episodes, which were also afforded top-class directing and writing talent. But the most fruitful decision concerning the adaptations was the choice of the actor David Morrissey to play the tenacious protagonist. The fact that the actor was a touch too young for the role was more than compensated for by the intensity of his performance – hardly surprising given that Morrissey is one of the most respected and versatile actors in the UK, who can move from Dickens to contemporary parts such as this with dexterity.

The first Thorne novel to be adapted – as three episodes – was *Sleepyhead* (it was, in fact, initially shown cut together as one complete film at an event put together by the British Film Institute at the National Film Theatre in London). Given that the filmmaking ethos of *Sleepyhead* (not to mention its superlative production values) was unquestionably on a cinematic level rather than a more modest TV scale, the cinema was perhaps a more natural home for this adaptation. Showing an intelligent regard for the source material, a great deal of what Billingham had originally created managed to find its way onto the screen – not least Thorne's tricky, non-consensual nature (perfectly caught in Morrissey's edgy performance), with many of the minor characters given a rich and interesting life (again, the casting here was a considerable asset, with such reliable character actors as Eddie Marsan providing solid backup for Morrissey's eye-catching performance). If not quite finding a film equivalent for the idiosyncratic quality of Billingham's original (the films are often efficiently generic rather than innovative), the director Stephen Hopkins demonstrated a particular skill for the urban setting, managing to make London look simultaneously threatening, rundown and beautiful. In fact, the milieu was one of the determining factors in these adaptations, with the detective's rather splendid flat and its canalside setting contrasting with the other equally well-chosen (if less telegenic) locations.

The films' use of editing to accentuate the tension has at times an almost surreal, off-kilter intensity and manages to cover the occasional ill-focused piece of writing in which Billingham's original has been left some distance behind.

A particular asset is the performance of Aiden Gillen as medical examiner Phil Hendricks, the sardonic gay character who was one of the triumphs of the original Billingham series. Also particularly well characterised is the killer's 'living-dead' victim played by Sara Lloyd Gregory, whose performance lies almost entirely in voice-over, creating a poignancy to offset the more action-based aspects of the narrative. If the revelation of the killer is less effective, this is one of several aspects of the series where the filmmakers really did not find the most apposite equivalent to Billingham's pungent prose, but the adaptation is nevertheless successful – certainly far more successful than the contemporaneous adaptations of Peter Robinson's DCI Banks novels, in which a miscast Stephen Tompkinson is notably adrift as a similarly short-tempered copper.

The second film in the series, an adaptation of *Scaredy Cat* (directed by Benjamin Ross), took liberties with the original material, but manages to balance the caustic inter-office politics involving Thorne and his ex-partner Tughan (played by Eddy Marsan) with its pursuit-of-serial-killer plot.

Billingham had been advised by many other writers to stay well away from any TV adaptation and had been told that 'being out of the loop' was the safest place to be. 'It was a win/win situation, I was assured', Billingham told me. 'If the TV series turns out to be terrible you can say, "nothing to do with me" and if it wins a hatful of BAFTAs you can tell people, "that's based on my book, you know".' As it turned out, Billingham did become involved and is delighted that he did:

> It was very much a collaboration ... between myself and David Morrissey who was the actor I had always wanted to play Thorne. As an executive producer on the series I was not only closely involved with scripts and casting, but spent time on the set and was sent rushes every day. I was consulted about every change in the transition from book to script and, nine times out of ten, was happy to approve them. Having worked as a TV writer myself, I'm very aware that things have to change, and though some readers have pronounced themselves unhappy with some of the changes, I can assure them that each one was absolutely necessary. The fact that Thorne did not have a cat, or the change in setting from north to east London is far less important to me than the calibre of the cast or script or the quality of the direction. There are things you can do in a book that simply do not translate onto the screen and you have to find a new way to come at the story. In many ways it is futile to compare a book with its television adaptation. They are completely different animals. All I ever wanted with *Thorne* was to make a good piece of television and, thanks to Stephen Hopkins' kinetic direction and the amazing cast we managed to assemble, I am confident that we did that.

The writer is currently working on scripts for a second series of *Thorne* that will be based on the next three books in the series: *Lazybones*,

The Burning Girl and *Lifeless*, with lead writer Simon Donald (who has worked on *Low Winter Sun*, *Wallander* and *The Deep*), who is currently plotting the story arcs for Thorne, Hendricks, Holland and the others across nine hours of television. At the same time, the BBC have optioned Billingham's standalone novel *In the Dark* and are looking towards a possible series based around its central character, Helen Weeks. As readers of the recent Thorne novel, *Good as Dead*, will be aware, Tom Thorne and Helen Weeks may well be spending some time together in future books.

Appendix 3: Crime and Espionage

While espionage has long been one of the most reliably engross-
ing of literary genres, it has simultaneously been a godsend to the
cinema – where the dark psychological areas explored by the great
spy novelists can find the perfect visual equivalents (along with the
excitement of the less thoughtful spy movies, of course). However,
psychological complexity was conspicuous by its absence in early
British cinema's flirtation with the genre.

Such once-popular films as *The Return of Bulldog Drummond* (1934)
and *Bulldog Drummond at Bay* (1937), directed, respectively, by Walter
Summers and Norman Lee, are two fascinatingly dated curios. The
proto-Bond Hugh 'Bulldog' Drummond films were inspired by the
popular series of thrillers based on H.C. 'Sapper' McNeile's novels
(desperately un-PC by twenty-first-century standards) about a two-
fisted ex-military man and soldier of fortune, Captain Hugh 'Bulldog'
Drummond. Drummond is the template for right-wing clubland
heroes (Ian Fleming transposed elements into the contemporary ethos
of James Bond and injected the sexuality totally absent from Sapper's
originals); Norman Lee's *Bulldog Drummond at Bay* features the forgotten John Lodge in the adaptation considered to be the one that most
captures the spirit of the original books, and offers a snapshot of perhaps antediluvian class attitudes (though the anti-Semitic strains of the
books are absent), while *The Return of Bulldog Drummond* showcases the
starrier names of Ralph Richardson and Ann Todd, in a lively but antediluvian curtain-raiser to their re-teaming in David Lean's *The Sound
Barrier*. However, it was to be some 30 years before the British cinema
took on board the psychological striations of literary espionage.

An examination of the work of one of the progenitors of the genre
(not too far from – but far superior to – the Bulldog Drummond
ethos) is instructive. Without John Buchan's *The Thirty Nine
Steps* (1915) we would be missing such classic novels as Geoffrey
Household's *Rogue Male*. Or Hitchcock's matchless British film version (not to mention his American remake in-all-but-name, *North by
Northwest*). Or, for that matter, the spy thriller in the Ian Fleming vein
(even though the latter adds a libido to John Buchan's upper-crust

English hero). And the most famous novel by Buchan is as much of a delight as when it was written – and remains one of the greatest espionage thrillers ever written. Concise and kinetic, Buchan's story has his mining engineer protagonist returning, at a loose end, from Rhodesia, as the Balkan conflict bubbles away. Hannay is falsely accused of killing an American spy engaged in the Balkan intrigue and is soon on the run (across a brilliantly realised Scotland – this is the ultimate picaresque thriller) from both police and enemy agents. Those who feel they know Buchan's tale too well from the numerous adaptations should really go back to the irresistible source novel. Alfred Hitchcock's British-made *The 39 Steps* (1935) was the blueprint for many of his subsequent films (*North by Northwest*, *Saboteur* and *Torn Curtain*), and this is one of that rare breed of films (like Michael Curtiz's *Casablanca*) in which absolutely every element (screenplay, direction, cinematography and playing) is burnished to perfection. Robert Donat is perfectly cast as the very British hero, and the customary Hitchcockian balance of suspense and sardonic humour gets its most adroit workout in the director's English period before he succumbed to the temptations of Hollywood. Subsequent remakes (with Kenneth Moore and Robert Powell) were efficient enough but were not remotely in the same league as Hitchcock's original. And the template for the Bond films is here in embryo – though the same director's *North by Northwest* was to provide a more direct inspiration.

John le Carré's *The Spy Who Came in from the Cold* (1963) remains the finest of all modern espionage novels. The narrative of the tragic British spy Alec Leamas achieves a genuine tragic dimension, and there is not another novel in the genre that has plotting as consummate as this, with every piece of sleight of hand played on both the characters and the reader being supremely satisfying. Finally, though, it is the not-a-wasted-word economy of the book that astonishes. It is interesting to speculate how much of his massive popularity John le Carré owes to Martin Ritt's perfectly honed adaptation of his classic novel. Le Carré enjoyed immense success, but that final plateau of celebrity may be down to Martin Ritt's movie. All the key elements of the source novel are incorporated in the top-notch Paul Dehn screenplay, while those elisions necessary are seamlessly done – it's hard to imagine a more copacetic adaptation. The icing on the cake is, of course, Richard Burton as Leamas. Too often the actor made unfortunate choices in his film roles – a fact he was all too aware of. Thankfully, he seized this opportunity with both hands.

If le Carré had never written the epic spy sagas that have occupied him for the last 20 years, his place in espionage literature would still have been assured by such books as *Call for the Dead* (1961), one of the perfectly honed, utterly economical books of his early years. Thriller writer Nicholas Blake (whose alter ego was Poet Laureate C. Day-Lewis) famously said of *Call for the Dead* that 'it makes most cloak-and-dagger stuff taste of cardboard', and this assessment is as appropriate as ever. George Smiley deals with both the parlous state of his marriage to the aristocratic Lady Anne and betrayal by close friends from the past with the quiet authority (and self-effacing demeanour) that marks him out from most literary spies; the structure of the book is masterly in its craftsmanship. Sidney Lumet's accomplished film adaptation, *The Deadly Affair* (1966), was a winner. Film riffs on le Carré novels have been hit-or-miss affairs (such as the low-voltage filmic takes on *The Little Drummer Girl* and *The Looking Glass War*), but everything clicked into place beautifully here: masterful direction by Sidney Lumet, a script (Paul Dehn) that strip-mines the choicest elements of the original novel and (best of all) consummate playing. One could make the case that James Mason's George Smiley (re-named Dobbs in the film) is every inch the equal of the more acclaimed Alec Guinness incarnation of the character, and Ingmar Bergman favourite Harriet Andersson gives her best performance in a non-Swedish film. And when the other players include Simone Signoret, Maximillian Schell and Harry Andrews, the quality is assured.

It is hard to realise today what an impact Len Deighton's remarkable spy novel *The Ipcress File* (1962) had on its first appearance in the 1960s. Like le Carré, Deighton was reacting against the glossy, unrealistic depiction of espionage in the novels of Ian Fleming (a certain Puritanism was a factor at the time, something that is less apropos these days now that Fleming's considerable virtues have been recognised). But certainly, *The Ipcress File*, with its insolent working-class hero and low-key treatment of all the quotidian details of a spy's life (endless futile requisitions for petty cash, a decidedly unglamorous secret service HQ), was astonishingly fresh, while the first-person narrative was a sardonic Londoner's refraction of Chandler's Marlowe-speak. Another radical touch was the refusal to neatly tie up the narrative with a cathartic death for the villain – the shadowy opponent of Deighton's unnamed protagonist is – for political reasons – unpunished. A series of novels in the same vein followed, none quite as impressive as this debut, but all highly accomplished. In Sydney Furie's celebrated film adaptation of 1965, the director's reliance on eccentric camera angles may look a touch mannered today, but it is worth remembering that this was remarked on at the time of the film's initial release. In fact, camera angles and all, this is a career-best for Furie – a perfect reworking of Deighton's quirky anti-Bond novel, with the inspired casting of Michael Caine as the low-rent (yet epicurean) spy. The dingy sets are by Ken Adam – hard to believe, given the elaborate work he was simultaneously doing on the Bond films for producer Harry Saltzman (whose project this was) and 007 composer John Barry was also on board. But almost the single most cherishable element (in a film crammed with subtle pleasures) is the late character actor Nigel Green as Caine's supercilious, pernickety boss – another career best.

In the cinema of the twenty-first century, the espionage genre has shown great durability. The Bond films have now banished the kitsch of the Roger Moore era and regained the essence of Ian Fleming, while the Bourne franchise (more sophisticated than the Robert Ludlum originals) has set down a conflicted spy in a carefully located modern milieu. Interestingly, it was some time after the renewed, post-Cold War literary acclaim of John le Carré that the success of adaptations of his work in the cinema was to be repeated, notably with the new film version of *Tinker Tailor Soldier Spy* (2011), with Gary Oldman making the part of the elderly spymaster George Smiley his own, despite the lengthy shadow thrown by Alec Guinness in the much-loved television adaptation. More controversial than Oldman's casting, however, was the choice of director. Tomas Alfredson had made a considerable mark with his adaptation of John Ajvide Lindqvist's modern-day supernatural novel *Let the Right One In* and seemed an eccentric choice for this markedly British tale of betrayal set largely in a clubland/Oxbridge milieu. In the event, the director demonstrated that he had the full measure of the material and created something very different from (but also as complex as) the original, Alfredson having the courage to take his time with the material, handled in long-breathed fashion (and single-mindedly avoiding the injection of any spurious suspense sequences). He also encouraged his leading performer to bring a harder, crueller edge to the otherwise avuncular George Smiley (although it should be remembered that Alec Guinness did not neglect this aspect of the character). As with many foreign directors casting a cool eye on British class and mores, Alfredson has the ability to illuminate unexpected facets in his narrative, notably a peculiarly English melancholia and the strange torpor that descends on the central characters, even though the stakes are of the highest order. John le Carré himself, never a man to mince his words, declared himself pleased with this radical reimagining of his novel – a verdict which must have occasioned several sighs of relief.

Appendix 4: Films, TV and Books

Films

Accident, 1967, directed by Joseph Losey
Adulthood, 2008, directed by Noel Clarke
Age of Consent, 1969, directed by Michael Powell
Alfie, 1966, directed by Lewis Gilbert
All Coppers Are..., 1972, directed by Sidney Hayers
And Then There Were None, 1945, directed by René Clair
Angel, 1982, directed by Neil Jordan
Apocalypse Now, 1979, directed by Francis Coppola
Assault on Precinct 13, 1976, directed by John Carpenter
Attack the Block, 2011, directed by Joe Cornish
Bear Island, 1979, directed by Don Sharp
Beat Girl, 1960, directed by Edmond T. Gréville
Bicycle Thieves, 1948, directed by Vittorio De Sica
Black Narcissus, 1946, directed by Michael Powell and Emeric Pressburger
Blackmail, 1929, directed by Alfred Hitchcock
Blind Date, 1959, directed by Joseph Losey
The Blue Lamp, 1950, directed by Basil Dearden
Bob le Flambeur, 1955, directed by Jean-Pierre Melville
Bonnie and Clyde, 1967, directed by Arthur Penn
The Boys, 1961, directed by Sidney J. Furie
Breaking Away, 1979, directed by Peter Yates
A Bridge Too Far, 1977, directed by Richard Attenborough
Brighton Rock, 1947, directed by John Boulting
Brighton Rock, 2010, directed by Rowan Joffe
Bulldog Drummond at Bay, 1937, directed by Norman Lee
Bullet Boy, 2004, directed by Saul Dibb
Bullitt, 1968, directed by Peter Yates
Bunny Lake is Missing, 1965, directed by Otto Preminger
The Butcher Boy, 1997, directed by Neil Jordan
Cabaret, 1972, directed by Bob Fosse
A Canterbury Tale, 1944, directed by Michael Powell and Emeric Pressburger
Cape Fear, 1962, directed by J. Lee Thompson
Carrington VC, 1954, directed by Anthony Asquith
Casablanca, 1942, directed by Michael Curtiz
The Case of Charles Peace, 1949, directed by Norman Lee
Cash on Demand, 1961, directed by Quentin Lawrence
The Challenge, 1960, directed by John Gilling (aka *It Takes a Thief*)
Chinese Boxes, 1984, directed by Chris Petit

Circus of Horrors, 1960, directed by Sidney Hayers
City of God, 2002, directed by Fernando Meirelles
A Clockwork Orange, 1971, directed by Stanley Kubrick
The Clouded Yellow, 1950, directed by Ralph Thomas
The Company of Wolves, 1984, directed by Neil Jordan
The Cook, The Thief, His Wife and Her Lover, 1989, directed by Peter Greenaway
Cosh Boy, 1953, directed by Lewis Gilbert
The Cottage, 2008, directed by Paul Andrew Williams
The Criminal, 1960, directed by Joseph Losey
The Crooked Road, 1965, directed by Don Chaffey
Croupier, 1998, directed by Mike Hodges
The Crying Game, 1992, directed by Neil Jordan
Cul-de-Sac, 1966, directed by Roman Polanski
The Damned, 1961, directed by Joseph Losey
Dance with a Stranger, 1985, directed by Mike Newell
Danger Route, 1967, directed by Seth Holt
The Day the Earth Caught Fire, 1961, directed by Val Guest
The Day They Robbed the Bank of England, 1960, directed by John Guillermin
Dead of Night, 1945, directed by Alberto Cavalcanti, Basil Dearden, Robert
  Hamer and Charles Crichton
Deadfall, 1968, directed by Bryan Forbes
The Deadly Affair, 1966, directed by Sidney Lumet
Deadly Strangers, 1976, directed by Sidney Hayers
Death in Venice, 1971, directed by Luchino Visconti
Death on the Nile, 1978, directed by John Guillermin
Death Wish, 1974, directed by Michael Winner
Deep End, 1970, directed by Jerzy Skolimowski
Dentist in the Chair, 1960, directed by Don Chaffey
The Devil's Business, 2011, directed by Sean Hogan
Les Diaboliques, 1954, directed by Henri-Georges Clouzot
The Diamond Mercenaries, 1976, directed by Val Guest (aka *Killer Force*)
Die Screaming Marianne, 1971, directed by Pete Walker
Dirty Harry, 1971, directed by Don Siegel
The Disappearance of Alice Creed, 2009, directed by J. Blakeson
Don't Bother to Knock, 1952, directed by Roy Ward Baker
Down Terrace, 2009, directed by Ben Wheatley
Dr Crippen, 1962, directed by Robert Lynn
Dracula, 1958, directed by Terence Fisher
80,000 Suspects, 1963, directed by Val Guest
Empire State, 1987, directed by Ron Peck
The End of the Affair, 1954, directed by Edward Dmytryk
Evil Under the Sun, 1982, directed by Guy Hamilton
Excalibur, 1981, directed by John Boorman
Face, 1997, directed by Antonia Bird
The Face of Fu Manchu, 1965, directed by Don Sharp
The Falconer, 1997, directed by Chris Petit

The Fallen Idol, 1948, directed by Carol Reed
Falling Down, 1993, directed by Joel Schumacher
Father Brown, 1954, directed by Robert Hamer
The FBI Story, 1959, directed by Mervyn LeRoy
Flame in the Streets, 1961, directed by Roy Ward Baker
The Flamingo Affair, 1948, directed by Horace Shepherd
Flash Gordon, 1980, directed by Mike Hodges
The Flesh is Weak, 1957, directed by Don Chaffey
Flight to Berlin, 1983, directed by Chris Petit
Fourteen Hours, 1951, directed by Henry Hathaway
Frieda, 1947, directed by Basil Dearden
The Friends of Eddie Coyle, 1973, directed by Peter Yates
Frightmare, 1974, directed by Pete Walker
Gangster No. 1, 2000, directed by Paul McGuigan
Get Carter, 1971, directed by Mike Hodges
Gideon's Day, 1958, directed by John Ford
The Godfather, 1972, directed by Francis Ford Coppola
The Good Father, 1986, directed by Mike Newell
The Good Thief, 2002, directed by Neil Jordan
Goodbye Charlie Bright, 2001, directed by Nick Love
Gran Torino, 2008, directed by Clint Eastwood
Great Expectations, 1946, directed by David Lean
The Grissom Gang, 1971, directed by Robert Aldrich
Gumshoe, 1971, directed by Stephen Frears
Guns of Darkness, 1962, directed by Anthony Asquith
The Guns of Navarone, 1961, directed by J. Lee Thompson
The Halfway House, 1944, directed by Basil Dearden
The Hamburg Cell, 2004, directed by Antonia Bird
Happiness, 1998, directed by Todd Solondz
The Hard Case, 1995, directed by Guy Ritchie
The Hard Way, 1979, directed by Michael Dryhurst
Hardcore, 1979, directed by Paul Schrader
Harry Brown, 2009, directed by Daniel Barber
Hell Drivers, 1957, directed by Cy Endfield
Hell is a City, 1960, directed by Val Guest
Hennessy, 1975, directed by Don Sharp
Henry V, 1944, directed by Laurence Olivier
High Spirits, 1988, directed by Neil Jordan
A High Wind in Jamaica, 1965, directed by Alexander Mackendrick
Hit Man, 1972, directed by George Armitage
The Hot Rock, 1972, directed by Peter Yates (aka *How to Steal a Diamond in Four Uneasy Lessons*)
The Hound of the Baskervilles, 1959, directed by Terence Fisher
House of Mortal Sin, 1975, directed by Pete Walker
House of Whipcord, 1974, directed by Pete Walker
I Start Counting, 1969, directed by David Greene

I Want to Live!, 1958, directed by Robert Wise
I'll Sleep When I'm Dead, 2003, directed by Mike Hodges
I'm All Right Jack, 1959, directed by John Boulting
if..., 1968, directed by Lindsay Anderson
Ill Manors, 2012, directed by Ben Drew
Inferno, 1953, directed by Roy Ward Baker
The Ipcress File, 1965, directed by Sidney J. Furie
It Always Rains on Sunday, 1947, directed by Robert Hamer
The Italian Job, 1969, directed by Peter Collinson
Jack the Ripper, 1958, directed by Robert S. Baker
Jamaica Inn, 1939, directed by Alfred Hitchcock
Jason and the Argonauts, 1963, directed by Don Chaffey
Jigsaw, 1962, directed by Val Guest
Joe Macbeth, 1955, directed by Ken Hughes
Kick-Ass, 2010, directed by Matthew Vaughn
Kidulthood, 2005, directed by Menhaj Huda
Kill List, 2011, directed by Ben Wheatley
Kind Hearts and Coronets, 1949, directed by Robert Hamer
Kiss of Death, 1947, directed by Henry Hathaway
The Kiss of the Vampire, 1963, directed by Don Sharp
The Krays, 1990, directed by Peter Medak
The L-Shaped Room, 1962, directed by Bryan Forbes
The Lady Vanishes, 1938, directed by Alfred Hitchcock
The Ladykillers, 1955, directed by Alexander Mackendrick
The Lavender Hill Mob, 1951, directed by Charles Crichton
Layer Cake, 2004, directed by Matthew Vaughn
The League of Gentlemen, 1960, directed by Basil Dearden
The Leather Boys, 1963, directed by Sidney J. Furie
Let the Right One In, 2008, directed by Tomas Alfredson
Life for Ruth, 1962, directed by Basil Dearden
The List of Adrian Messenger, 1963, directed by John Huston
The Little Drummer Girl, 1984, directed by George Roy Hill
Lock, Stock and Two Smoking Barrels, 1998, directed by Guy Ritchie
The Lodger, 1926, directed by Alfred Hitchcock
Lolita, 1961, directed by Stanley Kubrick
The Long Good Friday, 1980, directed by John Mackenzie
The Long Memory, 1952, directed by Robert Hamer
Look Back in Anger, 1959, directed by Tony Richardson
The Looking Glass War, 1969, directed by Frank R. Pierson
Lost in Space, 1998, directed by Stephen Hopkins
Mad Love, 1995, directed by Antonia Bird
The Magic Box, 1951, directed by John Boulting
The Man Between, 1953, Carol Reed
The Man in the White Suit, 1951, directed by Alexander Mackendrick
The Man Upstairs, 1958, directed by Don Chaffey
The Man Who Fell to Earth, 1976, directed by Nicolas Roeg

The Man Who Finally Died, 1962, directed by Quentin Lawrence
The Man Who Knew Too Much, 1934, directed by Alfred Hitchcock
Michael Collins, 1996, directed by Neil Jordan
Mine Own Executioner, 1947, directed by Anthony Kimmins
Ministry of Fear, 1944, directed by Fritz Lang
The Mirror Crack'd, 1980, directed by Guy Hamilton
Mona Lisa, 1986, directed by Neil Jordan
Morons from Outer Space, 1985, directed by Mike Hodges
Mother, Jugs and Speed, 1976, directed by Peter Yates
Murder, 1930, directed by Alfred Hitchcock
Murder by Decree, 1978, directed by Bob Clark
Murder on the Orient Express, 1974, directed by Sidney Lumet
The Nanny, 1965, directed by Seth Holt
Never Let Go, 1960, directed by John Guillermin
Never Take Sweets from a Stranger, 1960, directed by Cyril Frankel
Night and the City, 1950, directed by Jules Dassin
Night Must Fall, 1937, directed by Richard Thorpe
Night Must Fall, 1964, directed by Karel Reisz
Night of the Eagle, 1962, directed by Sidney Hayers
Night of the Hunter, 1955, directed by Charles Laughton
Night Train to Munich, 1940, directed by Carol Reed
Nighthawks, 1978, directed by Ron Peck
Nil by Mouth, 1997, directed by Gary Oldman
No Orchids for Miss Blandish, 1948, directed by St John Legh Clowes
Noose, 1948, directed by Edmond T. Gréville
North by Northwest, 1959, directed by Alfred Hitchcock
Nowhere to Go, 1958, directed by Seth Holt
Number Seventeen, 1932, directed by Alfred Hitchcock
Obsession, 1948, directed by Edward Dmytryk
The October Man, 1947, directed by Roy Ward Baker
Odd Man Out, 1946, directed by Carol Reed
Offbeat, 1960, directed by Cliff Owen
The Offence, 1972, directed by Sidney Lumet
Oliver!, 1968, directed by Carol Reed
Oliver Twist, 1948, directed by David Lean
On Friday at Eleven, 1961, directed by Alvin Rakoff (aka *The World in My Pocket*)
On the Waterfront, 1954, directed by Elia Kazan
One Million Years B.C., 1966, directed by Don Chaffey
Ooh... You Are Awful, 1972, directed by Cliff Owen
Orders to Kill, 1958, directed by Anthony Asquith
Our Man in Havana, 1959, directed by Carol Reed
The Party's Over, 1963, directed by Guy Hamilton
The Patriot, 2000, directed by Roland Emmerich
Payroll, 1961, directed by Sidney Hayers
Peeping Tom, 1960, directed by Michael Powell
Performance, 1970, directed by Donald Cammell and Nicolas Roeg

Piccadilly Third Stop, 1960, directed by Wolf Rilla
Pickup on South Street, 1953, directed by Samuel Fuller
Pink String and Sealing Wax, 1945, directed by Robert Hamer
Pit of Darkness, 1961, directed by Lance Comfort
Playback, 1962, directed by Quentin Lawrence
The Pleasure Garden, 1925, directed by Alfred Hitchcock
Pool of London, 1950, directed by Basil Dearden
A Prayer for the Dying, 1987, directed by Mike Hodges
Priest, 1994, directed by Antonia Bird
A Prize of Arms, 1961, directed by Cliff Owen
Prostitute, 1980, directed by Tony Garnett
The Prowler, 1951, directed by Joseph Losey
Psycho, 1960, directed by Alfred Hitchcock
The Public Enemy, 1931, directed by William A. Wellman
Pulp, 1972, directed by Mike Hodges
Puppet on a Chain, 1970, directed by Geoffrey Reeve (one sequence by Don
   Sharp)
Pygmalion, 1938, directed by Anthony Asquith
The Quatermass Xperiment, 1955, directed by Val Guest
Radio On, 1979, directed by Chris Petit
The Rasp, 1932, directed by Michael Powell
The Red Shoes, 1948, directed by Michael Powell and Emeric Pressburger
The Return of Bulldog Drummond, 1934, directed by Walter Summers
Revenge, 1971, directed by Sidney Hayers
Revolver, 2005, directed by Guy Ritchie
Rich and Strange, 1932, directed by Alfred Hitchcock
Rififi, 1955, directed by Jules Dassin (aka *Du Rififi Chez les Hommes*)
Robbery, 1967, directed by Peter Yates
Room at the Top, 1958, directed by Jack Clayton
Run for the Sun, 1956, directed by Roy Boulting
The Run of the Country, 1995, directed by Peter Yates
The Running Man, 1963, directed by Carol Reed
Saboteur, 1942, directed by Alfred Hitchcock
Safe, 1993, directed by Antonia Bird
Sands of the Kalahari, 1965, directed by Cy Endfield
Sapphire, 1959, directed by Basil Dearden
Saraband for Dead Lovers, 1948, directed by Basil Dearden
Saturday Night and Sunday Morning, 1960, directed by Karel Reisz
Scarface, 1932, directed by Howard Hawks
Scarface, 1983, directed by Brian De Palma
School for Scoundrels, 1960, directed by Robert Hamer
Scum, 1979, directed by Alan Clarke
Sea Fury, 1958, directed by Cy Endfield
Sebastian, 1968, directed by David Greene
A Sense of Freedom, 1979, directed by John Mackenzie
The Servant, 1963, directed by Joseph Losey

Seven Days to Noon, 1950, directed by John and Roy Boulting
Severance, 2006, directed by Christopher Smith
Sexy Beast, 2000, directed by Jonathan Glazer
The Shakedown, 1959, directed by John Lemont
Shallow Grave, 1994, directed by Danny Boyle
Sherlock Holmes, 2009, directed by Guy Ritchie
Sherlock Holmes: A Game of Shadows, 2011, directed by Guy Ritchie
Shopping, 1994, directed by Paul Anderson
The Shuttered Room, 1967, directed by David Greene
The Siege of Sidney Street, 1960, directed by Robert S. Baker and Monty Berman
The Singer Not the Song, 1961, directed by Roy Ward Baker
Sket, 2011, directed by Nirpal Bhogal
The Sleeping Tiger, 1954, directed by Joseph Losey
The Small Back Room, 1949, directed by Michael Powell and Emeric Pressburger
The Small World of Sammy Lee, 1963, directed by Ken Hughes
Snatch, 2000, directed by Guy Ritchie
Soho Incident, 1956, directed by Vernon Sewell
The Sound Barrier, 1952, directed by David Lean
The Sound of Fury, 1950, directed by Cy Endfield
Spare the Rod, 1961, directed by Leslie Norman
Sparrows Can't Sing, 1962, directed by Joan Littlewood
The Spider and the Fly, 1949, directed by Robert Hamer
The Spy in Black, 1939, directed by Michael Powell
The Spy Who Came in from the Cold, 1965, directed by Martin Ritt
The Stars Look Down, 1939, directed by Carol Reed
Station Six-Sahara, 1962, directed by Seth Holt
Stormy Monday, 1988, directed by Mike Figgis
The Story of Temple Drake, 1933, directed by Stephen Roberts
The Strange Affair, 1968, directed by David Greene
Strangers on a Train, 1951, directed by Alfred Hitchcock
The Stranglers of Bombay, 1959, directed by Terence Fisher
Straw Dogs, 1971, directed by Sam Peckinpah
Strongroom, 1961, directed by Vernon Sewell
A Study in Scarlet, 1914, directed by George Pearson
A Study in Terror, 1965, directed by James Hill
Summer Holiday, 1963, directed by Peter Yates
Suspect, 1960, directed by John and Roy Boulting
Suspicion, 1941, directed by Alfred Hitchcock
Sweet Smell of Success, 1957, directed by Alexander Mackendrick
Swept Away, 2002, directed by Guy Ritchie
The Tales of Hoffmann, 1951, directed by Michael Powell and Emeric Pressburger
A Taste of Excitement, 1970, directed by Don Sharp
Taste of Fear, 1961, directed by Seth Holt (aka *Scream of Fear*)
The Terminal Man, 1974, directed by Mike Hodges
That Riviera Touch, 1966, directed by Cliff Owen

They Drive by Night, 1938, directed by Arthur Woods
They Made Me a Fugitive, 1947, directed by Alberto Cavalcanti
The Thief of Bagdad, 1940, directed by Michael Powell, Ludwig Berger and Tim Whelan
The Third Man, 1949, directed by Carol Reed
The 39 Steps, 1935, directed by Alfred Hitchcock
The Thirty Nine Steps, 1978, directed by Don Sharp
This Gun for Hire, 1942, directed by Frank Tuttle
Thunder Rock, 1942, directed by Roy Boulting
Tiger Bay, 1959, directed by J. Lee Thompson
Tiger in the Smoke, 1956, directed by Roy Ward Baker
Tinker Tailor Soldier Spy, 2011, directed by Tomas Alfredson
Torn Curtain, 1966, directed by Alfred Hitchcock
A Town Like Alice, 1956, directed by Jack Lee
Town on Trial, 1956, directed by John Guillermin
Trainspotting, 1996, directed by Danny Boyle
Treasure Island, 1950, directed by Byron Haskin
Trent's Last Case, 1952, directed by Herbert Wilcox
The Trials of Oscar Wilde, 1960, directed by Ken Hughes
The Trollenberg Terror, 1958, directed by Quentin Lawrence
Twisted Nerve, 1968, directed by Roy Boulting
2001: A Space Odyssey, 1968, directed by Stanley Kubrick
An Unsuitable Job for a Woman, 1981, directed by Chris Petit
Vertigo, 1958, directed by Alfred Hitchcock
Victim, 1961, directed by directed by Basil Dearden
Village of the Damned, 1960, directed by Wolf Rilla
Villain, 1971, directed by Michael Tuchner
Violent Playground, 1958, directed by Basil Dearden
The Wages of Fear, 1953, directed by Henri-Georges Clouzot
The Warriors, 1979, directed by Walter Hill
We Shall See, 1964, directed by Quentin Lawrence
The Weak and the Wicked, 1953, directed by J. Lee Thompson
Went the Day Well?, 1942, directed by Alberto Cavalcanti
We're No Angels, 1989, directed by Neil Jordan
Whistle Down the Wind, 1961, directed by Bryan Forbes
The Winslow Boy, 1948, directed by Anthony Asquith
Witchcraft, 1964, directed by Don Sharp
Witchfinder General, 1968, directed by Michael Reeves
Woman in a Dressing Gown, 1957, directed by J. Lee Thompson
The Woman in Question, 1950, directed by Anthony Asquith
The World Ten Times Over, 1963, directed by Wolf Rilla
The Wrong Arm of the Law, 1962, directed by Cliff Owen
The Yellow Balloon, 1952, directed by J. Lee Thompson
Yield to the Night, 1956, directed by J. Lee Thompson
Young and Innocent, 1937, directed by Alfred Hitchcock
Zulu, 1964, directed by Cy Endfield

Television crime

The Adventures of Sherlock Holmes, 1984–1985, Granada Television for ITV
The Agatha Christie Hour, 1982, Thames Television for ITV
Agatha Christie's Poirot, 1989–, LWT for ITV (David Suchet as Poirot)
The Avengers, 1961–1969, ABC Television for ITV
The Baron, 1965–1966, ITC for ITV
The Blackheath Poisonings, 1992, Central Television for ITV
Callan, 1967–1972, ABC Television/Thames Television for ITV (Callan first
    appeared in 'A Magnum for Schneider', *Armchair Theatre*, 1967)
The Case-Book of Sherlock Holmes, 1991–1993, Granada Television for ITV
Colonel March of Scotland Yard, 1956–1957, Fountain Films for ITV
Dalgliesh, 1983–1998, Anglia Television for ITV (Roy Marsden as Dalgliesh)
Dalgliesh, 2003 and 2005, BBC (Martin Shaw as Dalgliesh)
Danger Man, 1960–1961 and 1964–1967, ITC for ITV
The Four Just Men, 1959–1960, Sapphire Films for ITC
Gideon's Way, 1964–1965, ITC
Inspector Morse, 1987–2000, Zenith Productions/Carlton Television for ITV
The Long Firm, 2004, BBC
Marple, 2004–2009, ITV (Geraldine McEwan as Miss Marple)
Marple, 2009–, ITV (Julia McKenzie as Miss Marple)
The Memoirs of Sherlock Holmes, 1994, Granada Television for ITV
Miss Marple, 1984–1992, BBC (Joan Hickson as Miss Marple)
The Persuaders!, 1971–1972, ITC for ITV
The Prisoner, 1967–1968, Everyman Films for ITC
Rebus, 2000–2001, STV Productions for ITV (John Hannah as John Rebus)
Rebus, 2006–2007, STV Productions for ITV (Ken Stott as John Rebus)
Red Riding, 2009, Channel 4
'Regan', *Armchair Theatre*, 1974, Euston Films/Thames Television for ITV
The Return of Sherlock Holmes, 1986–1988, Granada Television for ITV
The Rivals of Sherlock Holmes, 1971 and 1973, Thames Television for ITV
The Saint, 1962–1969, ATV/New World for ITC; Bamore for ITC
Sharman, 1995–1996, World Productions/Carlton TV
The Strange World of Planet X, 1956, ATV
The Sweeney, 1975–1978, Euston Films/Thames Television for ITV
Tom Thorne: Sleepyhead and *Scaredy Cat*, 2010, Sky1
The Trollenberg Terror, 1956, ATV
The Vice, 1999–2003, Carlton Television

Books mentioned in the text

Allingham, Margery, *The Tiger in the Smoke*, 1952
Ambler, Eric, *The October Man*, 1947
Arnott, Jake, *The Long Firm*, 1999
Balchin, Nigel, *Mine Own Executioner*, 1945

Balchin, Nigel, *The Small Back Room*, 1943
Bentley, E.C., *Trent's Last Case*, 1913
Billingham, Mark, *The Burning Girl*, 2004
Billingham, Mark, *Good as Dead*, 2011
Billingham, Mark, *In the Dark*, 2008
Billingham, Mark, *Lazybones*, 2003
Billingham, Mark, *Lifeless*, 2005
Billingham, Mark, *Scaredy Cat*, 2002
Billingham, Mark, *Sleepyhead*, 2001
Braine, John, *Room at the Top*, 1957
Buchan, John, *The Thirty Nine Steps*, 1915
Camus, Albert, *The Outsider [L'Étranger]*, 1942
Chase, James Hadley, *No Orchids for Miss Blandish*, 1939
Cheyney, Peter, *This Man is Dangerous*, 1936
Christie, Agatha, *And Then There Were None*, 1939
Christie, Agatha, *Death on the Nile*, 1937
Christie, Agatha, *Evil Under the Sun*, 1940
Christie, Agatha, *Murder on the Orient Express*, 1933
Christie, Agatha, *The Mirror Crack'd*, 1962
Clevely, Hugh Desmond, *The Gang-Smasher*, 1928
Clifford, Francis, *Act of Mercy*, 1959
Creasy, John, *Gideon's Day*, 1955
Cronin, A.J., *The Stars Look Down*, 1935
Curtis, James, *They Drive by Night*, 1938
Deighton, Len, *The Ipcress File*, 1962
Faulkner, William, *Sanctuary*, 1931
Green, F.I., *Odd Man Out*, 1945
Greene, Graham, 'The Basement Room', 1935 (short story, basis for *The Fallen Idol*)
Greene, Graham, *Brighton Rock*, 1938
Greene, Graham, *A Burnt-Out Case*, 1960
Greene, Graham, *The Comedians*, 1966
Greene, Graham, *The Confidential Agent*, 1939
Greene, Graham, *A Gun for Sale*, 1936
Greene, Graham, *The Heart of the Matter*, 1940
Greene, Graham, *The Man Within*, 1929
Greene, Graham, *The Ministry of Fear*, 1943
Greene, Graham, *Our Man in Havana*, 1958
Greene, Graham, *The Power and the Glory*, 1940
Greene, Graham, *The Quiet American*, 1955
Greene, Graham, *Stamboul Train*, 1932
Greene, Graham, *The Third Man*, 1950
Greene, Graham, 'The Lieutenant Died Last', 1940 (short story, basis for *Went the Day Well?*)
Hamilton, Patrick, *Twenty Thousand Streets Under the Sky* (trilogy: *The Midnight Bell*, 1929; *The Siege of Pleasure*, 1932; *The Plains of Cement*, 1934)

Harris, Thomas, *Red Dragon*, 1981
Harris, Thomas, *The Silence of the Lambs*, 1988
Herlihy, James Leo, *Midnight Cowboy*, 1965
Higgins, George V., *The Friends of Eddie Coyle*, 1970
Hogg, James, *The Private Memoirs and Confessions of a Justified Sinner*, 1824
Household, Geoffrey, *Rogue Male*, 1939
Hughes, Richard, *A High Wind in Jamaica*, 1929
James, P.D., *Original Sin*, 1994
James, P.D., *An Unsuitable Job for a Woman*, 1972
James, P.D., *Shroud for a Nightingale*, 1971
Janson, Hank (Stephen Daniel Francis), *When Dames Get Tough*, 1946
Jones, Elwyn and John Lloyd, *The Ripper File*, 1975
Kersh, Gerald, *Night and the City*, 1938
Kersh, Gerald, *Prelude to a Certain Midnight*, 1947
La Bern, Arthur, *It Always Rains on Sunday*, 1945
Lawrence, D.H., *Lady Chatterley's Lover*, 1928
le Carré, John, *Call for the Dead*, 1961
le Carré, John, *The Little Drummer Girl*, 1983
le Carré, John, *The Looking Glass War*, 1965
le Carré, John, *The Spy Who Came in from the Cold*, 1963
le Carré, John, *Tinker, Tailor, Soldier, Spy*, 1974
Leiber, Fritz, *Conjure Wife*, 1943 (basis for *Night of the Eagle*)
Lewis, Ted, *Jack's Return Home*, 1970
Lindqvist, John Ajvide, *Let the Right One In*, 2004
Lowndes, Marie, *The Lodger*, 1913
MacDonald, Philip, *The Rasp*, 1924
MacLean, Alistair, *Bear Island*, 1971
Mann, Thomas, *Death in Venice*, 1912
Maugham, Robin, *The Servant*, 1948
McCabe, Patrick, *The Butcher Boy*, 1922
Miller, Arthur, *Death of a Salesman*, 1949 (play)
Mitchell, James, *Death and Bright Water*, 1974
Mitchell, James, *A Magnum for Schneider*, 1969
Mitchell, James, *The Man Who Sold Death*, 1964
Mitchell, James, *Russian Roulette*, 1973
Orwell, George, 'Raffles and Miss Blandish', 1944 (essay)
Peace, David, *Nineteen Seventy Four*, 1999 (*The Red Riding Quartet*)
Peace, David, *Nineteen Seventy Seven*, 2000 (*The Red Riding Quartet*)
Peace, David, *Nineteen Eighty*, 2001 (*The Red Riding Quartet*)
Peace, David, *Nineteen Eighty Three*, 2002 (*The Red Riding Quartet*)
Pinter, Harold, *The Birthday Party*, 1957 (play)
Pinter, Harold, *The Dumb Waiter*, 1960 (play)
Powell, Anthony, *A Dance to the Music of Time*, 1951–1975
Rankin, Ian, *Exit Music*, 2007
Raymond, Derek, *He Died with His Eyes Open*, 1984
Raymond, Derek, *I Was Dora Suarez*, 1990

Sinclair, Iain, *Lights Out for the Territory*, 1997
Smith, Neville, *Gumshoe*, 1971
Stevenson, Robert Louis, *The Strange Case of Dr Jekyll and Mr Hyde*, 1886
Stoker, Bram, *Dracula*, 1897
Symons, Julian, *The Blackheath Poisonings*, 1978
Wellesley, Gordon, *Report on a Fugitive*
Welsh, Irvine, *Trainspotting*, 1993
Westerby, Robert, *Wide Boys Never Work*, 1937
Williams, Emlyn, *Night Must Fall*, 1935 (play)
Wyndham, John, *The Midwich Cuckoos*, 1957

Index